Humanistic Appr
Multiculturalism

Providing an overview of essential topics in multicultural psychology, *Humanistic Approaches to Multiculturalism and Diversity* focuses on the intersection of humanistic psychology and multiculturalism, including history, theory, research, and practice.

The authors examine the unique contributions of humanistic psychology to multicultural psychology on topics often ignored, such as cultural empathy and indigenous psychology and diversity. The book critiques and rectifies previous failures to adequately engage multicultural issues by providing methods for integrating multicultural psychology and humanistic therapy. Readers will find that each chapter advances scholarship through a dialogue with multicultural perspectives and builds a foundation for future scholarship and clinical practice.

This book will be of great interest to mental health professionals interested in humanistic and existential psychology.

Louis Hoffman, PhD, is a licensed psychologist in private practice. He provides training and supervision through the International Institute for Existential-Humanistic Psychology and teaches at Saybrook University.

Heatherlyn Cleare-Hoffman, PsyD, is a licensed psychologist originally from the Bahamas. She has worked as a faculty member, supervisor, and staff psychologist at various graduate and training programs in psychology.

Nathaniel Granger, Jr., PsyD, is a past president of the Society for Humanistic Psychology (APA Division 32), and a recipient of the Hari Camari Early Career Award. He also works as an adjunct professor at Saybrook University.

David St. John, PhD, is the executive director of FairSky Foundation, a nonprofit organization dedicated to the promotion of psychological, social, and ecological justice. He also teaches at the University of Detroit Mercy and Schoolcraft College.

"This excellent volume provides new and important perspectives on humanistic approaches to multicultural issues in clinical theory and psychotherapy. The authors embrace the foundations of humanistic psychology, and place at the core, the humanity and dignity of people. At the same time, they recognize the complex role of historical and ongoing social injustice and sociocultural identity on human experience. The volume expands humanistic psychology toward the inclusion of cultural humility as essential to empathy and connection in the psychotherapeutic relationship. It is an invaluable resource for therapists working with clients of any sociocultural background."

— **Usha Tummala-Narra**, PhD, associate professor in the Department of Counseling, Development, and Educational Psychology, Boston College, USA

"I have been so longing for this book to be written! It is a multi-perspectival consideration of the two leading approaches to psychotherapy that were formulated to maximize client empowerment in psychotherapy. Complexities related to how identity, social position, and relationship interact unfold in layer upon layer. Each chapter is a gentle invitation to become aware of another set of implicit beliefs, and by the end of reading you will more clearly understand your clients' lived experiences and gain new perspectives on how therapy can function."

— **Heidi M. Levitt**, professor of psychology, University of Massachusetts Boston, USA

"Shockingly honest, refreshing, and accessible to graduate students, academics, and seasoned clinicians, this book provides critical thinking and multifaceted realities. Through lived experiences, psychological literature, and suggested next steps, readers will be validated, challenged, and motivated to expand their theoretical orientation, research paradigms, case conceptualizations, and deepen their use of self in work and life."

— **Terri M. Davis**, director of the PsyD program and associate professor, University of Denver, USA

"The celebration of difference and diversity is at the very core of a humanistic ethic; yet humanistic psychology itself, has been woefully inadequate in addressing issues of multiculturalism, racism, and the dehumanisation of minority groups. The value of this book, therefore, is immense: taking our field right to the forefront of current debates and dialogues on these issues. In this respect, it deserves a place on the bookshelf of every humanistic psychologist."

— **Mick Cooper**, University of Roehampton, UK, and author of *Existential Therapies*

Humanistic Approaches to Multiculturalism and Diversity

Perspectives on Existence and Difference

Edited by Louis Hoffman, Heatherlyn Cleare-Hoffman, Nathaniel Granger, Jr., and David St. John

Routledge
Taylor & Francis Group

NEW YORK AND LONDON

First published 2020
by Routledge
52 Vanderbilt Avenue, New York, NY 10017

and by Routledge
2 Park Square, Milton Park, Abingdon, Oxon, OX14 4RN

Routledge is an imprint of the Taylor & Francis Group, an informa business

Library of Congress Cataloging-in-Publication Data
A catalog record has been requested for this book

ISBN: 978-0-8153-9582-9 (hbk)
ISBN: 978-0-8153-9583-6 (pbk)
ISBN: 978-1-351-13335-7 (ebk)

Typeset in Bembo
by Swales & Willis, Exeter, Devon, UK

To our students, past and present, who have served as inspiration and motivation in our writing, our careers, and our lives.

Contents

Foreword

This is not a comfortable book, but it is a brilliant and informative book. If you are looking for pat formulas and ready statements about the humanistic view of multiculturalism, you're reading the wrong book. This is a book that shakes the foundations of humanistic psychology's original quest: "what it means to be fully, experientially human and how that understanding illuminates the vital or fulfilled life." Speaking as a "lineage holder" and direct descendent of the founders, I once presumed that humanistic psychology had a quite comprehensive picture of the human predicament, of human striving and struggle; and that it was certainly heartier than many of our psychoanalytic and behavioral forebears. After all, we broke away from these forebears, enlarged upon their views, and beckoned them to follow our cutting edge path. Moreover, we took pride in the idea that our theories were deep, our practices empirically robust, and our treatment of fellow human beings sensitive, egalitarian, and integrative. We drew from some of the deepest wells of existential and humanistic philosophy, and had the backing of greats such as Socrates, Pascal, Kierkegaard, Nietzsche, and Sartre. And following these luminaries, we had the advocacy of some of the finest minds in psychiatry and psychology.

Yet what we didn't fully anticipate, and this text makes plain, is how culturally and ethnically bound we were—how delimited. At one level, this state of affairs makes sense. We strove for a new vision, a holistic vision that gave us the impression—some might say illusion—that we embraced a diversity of people; a cross-cultural core of human experience. We also became, like many practitioners and academics in the Western world, our own echo chamber. We spoke mainly to each other, and we referenced each other's research. Now to be sure, there were some among the founders in the humanistic movement who embraced the cause of social justice. Moreover, several of these activists, such as Rollo May, went on, at least partially, to incorporate their experiences into their theories. However, the very fact that the humanistic movement was (and still is to a notable degree) comprised of middle to upper class white men who are going to naturally apply their social sensitivity through the prism of their middle to upper class backgrounds is still a problem—particularly for a field that prides itself on elucidating what it means to be fully experientially human.

This book accordingly serves as a corrective of sorts, not just because it is rife with diverse authors, hailing from a remarkable range of ethnicities, genders, classes, and cultures, but also because it illuminates details about what it means to live as marginalized, devalued, and in many cases invisible individuals in mainstream Western society. On the other hand, the book illuminates the humanistic contributions of these populations— the genuine breakthroughs in our emerging understanding of self—in relation, embodiment, and spirituality. There is a depth and authenticity in this work that is rarely captured in texts about diversity. This is because the editors have carefully selected authors who speak from the inside about their subject matter, and who are impassioned about the human journey. I can think of no more fitting basis on which to forge a book about humanistic psychology and diversity.

To sum, I don't think any of us really knows where the multicultural seed will take us in humanistic psychology—or for that matter, psychology in general. What I do feel and share strongly with this book's contributors is that we need to step back, prepare the soil, and support that seed to blossom. Short of that our theories become impoverished relics, tools of a fractured inquiry, and subversions of our own mandate to intimately understand.

Kirk J. Schneider

Contributors

Sara K. Bridges, PhD, Co-Director Coherence Psychology Institute, Co-Director of Training, Counseling Psychology Program, The University of Memphis

Heatherlyn Cleare-Hoffman, PsyD, Staff Psychologist, Gallogy Recreation and Wellness Center, University of Colorado at Colorado Springs.

Joel Federman, PhD, Chair, Department of Transformative Social Change, Saybrook University, Pasadena, CA.

Nathaniel Granger, Jr., Rocky Mountain Humanistic Counsleing and Psychological Association; Saybrook University.

Myrtle Heery, PhD, Director, International Institute for Humanistic Studies, Petaluma, CA.

Dan Hocoy, PhD, President, SUNY Erie Community College, Western New York, NY.

Louis Hoffman, PhD, Executive Director, Rocky Mountain Humanistic Counseling and Psychological Association; Faculty, International Institute for Existential-Humanistic Psychology and the Existential-Humanistic Institute.

Theopia Jackson, PhD, The Association of Black Psychologists, Inc.; The Society for Humanistic Psychology; Co-Chair, Department of Humanistic & Clinical Psychology, Saybrook University, Pasadena, CA.

Zonya Johnson, PhD, Private Practice, Oakland, CA.

Michael Moats, PsyD, Private Practice, Colorado Springs, CO.

Christina M. New, MA, CAS, NCSP, Counseling Psychology Doctoral Student, The University of Memphis.

Jane Perlstein, MA, Co-director, Shambhala Meditation Center of Portland; Saybrook University.

Geneva Reynaga-Abiko, PsyD, Director, Counseling Services, California Polytechnic State University, San Luis Obispo.

Juliet Rohde-Brown, PhD, Chair, Depth Psychology: Integrative Therapy and Healing Practices Specialization, Pacifica Graduate Institute, Carpinteria, CA.

Kirk J. Schneider, PhD, President, Existential-Humanistic Institute, adjunct faculty, Saybrook University and Teachers College Columbia University.

Ilene Serlin, PhD, BC-DMT, Union Street Health Associates.

Drake Spaeth, PsyD, Psychology Chair, Humanistic and Clinical Psychology Department, Saybrook University.

David St. John, PhD, Executive Director, FairSky Foundation, Ferndale, MI; Adjunct Faculty at University of Detroit-Mercy and Saybrook University.

Louise Sundararajan, PhD, EdD, Founder and Chair, Indigenous Psychology Task Force.

Lisa Vallejos, PhD, the Humanitarian Alliance.

Alan G. Vaughan, PhD, JD, C.G. Jung Institute of San Francisco; Association of Black Psychologists; and Saybrook University, Oakland California.

Part I

History and Critique of Humanistic Psychology from a Multicultural Perspective

1   Introduction

*Louis Hoffman, Heatherlyn Cleare-Hoffman,
Nathaniel Granger, Jr., and David St. John*

Humanistic psychology emerged into prominence during the time leading up to the civil rights movement with both movements capitalizing on the spirit of the times (Grogan, 2013). The civil rights movement shared many foundational values with humanistic psychology. Concurrently, the Association of Black Psychology emerged, critiquing many of the same trends in psychology that humanistic psychology was rebelling against (see Chapter 4). Given these convergences, it seems these natural allies should have gravitated together to combine forces. Humanistic psychology was set up to be on the cutting edge of the early development of the civil rights and multicultural movements. Yet, this never happened, or at least only happened to a limited degree. While humanistic psychology was among the first to espouse a deep valuing of multiculturalism, it failed to actualize this value (Hoffman, 2016; Hoffman, Serlin, & Rubin, 2019).

Several notable attempts by humanistic psychologists to embrace multiculturalism can be identified. Carl Rogers, Maureen O'Hara, and three colleagues traveled to Brazil in 1977 to engage in cross-cultural dialogues and trainings in client-centered therapy (O'Hara, 1997). As O'Hara describes this trip, it prompted them to rethink earlier humanistic conceptions of empathy (see Chapter 9) in a direction that is more culturally sensitive and inclusive. Additionally, when Eleanor Criswell was president of the Society for Humanistic Psychology in 1999–2000, she attempted to draft and pass a statement on multiculturalism (Hoffman, 2016). Humanistic therapists attempted encounter groups focused on racial relations in the 1960s and 1970s (Grogan, 2013). Adelbert H. Jenkins, Ilene Serlin, Zonya Johnson, and others also contributed humanistic scholarship and trainings that sought to embrace multiculturalism. Despite these attempts, humanistic psychology continued to struggle with multiculturalism and diversity for many years, including some strong resistance to multicultural perspectives (Hoffman, 2016; Hoffman, Cleare-Hoffman, & Jackson, 2014).

Many therapists from diverse backgrounds did not find humanistic psychology to be a hospitable home. This is the basis for Geneva Reynaga-Abiko's reflections in Chapter 2. When we, the editors of this book, first began our involvement in humanistic institutions and organizations a little over ten years ago, these institutions were dominated by White therapists and scholars, particularly White males. Resistance, and sometimes outright hostility, was directed toward individuals presenting on multiculturalism and humanistic psychology, which was consistent with Boatright-Horowitz and Soeung's (2009) findings that teaching anti-racism and White privilege to a largely White audience often comes with a high cost. In the Society for Humanistic Psychology, women and people of color were less frequently recognized with awards and less likely to be elected to leadership roles (Hoffman, 2016). The contributions of these scholars, too, were cited less frequently and not recognized for their contributions. A notable example is Charlotte Bühler. Bühler was one of the most important early humanistic psychologists and could be considered a founder of the movement. Yet, her name is rarely included with Carl Rogers, Abraham Maslow, and others as a founder.

It is only within the last ten years that humanistic psychology has begun to embrace multicultural perspectives more consistently and on a deeper level. Hoffman (2016), in an article based on his 2013 presidential address to the Society for Humanistic Psychology, reviewed the history of multiculturalism and humanistic psychology in the United States, particularly within the Society of Humanistic Psychology, which is the most influential humanistic psychology organization in the United States. He noted that the transition to embracing multiculturalism in humanistic psychology was largely inspired by students and early career psychologists. Their voices helped establish the momentum for a multicultural movement in humanistic psychology. These emergent voices and leaders were committed to multicultural issues and recognized the necessity of embracing multicultural perspectives for humanistic psychology to survive. As Hoffman (2016) noted, if humanistic psychology does not embrace multiculturalism it will not, and should not, survive as a major force in psychology.

Along with the individuals who have been advocating for multicultural perspectives for many years, there are a number of emergent voices leading the way toward deepening humanistic psychology's commitment to multiculturalism, including Theopia Jackson, Lisa Vallejos, Roxanne Christensen, Monica Mansilla, Veronica Lac, Sarah Kamens, Gina Subia Belton, Nathaniel Granger, Jr., Derrick Sebree, Shawn Rubin, Donna Rockwell, and many others.

Contextualizing within Humanistic Psychology

Humanistic psychology is a term that has varying expressions within the field of psychology. At times, humanistic psychology is used broadly to refer to *the third force psychologies* that emerged after behaviorism and psychoanalysis, while at other times it refers more narrowly to psychologies that were developed from the writings of Carl Rogers, Abraham Maslow, Charlotte Bühler, and other early founders. In this book, we are referring broadly to the humanistic psychologies, but drawing more specifically from the contemporary practice of humanistic psychology. Existential-humanistic psychology is one branch of humanistic psychology that is particularly influential within contemporary practice in the United States (Byock et al., 2018; Paige et al., 2018), and many chapters draw heavily from an existential–humanistic framework as well.

Rooting Multiculturalism in Humanity

In this book, the contributors strive to root multicultural psychology in the humanity and dignity of all people. This may sound like a given; however, when reflecting upon the state of the world today it can be recognized as revolutionary. Racism, sexism, homophobia, and other forms prejudice and discrimination are often rooted in a *dehumanization* of groups of people. In contemporary times, this can be witnessed in efforts to characterize immigrants and refugees as morally corrupt criminals. It is often the most vulnerable people who have suffered extensively and have no platform to defend themselves that are dehumanized by those in power.

A true multicultural psychology must deeply embrace the humanity and basic rights of all people. This is not an easy task. Too often, in advocating for the humanity of one group, another group is forgotten or dehumanized. This can be seen even among multicultural activists, advocates, and allies. Frequently, divisions emerge even within the multicultural movement with criticisms that "they are not doing it right" (see Chapter 8). While it is important to engage in internal critique within the multicultural movement, including the multicultural movements within psychology and humanistic psychology, it is important that these critiques do not turn into unnecessary divisions or, worse yet, new forms of dehumanization. What is needed is a variety of humanistic approaches to combating discrimination and marginalization. Through a pluralism of approaches, humanistic psychology will be able to reach and impact more people. Yet, it is critical that all these approaches recognize the basic humanity and dignity of *all* people.

Embracing the humanity of all people has a number of implications. It means respecting the dignity and rights of all people. However, it also means recognizing that all people are finite, imperfect beings. All people have prejudicial beliefs, at times. Even advocates and allies are prone to having some unrecognized prejudices that may emerge, more often than not, in the form of microaggressions (see Chapter 7) or insensitivity to others.

Through embracing the humanity of all people with appropriate cultural humility, including human limitations, it becomes easier to embrace compassion and empathy for those who are different from oneself. Through recognizing the uniqueness of individuals and groups, it can be recognized that different tools, techniques, and tactics are required in different situations. At times, protest and confrontation are necessary. These strategies help identify and recognize problems that need to be addressed. However, confrontation and protest by themselves rarely lead to authentic change (Hoffman, Granger, & O'Neill, 2019). They may lead to compromise and concession; however, the most valuable outcome of confrontation and protest typically is beginning a conversation that can lead to deeper, more authentic change. Humanistic psychology teaches that relationship, empathy, and compassion are foundational for effective, lasting, authentic change.

This is not an easy ideal to live by, and it is one that can be misused. For example, too often people from marginalized groups and allies are criticized for being too forceful or angry in their advocacy and activism. They are told that they should not be so angry, forceful, or critical. They are told that if they just calmly advocated through the "proper channels," change would come. Yet, these deceptions have been disproven time and again. Comforting those in power often encourages the systemic harm and the status quo. Sometimes, confrontation is needed, even if confrontation alone will not bring about sustained, authentic change. Furthermore, placing more expectations upon marginalized groups in the form of expecting them to conform to the preferred approach to communication of the people in power—often while repressing their own pain and anger—is one more form of oppression and control. This repression can lead to negative physical and psychological consequences.

Conversations about multiculturalism and diversity are complex and uncomfortable for good reason. But if people are not willing to courageously venture into the uncomfortable conversations, it is unlikely that change will occur. Comfort protects the privileged.

Humanistic Approaches to Multiculturalism and Diversity is focused primarily on the therapeutic context, so the reader may be wondering why the introduction expounds on broader considerations of social change. In the end, it is not possible to separate the need for social change from the therapeutic context. The excessive focus on the individual and dispositional causations along with the minimization of social and systemic influences has been one of the greatest limitations of humanistic psychology. It is not that the focus on the individual is bad, but rather the focus on the individual to the neglect of the social, cultural, and systemic influences is an oversimplification of the human condition and experience. To embrace multiculturalism, it is necessary to recast humanistic psychology in a broader framework that considers the individual, the collective, and the system in ways that recognize and honor all these dimensions of the human experience. If therapists comfort their clients who experience prejudice, discrimination, and microaggressions in the therapy room while remaining unwilling to speak out against systemic forms of oppression, then they are not embracing the fullness of humanity in the therapy room. While the therapy room often is not the place to engage in debate and advocacy about multicultural issues, if being a therapist is reduced to what is done during the 50-minute hour then this is not a holistic psychology.

We are advocating that therapists must sharpen their multicultural competencies in the therapy room while also deepening their awareness of how social, cultural, and systemic issues impact their clients beyond the therapy office. Furthermore, we are suggesting that one cannot be multiculturally competent or proficient without engaging in advocacy and/or activism beyond the therapy room. To separate these is similar to the reductionism that humanistic psychology has stood against. In this book, we are asking readers to holistically look at the bigger picture. However, there is not one path that therapists need to take. For some, it may be engaging in protests while for others it may be educating people about multiculturalism or seeking out the type of conversations in the public sphere that may lead to positive social change.

We do not intend for this to be a comfortable book. Most readers will likely find some discomfort and points of disagreement in the book. However, we do not intend for it to be an attack on anyone either, including those who have been resistant to or struggling with multiculturalism and diversity. Rather, we hope that others will be willing to join with the editors and contributors in courageous conversations intended to help transform humanistic psychology and positively impact the world.

The Story of This Book

Humanistic Approaches to Multiculturalism and Diversity has been ten years in the making since we first began conversations about this book. In many ways, it is advantageous that the book has been slow in development. When we first began planning this book and recruiting authors, there was limited scholarship on multicultural perspectives in humanistic and existential psychology. Since then, this has changed. A good portion of the contemporary dialogues on multiculturalism began at the Society for Humanistic Psychology's Annual Conference, and gradually began emerging in the scholarly literature. Today, multicultural perspectives in humanistic psychology are beginning to thrive and there is a more solid basis for the scholarship represented in chapters included.

This book is divided into three parts. Part I focuses on the history and challenges of the multicultural movement in humanistic psychology. In many ways, the seeds for this book were planted in conversations that led to Chapter 2. Geneva Reynaga-Abiko, the author of Chapter 2, discusses her initial draw to humanistic psychology in graduate school followed by disillusionment when she began engaging the broader humanistic community. As a Latina psychologist, she did not find the home in humanistic psychology that she hoped would exist. In Chapter 3, Dan Hocoy provides a critique of humanistic psychology from a multicultural perspective. Unlike Reynaga-Abiko, Hocoy continues to identify with humanistic psychology, but also recognizes its limitations. A foundation of cultural competencies includes self-awareness and self-reflection rooted in cultural humility, which allows one to recognize their own biases as well as their limitations. The only way to write an authentic book on humanistic psychology and multiculturalism is to begin with an honest account of the past mistakes and current limitations. Chapters 2 and 3 are an important starting point in acknowledging humanistic psychology's problematic history.

Next, Theopia Jackson discusses the history of Black psychology and humanistic psychology in Chapter 4. Jackson has been emerging as a forceful voice in the leadership of humanistic psychology, challenging many of the barriers to a deeper embracing of multicultural perspectives. As noted in the outset of the chapter, Black psychology emerged concurrently, but separately, from humanistic psychology. Furthermore, while Black psychology frequently cites humanistic psychology, humanistic psychology has tended to neglect the scholarship of Black psychology, which continues today (Jackson, 2012, see also Chapter 4). In Chapter 5, Alan Vaughan explores sociopolitical issues with emphasis on the relevance of the history of social justice issues in the legal system and the Universal Declaration of Human Rights. This connects humanistic psychology to national and international trends and resources for considering the implications of a foundation of human dignity and social justice.

In Part II, the focus shifts to foundational issues relevant to cultural competencies. Each of these chapters includes a focus on mainstream perspectives as well as humanistic perspectives. Chapter 6 by Lisa Vallejos and Zonya Johnson focuses on cultural competencies. Johnson (2001) wrote the first article exploring cultural competency and humanistic psychology, which, sadly, has received limited attention in humanistic scholarship. Chapter 6 considers cultural competencies in the context of current humanistic and multicultural practice.

Chapters 7 and 8 focus on two of the more controversial topics in multicultural psychology today. First, Nathaniel Granger discusses microaggressions from a humanistic perspective. Microaggressions can be considered "the new racism," and represent unconscious and sometimes unintentional forms of racism that are pervasive in much of contemporary society. Granger provides a foundation for understanding microaggressions as well as guides on how to respond to them in a humanistic context. In Chapter 8, Michael Moats discusses White privilege. Privilege is frequently misunderstood and increasingly is a lightning rod for conflict. Moats provides a sympathetic understanding of White privilege that honors the importance of recognizing privilege while also warning of the dangers of using privilege as a weapon that may further polarize many individuals along racial and ethnic lines. While the chapter focuses specifically on White privilege, Moats approaches the chapter in a manner that encourages individuals to explore other forms of privilege, such as male privilege and Christian privilege.

The next two chapters focus on unique humanistic cultural competencies. In Chapter 9, Louis Hoffman discusses culture and empathy. He begins by clarifying the concept of empathy, including how it is often understood differently in humanistic psychology as compared to mainstream and psychoanalytic perspectives. Next, he discusses an inclusive humanistic approach to empathy that is more culturally sensitive than earlier conceptions while also considering the challenges to empathy across cultural groups. In Chapter 10, Heatherlyn Cleare-Hoffman, Louis Hoffman, and Jane Perlstein consider cultural myths, rituals, and festivals as a resource for culturally diverse clients, including consideration of Junkanoo as a Bahamian cultural festival and myth. This chapter builds from the framework of Rollo May's (1991) work on myth, which recognized myth as a foundational source of meaning. Cleare-Hoffman and colleagues build from May's ideas to include cultural rituals and festivals understood as embodied myths that carry memory and meaning.

Part II concludes with Chapter 11 by David St. John, and reviews the historical context of the current ecological and social crises facing the United States and the world. The identification of how traditional science's insistence on a detached, objective perspective contributes to our ecological and social predicament is highlighted. The need for psychology to integrate a humanistic and humanitarian ethics into its core, and for psychologists to openly advocate for psychological, social, and ecological justice for all, is promoted.

Part III shifts to focusing on specific applications, building upon the foundations set in the first two sections. Chapter 12 by Louise Sundararajan considers the place of indigenous psychology in multicultural discussions. Sundararajan established the Indigenous Psychology Task Force of the Society for Humanistic Psychology, which seeks to identify and advance indigenous perspectives that are often in conflict with the dominant Western perspectives on psychology. Indigenous psychology often is connected with international psychology; however, it is important that it is not reduced to being just another facet of international psychology or multicultural psychology. Rather, indigenous psychology provides a framework to critique the whole of psychology—including humanistic psychology, multicultural psychology, and international psychology—while recognizing, appreciating, and advancing unique psychologies of various indigenous groups.

Chapter 13 by Sara Bridges and Christina New considers issues of sexuality, including sexual identity and expression. The chapter addresses different forms of sexual expression as well as different gender and sexual identities. In Chapter 14, Juliet Rohde-Brown addresses one of the most neglected forms of diversity: disability. Too often, disability is seen as a specialty within psychology instead of recognizing it as an aspect of diversity. Next, Myrtle

Heery discusses aging from a humanistic perspective in Chapter 15. As baby boomers age, there is a larger population of older adults coming to therapy. Many clinicians are unprepared to work with these clients and the unique issues they sometimes bring with them, such as facing the end of one's life.

Another neglected form of diversity, religious and spiritual diversity, is considered by Drake Spaeth in Chapter 16. Even though religion and spirituality are commonly identified as aspects of diversity, religious and spiritual diversity often are not part of courses or books on multiculturalism. This may, in part, be due to the many different forms of religious and spiritual diversity that could easily be a course or book themselves. Spaeth discusses a more general framework for working with religious and spiritual diversity. This section closes with Chapter 17 on intersectionality by Joel Federman. Intersectionality recognizes that multiculturalism becomes more complex when considering how the various forms of diversity intersect. The discussion of intersectionality emphasizes that the topics and themes considered throughout this book cannot be understood in isolation. Instead, it is necessary to look at how the focus of all the different chapters in this book interact with each other. Federman considers both the challenges and opportunities within intersectionality.

We are pleased that two luminaries in humanistic psychology, Kirk Schneider and Ilene Serlin, contributed a Foreword and Afterword. Schneider, as noted by Jackson (2012), for many years was the name that most frequently emerged when searching the academic databases for multiculturalism and humanistic psychology. Many of these were his editorial introductions to the *Journal of Humanistic Psychology*, rather than his own scholarship, which reflects his role in inviting multicultural perspectives into the academic humanistic dialogues. Serlin, as noted previously, was one of the early voices advocating for multicultural and feminist perspectives in humanistic psychology and continues to be a leading voice advocating for diversity. Additionally, she has been instrumental in encouraging the recognition of important, neglected contributions of female humanistic psychologists. In her epilogue, Serlin reminds us of the early potential of humanistic psychology to be a voice in advocating for diversity and suggests a return to some of the roots of humanistic psychology may help actualize humanistic psychology's valuing of diversity.

Conclusion

We have many hopes and dreams for *Humanistic Approaches to Multiculturalism and Diversity*, but most importantly we hope that this book serves as the beginning of a conversation and a foundation for future scholarship. We recognize that humanistic psychology is late to joining this conversation, and that dialogues and language within multicultural psychology are rapidly evolving. What reflects cultural sensitivity today may be seen as naïve and short-sighted in the future, even the near future.

It is more valuable to view any important work in psychology as a stepping stone forward rather than the final word. We hope this book will be an important stepping stone for advancing humanistic conversations on multiculturalism and diversity. As this is a large, complex topic, no singular book can cover all the important topics, or cover them in sufficient depth. Thus, this book is best used as a starting point to delve more deeply into these and other related topics.

While humanistic psychology has come a long way in consideration of multicultural issues, it is vital that this conversation does not become stagnant and that humanistic psychology remains intentional about being inclusive. The book was designed so that it could serve as a multicultural textbook, including covering foundational concepts in multicultural psychology while also being relevant to professionals in the field seeking to strengthen their multicultural competencies. Therefore, we have approached this book in a manner that has broad appeal and does not assume that readers have a foundation in multicultural issues in psychology.

Since we first began work on this book, much has changed. Racial tensions have grown and there has been a significant increase in hate incidents and hate crimes (McCarthy, 2018). There is regression from some of the progress that had been made on multicultural issues in the United States. Yet, where these regressions have occurred there is also opportunity. The prevalence of prejudice, discrimination, and microaggressions is hard to deny in contemporary culture. The depth of the challenges encountered in the United States is increasingly evident. While this is painful to witness, it has helped make the *invisible visible* (see Chapter 7) and provided a clearer picture of contemporary realities. A starting point for authentic change begins from an honest appraisal of the current situation.

In multicultural psychology, there have been important advancements and challenges as well. The early waves of multicultural psychology tended to emphasize knowledge about cultures rather than skills and competencies in working with difference. This has evolved to a focus on multicultural competencies; however, this language has been misused. At times, multicultural competencies are viewed as something that one can attain through a course of study, while at other times they are used to justify the limited number of mental health practitioners who are people of color (Theopia Jackson, personal communication, March 6, 2019). It is important to recognize that cultural competencies are not something that one ever attains or masters; it is an ongoing process that requires continual reflection and growth. Comas-Diaz (2016) notes that, "instead of knowing facts, multicultural clinicians focus on understanding significant processes that occur during therapeutic encounters" (p. 163). A foundation of all cultural competencies is cultural humility, which represent a recognition that therapists never can be fully culturally competent. Rather, therapists need to remain intentional about reflections and learning, including about the evolving language in multicultural psychology. Mastering this book—and for that matter any book or collection of books—does not make one culturally competent. Instead, it represents a humble starting point or step in a lifelong journey of openness, introspection, and learning.

We have updated the language and added some concepts from when we first began writing this book. At the outset of the book, we focused on the language of *multicultural competency*. While this remains a focus, we have shifted the language from *multicultural competency* to *multicultural competencies*, and we have been more intentional about inclusion of the concept of cultural humility as a foundation. While cultural humility is sometimes pitted against the idea of cultural competency, consistent with Comas-Diaz (2016), we see it as foundational to any discussion of multicultural competency or competencies. The shift from the singular (competency) to the plural (competencies) is intended to emphasize that there is not a singular accomplishment that a practitioner attains to be multiculturally competent. The knowledge, skills, and attitudes are many and constantly expanding and evolving.

The idea of cultural humility is not new (Tervalon & Murray-García, 1998); however, as the discussion of multicultural competency/competencies evolves, it is has become more essential to emphasize this as a foundation of multicultural practice. In our view, *cultural humility is foundational to all multicultural competencies*. In their seminal article on cultural humility, Tervalon and Murray-García describe cultural humility in the following way: "Cultural humility incorporates a lifelong commitment to self-evaluation and critique, to redressing the power imbalances in the physician–patient dynamic, and to developing mutually beneficial and non-paternalistic partnerships with communities on behalf of individuals and defined populations" (p. 123). For many, cultural humility is implicit and essential to any discussion of multicultural competency/competencies; however, it is important that it becomes more explicit in these discussions to prevent the reduction or misuse of these concepts.

These evolutions in the language in multicultural psychology have lessons that are important to keep in mind as a framework for engaging this field. It is important to remain aware of how concepts can be misused and distorted—intentionally or unintentionally—in ways that can be detrimental to the mental health field and the people we serve. Second, this illustrates that there are good reasons for the evolving language. For some, the changing language can be tiring. It may even discourage some from trying to keep up with the current language. While sometimes it is best to retain the language and advocate for a deeper, evolving understanding of the concept, at other times the language has been compromised to where it has caused too much pain and harm to be redeemed. We believe that, at the time of this writing, *cultural competencies* can be redeemed, particularly through being more explicit about the incorporation of cultural humility and the recognition that cultural competencies are not a singular knowledge base or skill that one masters. However, this may change in the future.

Engaging in the construction of a book like this is a powerful process. We have learned much from the conversations and dialogues that have been part of the journey, and we are deeply thankful not only to the contributors, but to many others who have been part of the conversations that helped shape this book. We look forward to the many conversations—including the courageous and uncomfortable conversations—that we hope will continue.

References

Boatright-Horowitz, S. L., & Soeung, S. (2009). Teaching White privilege to White students can mean saying good-bye to positive student evaluations. *American Psychologist, 64*, 574–575.

Byock, G., Ellis, S., Falk, J., Godsey, M. L., Hoffman, L., O'Neill, J., Paige, J., Rathsack, J., Silveira, D., Sipes, G. S., Wamsley, D., Whitaker, A., & Vu, T. (2018, August). *Key authors and texts in humanistic psychology.* Poster presented at the 126th Annual Convention of the American Psychological Association, San Francisco, CA.

Comas-Diaz, L. (2016). Multicultural therapy. In H. S. Friedman (Ed.), *Encyclopedia of mental health* (2nd ed., pp. 163–168). Waltham, MA: Academic Press.

Grogan, J. (2013). *Encountering America: Humanistic psychology, sixties culture, and the shaping of the modern self.* New York, NY: Harper Perennial.

Hoffman, L. (2016). Multiculturalism and humanistic psychology: From neglect to epistemological and ontological diversity. *The Humanistic Psychologist, 44*, 56–71.

Hoffman, L., Cleare-Hoffman, H. P., & Jackson, T. (2014). Humanistic psychology and multiculturalism: History, current status, and advancements. In K. J. Schneider, J. F. Pierson & J. F. T. Bugental (Eds.), *The handbook of humanistic psychology: Theory, research, and practice* (2nd ed., pp. 41–55). Thousand Oaks, CA: Sage.

Hoffman, L., Granger, N. Jr., & O'Neill, J. (2019, March). *An existential–humanistic foundation for activism and social justice: Social, political, and clinical applications.* Paper presented at the 12th Annual Society for Humanistic Psychology Conference, Corvallis, OR.

Hoffman, L., Serlin, I. D., & Rubin, S. (2019). The history of existential–humanistic integrative psychology. In E. van Duerzen, K. Schneider, E. Craig, A. Langle, & D. Tatum (Eds.), *Wiley world handbook of existential therapy* (pp. 235–246). Hoboken, NJ: Wiley.

Jackson, T. (2012, March). *The tale of two cities: Humanistic psychology within a cultural context.* In L. Hoffman (Chair), *The collective and the individual in humanistic psychology: Implications of moving beyond the individualist bias.* Symposium presented at the 5th Annual Society of Humanistic Psychology Conference, Pittsburgh, PA.

Johnson, Z. (2001). Cultural competency and humanistic psychology. *The Humanistic Psychologist, 29*, 204–222.

May, R. (1991). *The cry for myth.* New York, NY: Delta.

McCarthy, N. (2018, November 14). FBI: hate crimes have increased for the third straight year. Forbes. Retrieved from: www.forbes.com/sites/niallmccarthy/2018/11/14/fbi-hate-crimes-have-increased-for-the-third-year-straight-info graphic/#6434fd641701

O'Hara, M. (1997). Relational empathy: Beyond modernism egocentricism to postmodern holistic contextualism. In A. C. Bohart, & L. S. Greenberg (Eds.), *Empathy reconsidered: New directions in psychotherapy* (pp. 295–319). Washington, DC: American Psychological Association.

Paige, J., Byock, G., Ellis, S., Falk, J., Godsey, M. L., Hoffman, L., O'Neill, J., Rathsack, J., Silveira, D., Sipes, G. S., Wamsley, D., Whitaker, A., & Vu, T. (2018, August). *Who practices humanistic psychology? Clarifying demographics.* Poster presented at the 126th Annual Convention of the American Psychological Association, San Francisco, CA.

Tervalon, M., & Murray-Garćia, J. (1998). Cultural humility versus cultural competency: A critical distinction in defining physical training outcomes in multicultural education. *Journal of Health Care for the Poor and Underserved, 9*(2), 117–125.

2 Why I Left Humanistic Psychology

Geneva Reynaga-Abiko

It's 1998. I am taking my first humanistic psychology course as a master's student with one of my favorite professors, Dr. David Elkins. I love it. I feel seen by Dr. Elkins. Fast forward to 2002. I am now a third-year doctoral student and finishing up my degree with a year-long course in Humanistic/ Existential Psychology, again with Dave Elkins. I love it. I regularly incorporate Viktor Frankl and Martin Buber in my work with clients. I do not question, or even think about, why all of the people we are reading are men of European descent as I feel very welcomed and supported not only by Dave Elkins but by my multicultural classmates in general.

Then I progress onto internship and complete my doctorate, leaving the protective bubble of my private graduate institution. I remain on various humanistic listservs and start attending conferences with others who identify with this particular form of psychology. Why is everyone European American? Why are they only talking about things from an upper class, European American perspective? Where do I, a Latina Muslim originally from a lower socioeconomic background who just happens to be a radical feminist multiculturalist practicing a blend of intersubjective-psychodynamic-humanistic psychology, fit in? Where is the critical consciousness I remembered from my classmates in graduate school? Why have I suddenly become invisible?

I experienced this several times before finally realizing that I just did not feel like I fit into the humanistic psychology circles available in the early 2000s. This took me some time to realize because every person I met in these spaces was very kind and open-minded. The conversations went just fine as long as we stayed to topics they could understand: unconditional positive regard, accepting people for who they are, and working in an authentic and congruent fashion with our clients. What about the difficulty of maintaining unconditional positive regard if you are experiencing racism in the room, or the effects of a legacy of racism? What about the arrogance of the tolerance model, which implies that one merely tolerate but not necessarily question systematic and historic oppressions, particularly for those people who have been otherized and ostracized in clinical and counseling psychology? How does one maintain an authentic relationship with a client if they are unintentionally offending the client by being ignorant of salient cultural factors present in the room? Ultimately, it was the prevailing opinion that there was no need to focus on issues of diversity because everyone was accepted as an individual, that ended up pushing me out. I felt like the values of my collectivistic cultures had no place here.

To be fair, I do not believe that anyone intended this to be the case. It is my opinion, with all due respect, that their own privileged social identities prevented these very caring people from understanding the impact on a person whose identities were not considered of the majority in the United States. Over time I realized that I simply did not fit in with this crowd. Their reality was not my reality. Their history was not my history. I could not pretend that the struggles and traumas related to my intersubjectivity could be squished into one box that unconditional positive regard could magically heal. I could not accept the apparent lack of critical consciousness in humanistic psychology.

So I left. I found a way to get my own needs met by reading and re-reading old favorites of multicultural feminist work that was incredibly human-centered and authentic (e.g., *This Bridge Called My Back* (Moraga & Anzaldua, 2015), *Haciendo Caras* (Anzaldua, 1990), and anything by Gloria Anzaldua, Aida Hurtado, Hope Landrine, Lillian Comas-Diaz, bell hooks, or Alice Walker). In fact, there was an incredible thing happening in the feminist multiculturalist movement wherein many writers were becoming more humanistic. I maintained my friendship with old favorites (e.g., Frankl, Buber) and was happy to add perspectives to these concepts that spoke so powerfully to the center of my being.

At this time, it is the mid-2000s and many people of color are gaining interest in humanistic psychology. I am aware that there is work presented and published that attempts to expand humanistic psychology. I appreciate this and want to get more involved but am nervous to open myself up to the same experience as before. Ultimately, the realities of a busy personal and professional life keep me from fully exploring the emerging possibilities.

In 2013, I am invited to be one of the keynote speakers at the Sixth Annual Society for Humanistic Psychology Conference and accept with nervous excitement, wondering what I can say to a group I had spent nearly ten years away from. The experience proved reminiscent of my graduate school years, enjoying time with old friends and having fun making new ones. There is still a dominant-culture feel to the conference, although I see additional glimmers of hope that we may expand our perspectives, communication styles, and values to begin to approach a social justice perspective. There are more people of color than I ever saw in previous humanistic gatherings, even though we are in the highly affluent area of Santa Barbara, California. I feel seen. I leave the conference with hope and a promise to the members to re-join.

I love the ideals of humanistic psychology. I have always believed in its unique power to positively transform the deepest of human struggles. I want to come back. I want to be seen. When will I feel included? When will I see mirrors of even some of my identities in its theories and texts? I hope soon.

References

Anzaldua, G. (Ed.). (1990). *Making face, making soul/Haciendo caras: Creative and critical perspectives by feminists of color*. San Francisco, CA: Aunt Lute Books.

Moraga, C., & Anzaldua, G. (Eds.). (2015). *This bridge called by back: Writings by radical women of color* (4th ed.). Albany, NY: SUNY Press.

3   The Challenge of Multiculturalism to Humanistic Psychology

Dan Hocoy

As existential–humanistic psychology became prominent in the mid-20th century largely as a departure from both psychoanalytic and behaviorist movements, it became known as the third force or wave in psychology (e.g., Benjafield, 2010). With its emphasis on human potential, creativity, and wholeness, existential–humanistic psychology was considered a fresh approach to human experience and behavior at the time. Today, however, there is considerable literature questioning the continued relevance of this third force (e.g., Diaz-Laplante, 2007; Hanks, 2008) in the contemporary context. The criticisms concern new understandings of the role of culture in human experience and concepts of the self. Kvale (1999) argued that "humanistic psychology (has) remained outside the postmodern discourse" (p. 45) in which knowledge is inherently ambiguous, perspectival, and open. Others have challenged the universality of some of the assumptions, values, and tenets of existential–humanistic psychology (e.g., Waterhouse, 1993).

The applicability and continued relevance of existential–humanistic psychology in light of the insights of multicultural psychology presents some significant challenges, challenges that are especially pertinent today, given the dramatically changing demographics of the United States (U.S. Bureau of the Census, 2011) and projections of further diversification in the U.S. population as well as in almost every country in the world.

The Fourth Force: Multicultural Psychology

Paul Pedersen (1999) among many others argued that multiculturalism is the "fourth force" in psychology, which represents a fundamental paradigm shift in the way we think about human experience and behavior. Culture is broadly defined by Pedersen (1999) as "any and all potentially salient ethnographic, demographic, status, or affiliation identities" (p. 3), which thus includes race, ethnicity, spirituality, language, sexual orientation, physical issues, age, socioeconomic status and any group that share an affiliation for some common aspect of identification. Multicultural psychology is defined as the systematic study of human behavior as it takes place in settings in which individuals of different cultural backgrounds interact or have contact with one another (e.g., Bochner, 1999). Multicultural psychology has grown in prominence with the growing recognition that diversity characterizes the human condition and as the populations in most of the world's countries have experienced a rapidly increasing diversification, due to economic globalization and various migration forces. The central assertion of multicultural psychology is that all aspects of human behavior are learned and expressed in a cultural context and, to comprehensively and accurately understand a person's experience or behavior, it is necessary to understand the cultural context.

As an application of multicultural psychology to the clinical setting, Sue, Ivey, and Pedersen (1996) proposed some basic assumptions of multicultural counseling and therapy. Chief assumptions assert that therapist and client identities are formed and embedded in multiple levels of biopsychosocial experiences and contexts. These identities then shape attitudes toward oneself and others, and are impacted by cultural status dynamics. They posit that the efficacy of therapy is enhanced when the therapist uses modalities and defines goals consistent with the client's life experiences and cultural values, and that there are multiple helping roles involving social units beyond the one-on-one dyad. Their approach emphasizes an expansion of consciousness that is contextual in orientation and draws from traditional healing practices from many cultures. The paradigm shift offered by multicultural psychology is evidenced by the various divisions of the American Psychological Association (APA) that are now concerned with diversity issues (Divisions 9, 17, 27, 35, 36, 44, 45, 48, and 51). As well, APA's Ethical Principles of Psychologists and Code of Conduct (APA, 2002) now contain a General Principle E that recommends that psychologists

> are aware of and respect cultural, individual, and role differences, including those based on age, gender, gender identity, race, ethnicity, culture, national origin, religion, sexual orientation, disability, language, and socioeconomic status, and consider these factors when working with members of such groups. Psychologists try to eliminate the effect on their work of biases based on those factors, and they do not knowingly participate in or condone activities of others based upon such prejudices.
>
> (p. 1063)

The APA also issued Guidelines on Multicultural Education, Training, Research, Practice, and Organizational Change for Psychologists (2003) that reflects the skills, knowledge, and attitudes required by psychologists in all areas of the field to competently work in a culturally diverse society. It is clear from just the impact of multicultural psychology on APA that Pedersen (1999) is correct in his claim that it is the true fourth force or wave in the field of psychology.

The Multicultural Critique of Existential–Humanistic Psychology

The critique inherent in multicultural psychology suggests that the theory, research, and practice of any orientation in Western psychology has the potential to perpetuate Western cultural dominance and even imperialism. The experiences, behaviors, and conceptualizations of other cultures have often been characterized as pathological or otherwise neglected or marginalized. The legacy of a "monocultural universalism" (Fowers & Richardson, 1996, p. 609) undermines the validity of any orientation in Western psychology that has failed to recognize this ethnocentric bias.

Culture Bound and Culture Blind

Although existential–humanistic psychology was explicitly developed with the intention of human emancipation and may be less culture bound than other psychological perspectives, it remains inescapably limited by its cultural and historical context (Hoffman, Cleare-Hoffman, & Jackson, 2014). Its approach derives from a specific set of cultural constructions, assumptions, and values that are uniquely Euro-American in origin. Existential–humanistic psychology inevitably reflects, perpetuates, and privileges a particular "cultural worldview" (Ibrahim, 1991, p. 13). An awareness and recognition of its cultural underpinnings is critical for it to recognize the limitations of its applicability to individuals of different cultural backgrounds (Yang & Hoffman, 2014). Existential–humanistic psychology may be culture bound, but it cannot afford to be culture blind.

The consequences of being culture blind may be especially serious for the applications of an existential–humanistic approach in clinical practice (e.g., Johnson, 2001). An existential–humanistic therapist that is culture blind treats all clients the same, without consideration of their cultural background. This culture blindness could result in the therapist misinterpreting or ignoring critical information in the assessment and treatment of an individual of another cultural origin, leading potentially to the mistreatment of the individual. A culture blind therapist may be working outside his or her area of competence when working with a client from another culture (Acton, 2001), and thus potentially unethical, as he or she may unknowingly serve as an agent of Euro-American cultural assimilation (Gerity, 2000) or cultural malpractice.

Critique of Existential–Humanistic Constructs

Do the existential–humanistic constructs of "actualization," "wholeness," or "self" have the same meaning or relevance for someone from another culture? Is the presumption of individuality valid or valued by someone from another culture? Is individual psychotherapy as an enterprise culturally congruent with someone from another culture? Since cultures may have different ways of organizing, prioritizing, and experiencing human phenomena, these constructs, assumptions, and values of existential–humanistic psychology cannot be assumed to be universal.

Cross-cultural research has demonstrated that various constructions specific to Western cultures may not have any correspondence in other cultures. For instance, Markus and Kitayama (1991) have shown that many of the constructs assumed in existential–humanistic psychotherapy may not even exist in Asian cultures; as an example, the concept of "self-esteem," which has meaning within an individualistic society in the West, does not have validity or the same meaning in a collectivistic society (like Japan) in the East. Similarly, the concepts of "self" and "free will" are predicated on a Euro-American individualistic paradigm and may not have the same meaning or equivalence for other cultures (see Hoffman, Stewart, Warren, & Meek, 2014).

Cross-cultural researchers have determined that for a construct such as "self-actualization" to constitute a universal, "dimensional identity" (Duijker & Frijda, 1960, p. 23) must be established for the construct (Poortinga, 1983). Dimensional identity is established by demonstrating that "self-actualization" has at least *conceptual* and *functional equivalence* in another culture (e.g., Berry & Dasen, 1974; Poortinga & Malpass, 1986). Conceptual equivalence points to the sameness of meaning or understanding of a particular construct (Sears, 1961), while functional equivalence refers to the commonness of purpose the construct serves across cultures (Frijda & Jahoda, 1966). It is quite likely that these criteria for construct equivalence are not fulfilled for various concepts of existential–humanistic psychology. The established research methods of cross-cultural psychology would be useful in formally testing the validity of existential–humanistic constructs in other cultures. For instance, the "forward–backward interpretation technique" (Brislin, 1970, p. 186), could be used to determine whether a particular construct in existential–humanistic psychology is valid in another culture.

Critique of Existential–Humanistic Psychotherapy

Existential–humanistic psychology is probably most celebrated for its clinical applications; the contributions of Maslow and Rogers are still felt today. However, the process and structure found in existential–humanistic psychotherapy may be problematic for individuals of non-Euro-American cultures. For one, psychotherapy itself may not constitute a naturally occurring construct from those in another culture. What then are the implications, ethically and culturally, that its application has for culturally different individuals? Does psychotherapy serve to undermine pre-existing forms of personal and group transformation? Does it serve to displace indigenous or local forms of healing and traditions that are essential for community identity and cultural integrity? Can psychotherapy serve as a tool of Euro-American assimilation or enculturation? As well, the open and unstructured process, which characterizes many existential–humanistic approaches, may lead to anxiety or confusion in some clients of different cultural backgrounds; the context of non-directive and ambiguous psychotherapy may be inconsistent with client expectations. Many clients from Asian, African, and Middle Eastern backgrounds have been found to prefer a more directed and authoritative style with clear and explicit relevance to the presenting problem (e.g., Samuda & Wolfgang, 1985). The process of psychotherapy can be viewed as a style of communication, one that may be foreign or even alienating to individuals of certain cultures. For instance, some clients may feel that one should only address intimate issues with someone with whom they have a close relationship (e.g., Laval, Gomez, & Ruiz, 1983).

A basic philosophical assumption implicit in existential–humanistic psychotherapy is the existence of the autonomous self (e.g., Alladin, 1999). This individualistic orientation may contradict the group orientation or emphasis on independent bonds found in collectivist cultures (e.g., many Asian cultures) (Pedersen, 1988). Since an individual's growth and problem-solving are rooted in familial and societal relationships in these cultures, self-exploration and decision-making based on one's individual desires may be experienced as self-indulgent and a threat to the community's social matrix; therefore, "there may be a great degree of shame and stigma associated with leaving the community and seeking professional help" (Hocoy, 1999a, p. 196). Consequently, the therapeutic goals of existential–humanistic psychotherapy, which are often premised on a value for self-determination, may not apply to individuals from collectivist cultures. For instance, existential–humanistic therapists encourage clients to "come to their own decision" about a life dilemma; however, this may not be desirable for someone from a culture in which the input of family and community are paramount in personal decision-making. An individual that may not embrace such an individualistic approach may be diagnosed pejoratively as not having a strong sense of self or "enmeshed" in his or her family dynamics.

In addition, existential–humanistic psychotherapy may privilege a socioeconomic class of individuals in the United States who can afford this particular type of treatment, one not usually provided or covered by insurance companies. This orientation of intervention, which may exclude many who cannot pay out-of-pocket for prolonged care, is likely to disproportionately impact the culturally different more than individuals in the dominant culture as individuals from minority groups (e.g., Latino Americans, African Americans, Native Americans) are overrepresented in the lower socioeconomic strata of the nation (U.S. Bureau of the Census, 2011). The question needs to be asked whether the expense of existential–humanistic psychotherapy constitutes a financial priority for individuals in the lower socioeconomic strata? Or framed another way: Is existential–humanistic psychotherapy based in the values particular to the middle and upper classes, which have the resources of money and time to pursue Maslow's top tier of self-actualization without concern for meeting basic survival needs?

When Carl Rogers (e.g., 1951, 1961) discussed the factors that were critical to good therapeutic outcomes, he, not unlike others of his generation, neglected the critical role culture plays in psychotherapy. Since his time, evidence from clinical outcome studies as well as client testimony has accumulated, demonstrating that culture does play a significant role. For instance, Ramirez (1991) found that clients generally prefer their therapist to have the same cultural origins. Some cultural factors that impinge on the psychotherapeutic relationship include: congruity between verbal and non-verbal communication (Jenkins, 1982), age or gender as indicators of wisdom or authority (Samuda & Wolfgang, 1985). As well, the client's own history and the therapist's cultural group (and therapist's with the client's) are likely to invoke transference (and countertransference) issues of a cultural nature that will have an impact in psychotherapy. Existential–humanistic approaches to clinical practice could benefit from adopting the recommendations of Sue, Ivey, and Pedersen (1996) for multicultural counselling and psychotherapy.

Degree of Acculturation

Since the cultural identity of an individual is likely to be of therapeutic importance (e.g., Hocoy, 1999a), an assessment of the client's cultural identity or degree of individual acculturation may be required for existential–humanistic psychotherapy to be an appropriate or effective intervention. Acculturation relates to the psychological processes of an individual that take place during cross-cultural contact, which can include: cultural identity, self-esteem, and general mental health, as well as the individual's attitudes toward one's culture of origin relative to attitudes toward the dominant (Euro-American) culture. Redfield, Linton, and Herskovits (1936) formally identified "acculturation" as the cultural change that results from continuous, first-hand contact between two distinct cultural groups. Although the construct was initially proposed as a social phenomenon that took place at the level of a group, it is now commonly recognized as a phenomenon that takes place on the level of the individual (Graves, 1967). J. W. Berry (1998) provides the prevailing framework of understanding acculturation processes in an individual. The framework compares an individual's attitudes toward one's culture of origin relative his or her attitudes toward the dominant culture; it identifies four modes of acculturation (i.e., integration, separation, assimilation, marginalization) based on a person's attitudes towards: a) cultural identity maintenance and b) a relationship with the dominant (e.g., Euro-American) culture. An individual who is in "integration" maintains his or her culture of origin while also fully participating in the dominant culture. An individual in the "separation" mode maintains his or her culture of origin but rejects the dominant culture. Someone in the "assimilation" mode rejects his or her culture of origin and embraces the dominant culture. A person in "marginalization" has lost identification with both his or her culture of origin and the dominant culture (e.g., Hocoy, 1999b). The efficacy and appropriateness of existential–humanistic psychotherapy depends on the individual's mode of acculturation. A person's mode of acculturation can be identified in a variety of ways including the Berry Acculturation Measure (Berry, Kim, Power, Young, & Bujaki, 1989).

The Culturally Sensitive Art Therapist

Art therapy, like its counterpart talk therapy, when practiced across cultures seems at best to be a cautious enterprise. However, there are a few things the art therapist can do to maximize the likelihood of ethical and effective treatment of individuals from non-Euro-American cultures. First, the therapist would benefit from engaging in a rigorous and honest self-examination as to his or her cultural competency. This would involve an awareness of his or her own cultural lens as well as an awareness of the assumptions and values on which theory and technique in art therapy is based. The therapist may have to come to terms with one's own uneasiness with the appearance, smell, non-verbal behaviors, physical proximity, worldviews, accents, or limited English of people of other cultures. Personal work may be necessary with regard to addressing conscious and unconscious attitudes and biases towards diversity and difference.

This awareness is the first step in guarding against the imposition, subtle or otherwise, of dominant culture values and methods, and in cultivating a sensitivity and conscientiousness critical to a socially responsible practice of art therapy. Further steps include continual professional development in multi-cultural competency through reading, workshops, and consultation with members of the community in which the therapist is working. A broad-based knowledge of the culture and fluency in the language from which the client comes as well as an understanding of the culture's historic relationship with the dominant culture are critical factors in establishing rapport and trust (Hocoy, 1999a). An understanding of the community in which the client lives, its resources (e.g., religious organizations), and impinging issues (e.g., interpersonal violence, social problems, etc.) is critical for effective intervention (e.g., Douglas, 1993). An investigation of "if" and "how" art is utilized as a means of psychological healing in the client's culture of origin would also be invaluable (e.g., Acton, 2001). It is important, however, not to make stereotypical overgeneralizations, but rather use knowledge of group differences to merely elucidate an individual's situation, while maintaining an openness to individual variations within the group (Hocoy, 1999a). An idiographic approach that focuses on the client's perspective and personal experiences may be effective in honoring the client's particular cultural worldview and identity (Palmer, 2000).

In terms of actual practice, the art therapist would be prudent to: assess the suitability (e.g., mode of acculturation) of art therapy for the particular client, introduce the purpose and nature of art therapy and the role of the therapist, understand that any individual's artistic expression is rooted in socio-cultural factors, ensure that any assessment used adequately matches the cognitive style and cultural background of the client, take advantage of pre-existing indigenous means of transformation, continually assess his or her role and that of art therapy with that individual and in that community, ensure that art therapy does not serve as a Procrustean bed of enculturation, and be open to art therapy not being the only or best intervention for the client.

Recommendations for the Field

There are many implications for existential–humanistic psychology with respect to the human diversity issues discussed here. The field has experienced many challenges to its continued relevance in the 21st century, however, its ability to address issues of multiculturalism could make existential–humanistic psychology instantly contemporary and relevant. Three recommendations for the field include:

1)   A comprehensive re-examination of the theoretical constructs, assumptions, and values that undergird the existential–humanistic perspective from a cultural and diversity lens. An assessment of the validity and modification or qualification of individual constructs and practices is required before any construct can be applied to any particular culture.

2)   In terms of existential–humanistic psychotherapy, the field needs to evaluate and modify its practices and assumptions in light of the recommendations of Sue, Ivey, and Pedersen (1996) for multicultural counselling and psychotherapy. The existential–humanistic practitioner needs to evaluate his or her own competency to work with the client's particular culture and mode of acculturation as well as the appropriateness or validity of any particular practice or assumption with the individual's cultural background and identification.

3)   A new handbook of existential–humanistic psychology that includes a comprehensive review of the validity and applicability of constructs, assumptions, and values of the field and the subsequent modifications or qualifications required for various cultures.

References

Acton, D. (2001). The color blind therapist. *Art Therapy, 18*, 109–112.

Alladin, W. (1999). Models of counselling and psychotherapy for a multiethnic society. In S. Palmer & P. Laungani (Eds.), *Counselling in a multicultural society* (pp. 90–112). London: Sage Publications.

American Psychological Association. (2002). *Ethical principles of psychologists and Code of Conduct*. Washington, DC: APA.

American Psychological Association (2003). Guidelines on multicultural education, training, research, practice, and organizational change for psychologists. *American Psychologist, 58*(5), 377–402.

Benjafield, J. (2010). *A history of psychology* (3rd edition). Don Mills, ON: Oxford University Press.

Berry, J. W. (1998). Acculturation and health: Theory and research. In S. Kazarian & D. Evans (Eds.), *Cultural clinical psychology* (pp. 39–57). New York, NY: Oxford University Press.

Berry, J. W., & Dasen P. (Eds.) (1974). *Introduction to culture and cognition*. London: Methuen.

Berry, J. W., Kim, U., Power, S., Young, M., & Bujaki, M. (1989). Acculturation attitudes in plural societies. *Applied Psychology: An International Review, 38*, 185–206.

Bochner, S. (1999). Cultural diversity within and between societies: Implications for Multicultural Social Systems. In P. Pedersen (Ed.), *Multiculturalism as a fourth force*. Castleton, NY: Taylor & Francis.

Brislin, R. W. (1970). Back translation for cross-cultural research. *Journal of Cross-Cultural Psychology, 1*, 185–216.

Diaz-Laplante, J. (2007). Humanistic psychology and social transformation: Building the path toward a livable today and a just tomorrow. *Journal of Humanistic Psychology, 47*(1), 54–72.

Douglas, B. C. (1993, August). Psychotherapy with troubled African American adolescent males: Stereotypes, treatment amenability, and clinical issues. *Paper presented at the Annual Meeting of the American Psychological Association*, Toronto, Canada.

Duijker, H. C. J., & Frijda, N. H. (1960). *National character and national stereotypes*. Amsterdam: Noord-Hollandse.

Fowers, B. J., & Richardson, F. C. (1996). Why is multiculturalism good? *American Psychologist, 51*(6), 609–621.

Frijda, N. H. & Jahoda, G. (1966). On the scope and methods of cross-cultural research. *International Journal of Psychology, 1*, 110–127.

Gerity, L. A. (2000). The subsersive art therapist: Embracing cultural diversity in the art room. *Art Therapy, 17*, 202–206.

Graves, P. L. (1967). Psychological acculturation in a tri-ethnic community. *Southwestern Journal of Anthropology, 23*, 337–350.

Hanks, T. (2008). The Ubuntu paradigm: Psychology's next force? *Journal of Humanistic Psychology, 48*(1), 116–135.

Hocoy, D. (1999a). Working with Asian-American clients. In J. V. Diller (Ed.), *Cultural diversity: A primer for human service professionals*(pp. 189–205). Pacific Grove, CA: Brooks/Cole.

Hocoy, D. (1999b). The validity of Cross's model of Black racial identity development in the South African context. *Journal of Black Psychology, 25*, 131–151.

Hoffman, L., Cleare-Hoffman, H. P., & Jackson, T. (2014). Humanistic psychology and multiculturalism: History, current status, and advancements. In K. J. Schneider, J. F. Pierson & J. F. T. Bugental (Eds.), *The handbook of humanistic psychology: Theory, research, and practice* (2nd edition, pp. 41–55). Thousand Oaks, CA: Sage.

Hoffman, L., Stewart, S., Warren, D., & Meek, L. (2014). Toward a sustainable myth of self: An existential response to the postmodern condition. In K. J. Schneider, J. F. Pierson & J. F. T. Bugental (Eds.), *The handbook of humanistic psychology: Theory, research, and practice* (2nd edition, pp. 105–133). Thousand Oaks, CA: Sage.

Ibrahim, F. A. (1991). Contribution of cultural worldview to generic counseling and development. *Journal of Counseling & Development, 70*(1), 13–19.

Jenkins, A. H. (1982). *The psychology of the Afro-American.* New York, NY: Pergamon.

Johnson, Z. (2001). Cultural competency and humanistic psychology. *Humanistic Psychologist, 29,* 204–222.

Kvale, S. (1999). *Psychology and postmodernism.* London: Sage.

Laval, R. A., Gomez, E. A., & Ruiz, P. (1983). A language minority: Hispanics and mental health care. *The American Journal of Social Psychiatry, 3,* 42–49.

Markus, H. R., & Kitayama, S. (1991). Culture and the self: Implications for cognition, emotion, and motivation. *Psychological Review, 98*(2), 224–253.

Palmer, S. (2000). Developing an individual therapeutic program suitable for use by counselling psychologists in a multicultural society: A multimodal perspective. *Counselling Psychology Review, 15,* 32–50.

Pedersen, P. (1988). *A handbook for developing multicultural awareness.* Alexandria, VA: American Association for Counseling and Development Press.

Pedersen, P. (1999). *Multiculturalism as a fourth force.* Castleton, NY: Taylor & Francis.

Poortinga, Y. H. (1983). Psychometric approaches to intergroup comparison: The problem of equivalence. In S. H. Irvine, & J. W. Berry (Eds.), *Human assessment and cultural factors* (pp. 237–257). Boston, MA: Springer.

Poortinga, Y. H. & Malpass, R. S. (1986). Making references from cross-cultural data. In W. J. Lonner & J. W. Berry (Eds.) *Field methods in cross-cultural research* (pp. 17–36). Beverly Hills, CA: Sage.

Ramirez, M. III. (1991). *Psychotherapy and counseling with minorities.* Toronto: Pergamon.

Redfield, R., Linton, R., & Herskovits, M. J. (1936). Memorandum on the study of acculturation. *American Anthropologist, 38,* 149–152.

Rogers, C. R. (1951). *Client-centered therapy: Its current practice, implications and theory.* London: Constable.

Rogers, C. R. (1961). *On becoming a person: A psychotherapist's view of psychotherapy.* Boston, MA: Houghton Mifflin.

Samuda, R. J. & Wolfgang, A. (1985). *Intercultural counselling and assessment.* Toronto: C. J. Hogrefe Publishers.

Sears, R. R. (1961). Transcultural variables and conceptual equivalence. In B. Kaplan (Ed.) *Studying personality cross-culturally* (pp. 445–456). New York, NY: Row & Peterson Press.

Sue, D. W., Ivey, A. E., & Pedersen, P. (1996). *A theory of multicultural counseling and therapy* (A Clairemont book). Pacific Grove, CA: Brooks/Cole Pub.

U.S. Bureau of the Census (2011). *Population projections of the United States by age, sex, race, and Hispanic origin: 2000 to 2050.* (Current Population Reports P25-1002). Washington, DC: U.S. Government Printing Office.

Waterhouse, R. L. (1993). "Wild women don't have the blues": A feminist critique of "person-centered" counselling and therapy. *Feminism & Psychology, 3*(1), 55–71.

Yang, M., & Hoffman, L. (2014, August). *Training and practice in an international context.* In C. N. Shealy (Chair), International humanistic psychology: Implications and applications for research and practice. Symposium presented at the 122nd Annual Convention of the American Psychological Association, Washington, DC.

4 The History of Black Psychology and Humanistic Psychology

Synergetic Prospects

Theopia Jackson

It is relevant to position this chapter as a professional narrative intended to engage the reader in one clinician's journey of becoming a Black humanistic psychologist. This distinction is situated in an epiphany that emerged for me as a 4th year graduate student during a community meeting at the Wright Institute in Berkeley, California. This meeting was the culmination of increased unrest among predominantly European American students who were critical of an African American professor (one of only two in the program) for securing funding from the Institute to host monthly get-togethers for students of color. The primary criticism was that such an initiative was divisive and exclusionary; the same criticism that often can be heard today in various contexts. It was perplexing to note that these same colleagues presented clinical case material where they advocated for the benefits of their clients of color to attend ethnically representative self-esteem groups to augment their therapy; as if the colleagues were recognizing that their clients of color needed something more than what they as European Americans or their psychology could afford them. This phenomenon certainly mirrored my experience of not recognizing myself in my education/training, nor the experiences of those I know from Black communities, in the constant problem-saturated theories pertaining to Black folks. It was as if something about my blackness was being portrayed as less than and/or discounted and that I was being socialized into thinking about blackness through someone else's lens and the story was not favorable (internalized racism). The *Father of Pan-Africanism*, Dubois (1903), boldly articulated the experience of double-consciousness in his seminal publication, *The Souls of Black Folk*;

> It is a peculiar sensation, this double-consciousness, this sense of always looking at one's self through the eyes of others, of measuring one's soul by the tape of a world that looks on in amused contempt and pity. One ever feels his [their] twoness,—an American, a Negro; two souls, two thoughts, two unreconciled strivings; two warring ideals in one dark body, whose dogged strength alone keeps it from being torn asunder.
>
> (p. 13)

It became apparent that Western (Eurocentric) psychology could teach me to be an effective clinical psychologist yet could not teach me to be an effective *Black* psychologist. More was needed for me to make peace with my stepping into a field that historically (arguably, does so today) played a role in the oppression experienced by many Black folks, as evidenced by the plethora of "science" that perpetuated the inferiority model or deficit/deficiency model (Cokley, Palmer, & Stone, 2019; Jones, 2004; Robinson, 2012) and other scholarship that placed Blacks at the top of any bad list and the bottom of any good one, with no attention to the contributions of social situations.

In my professional impressionable state as a clinician-in-training, I knew that this duality was detrimental to my spirit (sense of self), as well as to those I planned to serve. I needed to actively seek out scholarship to counter this psychological assault. With this intention, like many other Black peers in predominately White institutions (PWIs), I stayed the course (not rocking the boat) in satisfying educational expectations and actively sought out teachings in Black psychology to help reconcile the internal struggle and give scholarly voice to speaking cultural truth. Upon reflection, this experience illuminated that what I had taken for granted in my undergraduate and master level training at Howard University in Washington, DC, a historical black college/university (HBCU). There I was critically exposed to dominate Western (Eurocentric) psychology through a culturally affirming lens of Black psychology that inoculated me against such psychological assaults and armed me with cultural critical thinking. It was also at Howard University where I was introduced to humanistic psychology, the same theoretical stance that my Wright Institute colleagues proclaimed informed their practice despite their resistance to affording their colleagues similar spaces. Carl Rogers's (1961, 1980) positing of humanistic psychology as a means for self-determination and person-centered liberation was inspiring as it renewed the potential for locating myself in the profession. Finally, this was a voice from within the academy that resonated with my spirit. Additionally, it was further reaffirming to draw upon the work of Adlebert Jenkins' (2005), the most acclaimed Black humanistic psychologist, and his heartfelt narrative for integrating his cultural-ness with his humanistic sense of self. In this chapter, in the legacy of Jenkins, I provide a brief history of the parallel and divergent processes of Black psychology (BP) and humanistic psychology (HP), consider the integration of tenets of multiculturalism into humanistic psychology, and humbly contribute to the future generations of Black (as well as other professionals of color) humanistic scholar-practitioners and cultural allies.

History of Black Psychology

The inception of Black psychology was sparked by the social issues of the times, including the civil unrest of the '60s, where many social science Black professionals were taking their disciplines to task regarding accountability for social change and cessation of perpetuating the problems. During the 1968 American Psychologist Association (APA) conference in San Francisco, California, a group of Black professionals and graduate students indicted APA with promoting the White racist character of United States (U.S.) society and failing to provide models and programs conducive to the solving of African American problems stemming from the oppressive effects of U.S. racism (Williams, 1974). Grogan (2008, 2013) provides a detailed account of the behind the scenes racist commentary that ensued from APA leadership. In response to APA's apathy, resistance, and hostility, many Black psychologists walked out of the conference, denounced their membership, and secluded themselves in deep discussion, contemplating the plight of Black Americans; the inherent institutional racism that informed their education, training, and research; the lack of representation in the field; and the desperate need for a paradigm shift. The outcome was the founding of the Association of Black Psychologists, Inc. (ABPsi) and the recognition of the formidable task of establishing scholarship centered in Black reality (Williams, 1974). These professionally diverse scholars strategically embarked on articulating what it meant to be healthy and whole from a culturally centered perspective. Nobles (2015) succinctly identified the scholar-warriors credited with the first two decades, culminating with the delineation of an African worldview, tenets of Black psychology, and African cosmology:

> During the next two decades, several Black psychologists, for example, King, Dixon, and Nobles (1976); Akbar (1984, 1990); Azibo (1989); Hilliard (1986); Nobles (1972, 1986a, 1986b, 1997); Myers (1988); Kambon (1992); Wilson (1993); Grills and Rowe (1998 joined in the excavating of African ideas as grounding for the reemergence and advent of the discipline of Black psychology.
>
> (p. 400)

Karenga (1992; see also Jamison, 2008; Jones, 2004) identified three overlapping schools of thought (Table 4.1) informing the critical discourse among the scholars. In countering systems of oppression in psychology, the *Resister* or *Traditionalist* scholars sought to humanize African Americans' experiences. They were focused on developing new theories to account for behaviors of African Americans and to change the mindset of European professionals about Black reality. The *Reformists* bridged the Resisters/Traditionalists and Radicalists. Their focus was the residuals of the American enslavement of Blacks and the ensuing identification of distinct reactive patterns of adaptation. Thus, their frame of reference for Black reality began as a reaction to the enslavement of Blacks. However, the *Radicalists* engaged in deconstruction, reconstruction, and construction efforts to determine culturally congruent or African-centered theories; establishing principles and assumptions that informed new theories in understanding and explaining African American

Table 4.1 Schools of Thought in Black Psychology

Schools	Black Scholars (Selective List)	Focus of Intervention	Focus of Scientific Inquiry
Resister or Traditionalist	Kenneth Clark Mamie Phipps-Clark Price Cobbs William Grier Alvin Poussaint	Explain Black behavior to Whites	To use traditional psychological theory in understanding and explaining the behavior of African Americans
Reformist	William Cross Joseph White Charles Thomas Nancy Boyd-Franklin	Change psychological policies and protocols aimed at African Americans	To develop new theory in understanding and explaining the behavior of African Americans
Radicalist	Na'im Akbar Francis Cressling Kobi Kambon Linda James Meyer Wade Nobles	To determine culturally congruent (African-centered) theories for application with Black people	To articulate (from the African intellectual past) a new set of principles from which to create new theory in understanding and explaining the behavior of African Americans

behaviors before the "New World" (Jones, 2004). This group focused on understanding Black behavior within the context of the African essence or nature; however, they were not preoccupied with changing White attitudes. Appreciating the scholarly diversity among them, these thought-leaders positioned ABPsi as the refuge in sustaining the excavation of knowledge centered in African/Black reality and analysis. Therefore, the development of the field and discipline are intimately connected with the resilience of ABPsi and the operationalizing of its mission as the liberation of the African Mind, empowerment of the African Character, and enlivenment and illumination of the African Spirit (www.abpsi.org). It served then, as it does now, as the "professional homecoming" for Black scholars/students and members of Black communities to congregate, exhale, rejuvenate, and strategize in addressing the complexities of the issues faced by persons of African ancestry as many felt isolated in their respective work settings. Despite their conceptual differences, the epistemology of African-centered values of collectivism, child-centered, and oneness of being which has led to such theories as optimal theory and belief systems analysis (Myers, 1988, 1992); NTU therapeutic response (Phillips, 1990); multi-systems model (Boyd-Franklin, 1989); Nguzo Saba (Karenga, 1977); and others grounded in philosophical solidarity.

In 2018, ABPsi celebrated its 50th anniversary, returning to its birthplace in Oakland, California. While much was celebrated in terms the gains made in Black psychology, much more was still needed. Globally, Black communities continue to be underserved, over/under medicated, disenfranchised, and dehumanized. Thus, Black psychology is poised to meet the mandate to expand the discourse in the establishment of a Pan-African psychology (Nobles, 2015), advocating for the ratification of "African notions of Pan African Humanness, indigenous knowledge systems and terminology as key to the illumination and reframing of a Pan African therapeutic engagement and the teaching and training of psychologists in the African worldview, ontology, and culture" (Nobles, Baloyi, & Sodi, 2016, p. 1). As many Black/ African scholars from across the Diaspora collaborate, it becomes apparent that the *myth of Black inferiority and White supremacy* plagued all persons of African ancestry—it just manifests itself differently based on the context. A global response in countering the residuals of this myth is an innovative community-defined practice is the Emotional Emancipation Circles[SM] that was envisioned by the Community Healing Network (CHN), Inc. and operationalized by ABPsi (Grills, Aird, & Rowe, 2016). These circles are a "bottom-up, grassroots mobilization effort to create safe spaces where Black people can work together to overcome and overturn the lie of Black inferiority" (p. 6). In other words, there are in-house or in-family conversations that need to happen among persons of African ancestry as we dissect internalized oppression, promote cultural/holistic wellness, and shore folks up in relation to historical/persistent racial oppression so they are less reactive and more intentional. Such cultural conversations across the diversity of persons of African ancestry may dismantle the dominate homogeny or psychological colonization and foster emancipatory processes. Arguably, to do so would shed insight for the academy in being able to generate pedagogies that accommodate diverse worldviews, integrate indigenous healing practices, promote culturally centered wellness, and minimize ethnocentricity if the academy was so inclined to engage such scholarship. A longstanding barrier for Black psychology—psychology in general—has been the need to raise up a Black psychologist workforce that can further develop this work. The 2017 profile of the typical psychology workforce in the U.S. was a 60-something years old White woman, whereas professionals of color (POC) represented about 15% of all psychologists—a percentage that has not changed significantly in the last decade. More profound is that, of the 15% POC, only 4% identified as Black/African American (APA, 2018). I submit that the quantitative deficiency of diversity in the workforce brings with it a lack of culturally congruent epistemological diversity and cultural wisdom. Subsequently, it can be deducted that the myth of African Americans or Blacks not being effective consumers of mental health services is more about the theories, practices, and interventions, as well as the face of the provider, not adequately reflecting their realities and/or not nurturing a deeper sense of cultural meaning-making. In other words, the onus is on the academy and the profession to rise to the occasion than on Black communities limiting themselves to care that may not fully reflect their realities.

Despite the emergence of Black psychology, it was not embraced as required knowledge in the academy, as evidenced by many Black students/practitioners, as well as general professionals, not being aware of its existence; which is still the case. Education, training, and research continued to be focused on African Americans yet limited attention to the implications of this scholarship. This has been perplexing to me in that it is quite likely that anyone professing to specialize in working with women would have at least interrogated the writing of feminist scholars about the experiences of women. However, this logic seemed not to follow when working with persons of African ancestry, seeking out what is written about Blacks by Blacks. As a Black psychologist contending with these complexities and wanting to effect change within the academy, principles of humanistic psychology resonated with me. Adelbert Jenkins' article, "A Humanistic Approach to Black Psychology," in Jones' (2004) seminal text, *Black Psychology*, was refreshingly enlightening. Jenkins positioned his power and privilege in challenging educational institutions to consider systemic flaws in teaching style and expectations that contribute to the achievement gap as opposed to suggesting that African American children cannot learn. This served as an impactful model of how humanistic principles that stressed that human potential could be utilized in pushing back on the plethora of negative memes and interpretations of children of African ancestry are limited without considering the situational context. Their behavior can be seen as *normal reactions to abnormal situations* versus their pathology. Comas-Diaz (2012) noted that if one is not aware of the social-political-economic-environmental contexts that inform the lives of those they serve, then they run the risk of preserving the social-political status quo. I contend that if one fails to interrupt such systems of oppression then one colludes with the dehumanization. Though humanistic psychology emerged as the Third Force in Western (European) psychology in drawing attention to freedom and choice, it was not immune from the ethnocentrism that plagued the academy; its blinders lie in the focusing on the individual, which is not the starting point for many cultural groups, and not targeting its responsibility for social change and conditions. In 1972, Carl Roger's personal reflections on his own cultural blinders elucidated for him the impact of context.

> We know how to carry out every aspect of what I have proposed in regard to our cities. The only element lacking is the passionate determination which says, "Our cities are inhuman. They are ruining lives and mental and physical health at a devastating rate. We are going to change this, even if it costs us money!"
>
> (p. 49)

Unfortunately, it appears that HP neglected to fully embrace this charge and instead remained focused on individual transformation and theoretical conceptualization of social and cultural issues within this context. In other words, despite good *intentions* it contributed to the negative *impact* upon Black people and other people of color by not locating their therapy in POC's worldview and social context. Despite the history, the relational roots between HP and BP have not been central in the HP academy. For example, I am curious of the possibilities for the evolution of HP if the realization that W. E. B. DuBois was a student of William James (Campbell, 1992) and if DuBois' work was prominent in HP studies and training, allowing for an acculturation of knowledge versus a nuance to be discovered of his connection to the lineage. It may have manifested in Black students/learners being able to see themselves in HP knowledge keepers, resulting in the preponderance of Black humanistic psychologists.

Black Psychology and Humanistic Psychology

Plausibly, there are lessons to be gleaned from considering the synergy or parallel processes between Black psychology and humanistic psychology. In 1962, the formation of the Association of Humanistic Psychology (AHP) sparked a plethora of interest in alternatives to mainstream psychological approaches. Similar to the plight of Black psychology, the humble beginning of humanistic psychology was met with visibility challenges, including HP being marginalized in the dominate required scholarship in the academy. Reportedly, Maslow was quite sensitive to the lack of professional recognition of HP in APA and his responses contributed to the establishment of Division 32 (now the Society for Humanistic Psychology) in 1971 under the stewardship of Gibbons (Grogan, 2008). From this perspective, it can be conceptualized that HP has worked diligently from within the belly of the beast in order to effect change despite the critique of its silence pertaining to the dehumanizing impact of systems of oppression. Greenleaf, Manivong, and Song (2016) skillfully documented this history, laying the foundations as to why more should be expected of HP. From their perspective, HP's omission of attending to classism and economic poverty has hindered its impact. In making these critiques, Greenleaf and colleagues also provide practical strategies in addressing such economic injustices.

Black scholars have maintained a double-consciousness in the pursuit of re-membering, re-claiming, and re-defining the wholeness and goodness of the African spirit while simultaneously remaining engaged in the dominate dis-course of APA and seeking to effect change from within. This duality can be professionally exhausting, whereas engagement in Black psychology can be rejuvenating and illuminating. This is a similar experience for humanistic scholars in the academy that struggle to manage the duality of positioning person–centered ways of being in relation to the prevalence of symptom reduction initiatives and privileged positivistic epistemologies. Many thought-leaders in Black psychology remained affiliated with the APA while grounded in their ABPsi family relatedness. These include scholars such as Boyd-Franklin (1989), Myers and Speight (2010), Neville, Tynes, and Utsey (2009), Parham, Ajamu, and White (2010), and Cokley (2015), to name just a few. Probably the most notable among them is the *Godfather of Black Psychology*, a founder of the

ABPsi, Joseph "Joe" White, who unexpectedly transitioned in 2018. He boldly convicted the academy with his *book smarts* and *street smarts* demeanor, and genuinely impacted the general field of psychology (Cokley, Palmer, & Stone, 2019). White is among the first to model for me how to speak truth to power in a way that power can listen and feel—keeping it real. His multicultural *freedom train* of scholars has the necessary blueprint to effect change within the academy for generations to come. Parenthetically, it should also be noted that some of the major scholar-intellectuals and architects of the discipline of Black psychology, like Wade Nobles, Na'im Akbar, and Kobi Kambon, have chosen to have absolutely no affiliation with the APA. In honor of the efforts of such scholars, I submit that the contributions of Black psychology paved the way for other culturally centered psychologies, serving as a model for the formation of other ethnic psychological associations that spawned reputable ethnically centered scholarship; however, the power imbalance and discourse in the field persists. To date, ABPsi remains the only ethnic psychological association that is completely independent of APA, whereas the other ethnic psychological associations have some interdependent relation. The APA website describes the mission of the Council of National Psychological Associations for the Advancement of Ethnic Minority Interests (CNPAAEMI; www.apa.org), which is made up of leadership from each of the ethnic psychological associations, including ABPsi. Within APA decision-making structure, CNPAAEMI is delegated to an advisory capacity, which adversely impacts its actualization as added value to APA. It logically follows that few APA members know it exists, are aware of its accomplishments, and how to benefit from its efforts. This critique is also applicable when considering the positioning of the revised APA 2017 Multicultural Guidelines. The task force consisted of several scholars who are concurrent members of ABPsi and APA, and are prominent authors in the field of Black psychology. The Task Force is to be commended for its directives with regard to education, training, and research, yet it is ironic that its implementation is advised versus required; they are guidelines instead of being positioned as ethical requirements. This passive stance colludes with the preponderance of unbound implicit bias, systemic oppression, and misaligned treatment approaches when working with communities of color, which is substantiated by the mental health care disparities between European (White) and Black clients (McGuire & Miranda, 2008).

Appreciating the inherent challenges in promoting humanistic principles throughout the field, HP is situated closer to the dominant discourse; thus, it is poised and privileged to influence future generations of practitioners. After all, it is the Third Force! In contrast, tenets of Black psychology are not so privileged in the academy, where many scholar-practitioners, especially those of African ancestry, are not aware of this culturally centered humanizing scholarship. This intellectual capitalistic context (e.g., the monetizing of what are required readings in academia and determining what is not required) contributes not only to the pervasive misunderstandings and missteps in the treatment of persons of African ancestry, it perpetuates the potential of socializing persons of African ancestry to always being "sick" or pathologized with well-intended practitioners as the uninformed agents in this cycle. You simply don't know what you don't know and you cannot consider or interrogate that which you have not been exposed to. The *Journal of Humanistic Psychology* (JHP) and *Journal of Black Psychology* (JBP) are well revered peer review journals that are the vanguard for publications related to HP and BP, respectively. Table 4.2 documents an informal key term search in both journals that may provide insight in the quality of discourse between HP and BP. For the period of 1961–2019, the term "Africans" yielded 171 hits in JHP, with an additional 21 for "African Americans," demonstrating interest in the experiences of persons of African ancestry. Understandably, JBP denotes a significantly higher attention to this diverse population with 736 hits for "Africans" and 465 hits for "African Americans" in the same period. However, what is most notable is the reference to "Black psychology" or its comparable term of "Africentric" as only one hit each in JHP (from the same article); whereas there were 39 hits for "humanistic" in JBP. It can be deduced that there may be a number of professionals of African ancestry exposed to humanistic psychology yet they are publishing research specific to persons of African ancestry in JBP versus JHP. The term "multiculturalism" yielded 33 hits for both JHP and JBP, yet there is a qualitative difference in that the majority of the JHP hits were editorial comments from the former editor, Kirk Schneider; whereas the JBP hits were dispersed almost exclusively among the varied articles. These results, coupled with numbers of persons of African ancestry receiving services, the limitation of ethnically congruent/culturally informed providers, and culturally uninformed ethnically diverse providers, underscores the necessity for psychology *to get it right*. It is quite probable that the potential for doing so lies in the synergy between Black psychology and humanistic psychology, grounded in multicultural principles. The cost to collective-actualization (Hanks, 2008) is too high to do otherwise.

Table 4.2 JBP/JHP Key Term Search from 1961–2019

	Journal of Humanistic Psychology	*Journal of Black Psychology*
Keyword (anywhere)		
Africans	171	736
African American	21	465
Multiculturalism	33	33
Black psychology	1	★
Africentric	1	★
Humanistic	★	39

Multicultural-Informed Humanistic Psychology

The infusion of tenets of multiculturalism and social justice with humanistic principles may in fact be the formula needed by the academy to foster a both/and approach in terms of expanding the conceptualization of treatment efficacy beyond quantifiable evidence-based standards to community-endorsed quality of life practices. Comas-Diaz (2012) states that "humanism is a cultural construct, and multiculturalism is infused with humanism. Such alliance anchors psychotherapy as a healing practice" (p. 1). Multiculturalism, the Fourth Force, brings attention to issues of cultural competencies. However, this is quite limiting as it further perpetuates the "othering" of peoples' cultural experiences and the "expert stance" of the provider in needing to know the other. It encourages a false sense of efficacy in that an ethnically/culturally diverse workforce is not warranted in the production of competent European American practitioners. In response to the limitations of cultural competence, attention to the interplay among power, privilege, and oppression and implications is imperative. Cultural equity provides a blueprint for a "systemic analysis of systems of domination and subordination across and within cultures" (Almeida, Hernández-Wolfe, & Tubbs, 2011, p. 49) that can be applied in education, training, and research to foster cultural accountability. In alignment with humanistic principles, cultural equity requires humility, not cultural competence. Tervalon and Murray-Garcia (1998) introduced the concept of cultural humility, which refers to life-long learning and self-reflection that counters "the false sense of security that stereotyping [or othering] brings" (p. 119); freeing us up from the need to know and settling into the engagement of knowing. The systemic analysis of cultural equity also draws upon the work of Black Feminist K. Crenshaw (1989) pertaining to intersectionality, which is a framework for critically considering how the multiple axes of identity are informed by aspects of who we are, situated in multiple systems of power, privilege, and oppression. To this end, cultural equity is a blueprint for action. It affords practitioners the ability to genuinely know the uniqueness of each in the matrix of systems of oppression so one can better serve the client as they examine the impact of such systems on their lived experiences and, as filtered through the lens of Black psychology, advance the possibility to be free and authentic. From a social justice perspective, we must *do* something with what we illuminate; not just be satisfied with the illumination or leaving the client alone to contend with the social ramifications. Hoffman, Granger, Vallejos, and Moats (2016) echo this stance:

> If existential–humanistic psychologists only battle these injustices inside the therapy room, then they will continue to fail to actualize the fullest potential of existential–humanistic principles in the world. It is time to say, "No more will we be silent!" If humanistic and existential–humanistic psychology truly value human dignity, compassion, and empathy, and practices the art of listening and valuing the

experience of others, including the marginalized and oppressed, then there is no authentic option but to speak.

(p. 608)

However, within the tenants of Nobles' (2013) notion of Skh Djr and Irt hr Sku, our charge would be more than "to speak" but to inspire, prescribe and inspire solutions and actions that will free humanity from both material and spiritual degradation (p. 295). To be clear, though not named as such, the essence or spirit of many of the concepts, terminologies, and discourse that are emerging in the dominate literature has been fortified in Black psychology since its inception. However, these concepts serve as a language for those Black psychologists who are committed to remaining in dialogue with potential cultural allies in the academy with the hope that such collaborative efforts could propagate collective-actualization (Hanks, 2008) as professionals charged with the psychological, spiritual, and physical care of societies. Language informs meaning which informs actions. For example, African Americans are not descendants of slaves; we are descendants of those Africans who were enslaved. Our children are not at-risk; they are at-potential in at-risk environments. Such intentional language places human experiences in a relational context that requires one to ask the question, *what happened to you?* and not *what is wrong with you?* What if practitioners and the field were to hold treatment accountable to impacting change in the context of where our clients live their lives, beyond simply in the client, symptom reduction? In doing so, as humanistic practitioners, we would be responding to Hoffman, Cleare-Hoffman, and Jackson's (2016) interpretation that social justice issues emerge on a collective level when groups are forced to confront aspects of the givens of existence due to social structures or impositions. However, Lemberger and Lemberger-Truelove (2016) add that "while sustaining the singular conviction of justice, humanistic practitioners must embrace havoc and uncertainty of social changes toward justice" (p. 575). They go on to delineate five propositions for a more social justice infused humanistic practice.

Summary

I remain grateful to Black psychology scholars for the culturally centered liberation, meaning-making, and illumination in the deepest sense, and to the founders of humanistic psychology for affording me the culturally transferable tenets of positive regard, empathy, self-determination, meaning-making, and self/collective-actualization that sustains me in a both/and versus either/or stance within the academy. For me, it epitomizes a proverbial commentary from Nobles (1985) regarding the duality of persons of African ancestry and descendants of American enslavement; *African by nature and American by nurture.* It is my hope that the reader has gained curiosity for culturally centered knowledge and meaning-making as epitomized by Back psychology, an appreciation for the ethical application of multiculturalism across theories, and indebtedness for humanistic psychology's responsibilities as theoretical change agents based on its epistemology. It is also my intention to "gift" the reader an introduction to Black scholars and scholarship that may not be prevalent in PWI psychology curriculum yet may give voice to folks' experiences. Rice (2015) admirably describes the history of humanistic psychology addressing social justice issues. This is not questioned. However, I maintain that more is needed; specifically, direct attention to the application of humanistic principles in action. To date, Carl Roger's (1972) call to action has not been realized as evidenced by the limited visibility in the *Journal of Humanistic Psychology* of social action guidelines, the observation that humanistic-informed scholars are moving such discourse in other journals such as the *Journal of Black Psychology*, and lack of centrality of multicultural discourse in humanistic psychology. The need to intentionally infuse and/or impose humanistic principles throughout the academy emerges as a unique opportunity to *do* humanistic psychology. In echoing Thrift and Sugarman's insistence that practitioners move beyond looking for "individual solutions to what are arguably social problems" (p. 11) and strategically consider intentional impact on social situations. It is toward this end that I offer the following for consideration.

- Centering cultural equity, humanistic psychologists should hone skills in responding to social-political contexts by accepting Lemberger and Lemberger-Truelove's (2016) invitation to "challenge, revise, and personalize" (p. 575) the five propositions they offered for a more social justice humanistic praxis.
- Humanistic psychologists should be modeling the engagement of scholarship with each of the ethnic psychological associations with the curiosity of what can be gleaned for HP, as well as other culturally centered groups, as keepers of wisdom knowledge.
- It is incumbent upon humanistic psychologists to strategically reach across the theoretical-divide within the academy/field in order to forge alliances, effect systemic change, and infuse humanistic principles throughout as society's humanism depends upon it.
- From a social justice multicultural stance, the intentional delineation of humanistic principles *in action* would further the influence of humanistic psychology in education, training, and practice. More specifically, humanistic scholars should target how to situate humanistic principles in complex clinical space such as crisis intervention, mandated reporting, psychiatric hospitalization, etc.; thereby establishing guidelines for holding an HP stance in spaces that can feel dehumanizing to those being served.

As a Black humanistic psychologist, I am encouraged by the next generation of HP scholar-practitioners who are armed with foundational humanistic roots and grounded in multicultural relativities. I am in awe of the contemporary HP vanguards who admirably answered the call to *sit in discomfort and breathe through to possibilities* (Jackson, 2015) regarding humanistic psychology's future in this vain. It is invigorating to witness such humanistic scholars embrace the charge so eloquently positioned by Hanks (2008):

> Complacent and afraid, we can choose to follow the masses in the direction of "traditional" psychology, or we can honor the vision of Maslow, May, and Rogers by blazing new paths and developing new paradigms firmly rooted in the humanistic dedication to the full expression of our humanness. If we are to be true to our convictions, that choice should be clear.
>
> (p. 117)

Being a cultural ally comes with risks as it means that one must be strategic in leveraging one's power and privilege with the potential for consequences (Lemberger & Lemberger-Truelove, 2016). In response to the conviction of Hoffman, Granger, Vallejos, and Moats (2016), contemporary HP scholars are ensuring that the history books record the courageous contributions of humanistic psychology's responsiveness to national and global civil unrest, boldly taking a stand against injustices. For example, in 2018, Division 32 Society for Humanistic Psychology commissioned an international Task Force on Hate Incidents. Many HP scholar-warriors, such as those in this text, are a testament to the possibilities of actualizing humanistic principles in the field and to the legacy of its founders. Drake Spaeth, in his statement to the board as president-elect during the 12th Annual Conference of the Society for Humanistic Psychology, valiantly proclaimed:

> Clearly, in humanistic psychology, it is no longer sufficient to settle for a concept of wholeness that rests on the privilege of mere self-expression as its benchmark of success. Being human also encompasses awareness of our inextricable embeddedness in communities. None of us are whole while any portion of us languishes in the struggle for survival and fails even to be seen. Moreover, macrocosm mirrors microcosm. We must bravely confront within ourselves that which we all too often are ready to attribute to being outside of ourselves as preparation to work collectively to right the wrongs we loathe so deeply.

In closing, I hope that this chapter has expanded the readers' knowledge, inspired curiosity for others, and sparked discussion for all. It is through such critical discourse that humanistic principles can remain relevant for diverse persons. It is through such critical discourse and deep interrogation of the science of African human functioning that humanistic psychology can honor the African meaning of being human, as well as other meanings relevant for diverse ethnic groups. As African proverbs teach us:

He {She} who begins a conversation, does not foresee the end

~African proverb

References

Almeida, R., Hernández-Wolfe, P., & Tubbs, C. (2011). Cultural equity: Bridging the complexity of social identities with therapeutic practices. *The International Journal of Narrative Therapy and Community Work, 3,* 43–56.

American Psychological Association. (2017). *Multicultural guidelines: An ecological approach to context, identity, and intersectionality.* Retrieved from: www.apa.org/about/policy/multicultural-guidelines.pdf.

American Psychological Association. (2018). *Demographics of U.S. Psychology Workforce* (Interactive data tool). Retrieved from: www.apa.org/workforce/datatools/demographics.aspx

Boyd-Franklin, N. (1989). *Black families: A multi-systems approach.* New York, NY: Guildford Press.

Campbell, J. (1992). DuBois and James. *Transactions of the Charles S. Pierce Society, 28* (3), 556–581.

Cokley, K. O. (2015). *The myth of black anti-intellectualism: A true psychology of African American students.* Santa Barbara, CA: Praeger/ABC-CLIO.

Cokley, K., Palmer, B., & Stone, S. (2019). Toward a black (and diverse) psychology: The scholarly legacy of joseph white. *Journal of Black Psychology, 45*(2), 112–121.

Comas-Diaz, L. (2012). Psychotherapy as a healing practice, scientific endeavor, and social justice action. *Psychotherapy, 49*(4), 473–474.

Crenshaw, K. (1989). Demarginalizing the intersection of race and sex: A Black feminist critique of antidiscrimination doctrine, feminist theory, and antiracist politics. *University of Chicago Legal Forum, 140,* 139–167.

Dubois, W. E. B. (1903). *The souls of Black folk.* Chicago, IL: A.C. McClurg & Co. University Press John Wilson & Son, Cambridge, USA.

Greenleaf, A. T., Manivong, J. R., & Song, S. Y. (2016). Rediscovering classism: The humanistic vision for economic justice. *Journal of Humanistic Psychology, 56* (6), 646–664.

Grills, C. N., Aird, E. G., & Rowe, D. (2016). Breath, baby, breathe: Clearing the way for the emotional emancipation of black people. *Cultural Studies-Cultural Methodologies, 16*(3), 1–11.

Grogan, J. L. (2008). A cultural history of the humanistic psychologist movement in America. Retrieved from: https://repositories.lib.utexas.edu/handle/2152/3855

Grogan, J. L. (2013). *Encountering America: Humanistic psychology, sixties culture, and the shaping of the modern self.* New York, NY: HarperPerennial.

Hanks, T. L. (2008). The ubuntu paradigm: Psychology's next force? *Journal of Humanistic Psychology, 48,* 116–135.

Hernandez-Wolfe, P., & McDowell, T. (2014). Bridging complex identities with cultural equity and humility in systemic supervision. In Thomas C. Todd, & Cheryl L. Storm (Eds.), *The complete systemic supervisor: Context, philosophy, and pragmatics* (2nd ed., pp. 43–61). Lincoln, NE: Authors Choice Press.

Hoffman, L., Cleare-Hoffman, H. P., & Jackson, T. (2016). Humanistic psychology and multiculturalism: History, current status, and advancements. In K. J. Schneider, & J. F. Pierson (Eds.), *The handbook of humanistic psychology: Leading edges of theory, research, and practice* (2nd ed., pp. 41–55). Thousand Oaks, CA: Sage.

Hoffman, L., Granger, Jr., N., Vallejos, L., & Moats, M. (2016). An existential-humanistic perspective on Black Lives Matter and contemporary protest movements. *Journal of Humanistic Psychology, 56*(6), 595–611.

Jackson, T. (2015, March). *Humanistic psychology, your house is on fire: There is no rest for the weary!* Keynote address presented at the 8th Annual Society for Humanistic Psychology Conference, Chicago, IL.

Jamison, D. (2008). A critical review of conceptual and methodological issues in Africology as seen through the paradigmatic lens of Black psychology. *The Journal of Pan African Studies, 2*(2), 96–117.

Jenkins, A. H. (2004). A humanistic approach to Black psychology. In R. Jones (Ed.), *Black psychology* (4th ed., pp. 135–155). Hampton, VA: Cobb & Henry.

Jenkins, A. H. (2005). The personal/psychological and the pursuit of a profession. In G. Yancy, & S. Hadley (Eds.), *Narrative identities: Psychologists engaged in self-construction* (pp. 191–207). London, UK: Jessica Kingsley Publishers.

Jones, R. L. (2004). *Black psychology* (4th ed.). Hampton, VA: Cobb & Henry Publishers.

Karenga, M.R. (1977). *Kwanzaa: Origin, concept, practice.* Inglewood, CA: Kawaida Publications.

Karenga, M. (1992). *Introduction to Black studies.* Los Angeles, CA: University of Sankore Press.

Lemberger, M. E., & Lemberger-Truelove, T. L. (2016). Bases for a more socially just humanistic praxis. *Journal of Humanistic Psychology, 56*(6), 571–580.

McGuire, T. G., & Miranda, J. (2008). Racial and ethnic disparities in mental health care: Evidence and policy implications. *Health Aff (Millwood), 27*(2), 393–403.

Myers, L. J. (1988, 1992). *Understanding an Afrocentric worldview: An introduction to optimal psychology.* Dubuque, IA: Kendall/Hunt.

Myers, L. J., & Speight, S. (2010). Reframing health and psychological well-being among persons of African descent: Africana/Black psychology meeting the challenges of social and cultural realities. *The Journal of Pan African Studies, 3*(8), 66–82.

Neville, H. B., Tynes, B., & Utsey, S. (Eds.) (2009). *Handbook of African American psychology.* Thousand Oaks, CA: Sage Publication.

Nobles, W. W. (1985). *Africanity and the black family: The development of a theoretical model* (2nd ed.). Oakland, CA: Institute for the Black Family Life.

Nobles, W. W. (2013). Fundamental task and challenge of Black psychology. *Journal of Black Psychology, 39,* 292–299.

Nobles, W. W. (2015). From black psychology to sakhu djaer: Implications for the future development of a pan African black psychology. *Journal of Black Psychology, 41*(5), 399–414.

Nobles, W. W., Baloyi, L., & Sodi, T. (2016). Pan African humanness and Saku Djaer as Praxis for indigenous knowledge systems. *Alternation Special Edition, 18,* 36–59.

Ojukwu, E., Erugo, S., & Adekoya, C. (2013). Social justice and access to justice. In Clinical legal education curriculum lessons and materials. Network of University Legal Aid Institution (NULAI Nigeria): Garki II Abuja.

Parham, A. P., Ajamu, A., & White, J. (Eds.). (2010). *Psychology of blacks: Centering our perspectives in the African consciousness* (4th ed.). London: Psychology Press.

Phillips, F. (1990). NTU psychotherapy: An Afrocentric approach. *Journal of Black Psychology*, *17*(1), 55–74.

Rice, D. (2015). Humanistic psychology and social action. In K. J. Schneider, & J. F. Pierson (Eds.), *The handbook of humanistic psychology: Leading edges of theory, research, and practice* (2nd ed., pp. 614–625). Thousand Oaks, CA: Sage.

Robinson, L. (2012). *Psychology for social workers: Black perspective on human development*. New York, NY: Routledge.

Rogers, C. (1961). *On becoming a person: A therapist's view of psychotherapy*. Boston, MA: Houghton Mifflin.

Rogers, C. (1972). Some social issues which concern me. *Journal of Humanistic Psychology*, *12*(2), 45–60.

Rogers, C. (1980). *A way of being*. Boston, MA: Houghton Mifflin.

Spaeth, D. (2019, March). Humanistic psychology in the Anthropocene: An invitation. President elect statement presented to the board of the APA Division 32 Society for Humanistic Psychology, Corvallis, Oregon.

Tervalon, M., & Murray-Garcia, J. (1998). Cultural humility versus cultural competence: A critical distinction in defining physician training outcomes in multicultural education. *Journal of Health Care for the Poor and Underserved*, *9*, 117–125.

Thrift, E., & Sugarman, J. (2019). What is social justice? Implications for psychology. *Journal of Theoretical and Philosophical Psychology*, *39*, 1–17.

Williams, R. (1974). A history of the association of black psychologists: Early formation and development. *Journal of Black Psychology*, *1*, 9–24.

5 Humanity and Inhumanity

Relational Themes in Humanistic–Existential Psychology and Multiculturalism Reflected in the United States Constitution, U.S. Constitutional Jurisprudence, and the United Nations Universal Declaration of Human Rights

Alan G. Vaughan

History and the dialogue between humanistic–existential psychology and multiculturalism demonstrates the need for a depth humanistic psychology to cultivate a dialectical and dialogic conversation with inhumanity to produce a greater sense of its wholeness and relevance within and beyond Western psychology, for individuals and the global collective. The inhumanity is continuous but varies in presentation across the arc of history. A prime example today is the social construction of the race fiction and pathological practices of racism in the 20th and 21st centuries. Humanistic psychology must encounter its own shadow and the shadow of inhumanity in Western history's treatment of people of color, and European American psychology's agency in this treatment. To do so promises a depth humanistic–existential psychology that engages the ethno-cultural layer of psyche and complex historiographies of multi-cultural populations, inclusive of those with diverse European ancestry beneath the shadowed covenant of whiteness. It offers a prism of hopeful insight and invites reflection on the intersections of important rich transdisciplinary and transcultural considerations of what it means to be human and what is required to create humane societies. What it means to be optimally human and detrimentally inhumane is the robust question answered in the dialogue across multiple cultures and in the context of their relational historiographies.

In moving from the subjective to the objective, I begin with a brief narrative reflection on my personal engagement with humanistic–existential psychology and its influence in my life. The journey first looks back, then forward to consider an emergent 21st century multiculturalism and its relevance for me, humanistic psychology, and humanity. This humanity is framed in dialectic opposition to inhumanity within the global macro-culture of micro-cultures, all sharing the common goals of survival, maintenance, and evolution of the human species; a human species in multiple cultures that lives in reverence to and in relation to the natural environment of planet Earth, and a consciousness expanded enough to recognize and manage its destructive forces, in the inhumanity that can and will destroy the environment that we all must share.

Personal Reflections on the Quest for Meaning during the Era of Apartheid in the United States

Dustin Hoffman, a young Jewish male, was starring in the popular Hollywood film *The Graduate* as I was coming of age as a young African American man graduating from a Jesuit university in the Pacific Northwest. I identified with his character's existential quest for purpose and life's meaning. My quest did not originate in Beverly Hills but from the segregated neighborhoods of central and west Los Angeles, in a family whose history is interwoven with the Great Migration from the south and the African American community. It offered a rich culture and life-transforming experiences. My grandparents, parents, and siblings, the church, and an extended community of neighbors were the "village it takes to raise a child." They took their responsibility seriously, offering gentle and tough love and nurturing our interests in creative pursuits, economic independence, and resourcefulness. We rode our bikes, skated, and played football and basketball on the streets and in driveways that connected our houses. We enjoyed a childhood of relative ease, comfort, security, and safety. We were sheltered by our parents and by the extended community from the policies of American apartheid, from the laws that institutionalized practices of inhumanity in racism, and from knowledge of discriminatory banking practices that redlined our neighborhoods. My father, a Navy veteran, and our mom, a nurse, bore the brunt of the stress and trauma relative to racism in the United States. They were courageous, loving, and resourceful despite this reality. Their experiences, and later mine, intersected with the Pan-African liberation movements, the U.S. civil rights movement, and the anti-Viet Nam War and free speech movements during the 1950s and 1960s.

From these lived experiences emerged my appreciation for the values that are embedded in the African worldview—a worldview later espoused in the mid-1980s and 1990s in the literature of African American history, Black psychology, sociology, the humanities, arts, and music. Daudi Ajania ya Azibo (1996) identified the African worldview of which African Americans became more conscious, in values such as oneness with God, fellowship as human beings, harmony with nature and community, and communalism rather than competition and attempts to control nature (Jones, 2004).

In retrospect, I now identify with these values in my desire for harmony with nature, derived from childhood camping and fishing trips to Yosemite

National Park. As a young adult my quest continued in extensive travels to the Caribbean, Africa, and Latin America, and the pressing need to map the historiography of the African diaspora; and to immerse myself in its common and diverse culture. I came to the realization that the rich and resonant stories, experiences, and cultures of the African diaspora and the values of an African American worldview were omitted from public and private school curricula, dismissed and buried in the shadow of cultural history in the United States beneath the mindscapes of the European American psyche.

Along with ethnic groups, African Americans have relied on the values of inclusiveness, collaboration, cooperation, collective economic and political consciousness, and extended community networks that nurtured my childhood and coming of age. Higher education was the mantra in my family, and our lives were organized around achievement. This was the righteous ongoing eros or libido as creative transformative life energy that fueled the civil rights movement in the United States and challenged the blatant practices of apartheid in which African Americans lived "separate and unequal."

Religion, and later African spirituality, grounded African American human relations and expanded consciousness. The Black church was the anchoring social institution that withstood the inhumanity in the violent oppression of slavery, with music programs that produced vocal powerhouses such as Aretha Franklin and Whitney Houston, education programs that inspired black scholars such as Cornel West and Martin Luther King, Jr., sports programs that produced legends such as Michael Jordon and Arthur Ashe, and financial services programs that tutored and inspired black businessmen and women. The Black Church has historically morphed into whatever cultural institutions were needed by the African American community from the period of captivity and enslavement through Jim Crow and apartheid.

My emerging consciousness understood the value of education and recognized school as a safe space—a place that became central to my personal quest and journey toward consciousness and optimal freedom. I watched the 1950s and 1960s televised programs that showed the brutality of the school desegregation movement following the U.S. Supreme Court decision in *Brown v. Board of Education of Topeka* (1954). I saw the resistance in the pathological faces of racism and rage as they emerged from the shadow across the nation in acts of violence and irrationality. I was cognizant of needing to understand human nature and behavior, the inhumanity underlying this racism and rampant violence in lynchings and murders, and to answer pressing questions: From where and why this inhumane behavior? Why were white folks so barbaric, cruel, and hateful? No discussions or answers to these questions were forthcoming in my introductory psychology class. The subject of racism, as a form of inhumanity, never arose in the lectures on aggression and violence in animal and human studies. I imagined that this quest for a higher, even transcendent consciousness would engender a deeper understanding of my own humanity, unleash my creativity, and be a catalyst for freedom from the system of apartheid in the United States. I hoped it would provide a foundation for the construction of an optimal, interesting life. As president of the Black Student Association, the Jesuit university did capitulate to the need for a curriculum that taught us about our African American history and affirmed our positive life experiences. It was in graduate school that I first encountered and embraced humanistic and existential psychology—initially, as a path to this deeper understanding and broader consciousness that later individuated toward analytical psychology and certification as a Jungian analyst.

Moving to New York to pursue doctoral studies in clinical psychology, I found among the European theorists companions and compatible ideas in writings of Rollo May, Carl Rogers, Abraham Maslow, Jean Paul Sartre, Simone de Beauvoir, Sigmund Freud, Donald Winnicott, Ronald Fairbairn, Harry Guntrip, and Harry Stack Sullivan. Among African diaspora scholars, the works of Francis Cress Welsing, Wade Nobles, Frantz Fanon, and Cheikh Anta Diop grounded my African worldview and profiled the systemic nature and bias of racism in European American theory, research, and clinical practice among the dominant Jewish faculty at the university. The African worldview as a counterpoint to Eurocentrism allowed me to gain perspective on the emergence of the ethnocultural psychology that preceded multicultural psychology. Del Jenkins, my dissertation chair at New York University and the sole African American faculty in the psychology department, brought humanistic psychology into sharper focus in his later paper on humanistic psychology and multiculturalism (2001), and aligned it with the liberation goals and struggles of the U.S. civil rights movement, and the Pan-African Liberation Movement.

Contemporary Definitions: Humanistic Psychology, Existential Psychology, and Multicultural Psychology

Moss (2001) notes that, "from the beginning, humanistic psychologists have cared deeply about what it means to be fully human and have sought pathways and technologies that assist humans in reaching full humanness" (p. 5). Schneider, Bugental, and Pierson (2001) suggest that humanistic psychology raises two important questions that engage and define the humanistic approach to psychology: "What does it mean to be fully and experientially human? How does that understanding illuminate the fulfilled or vital life?" (p. xx). They define what I would call a depth humanistic psychology as a "concerted brew of existential, transpersonal and constructivist theorizing, and encompasses a breathtaking investigative range" that can be thought of as experiential humanism, one that embraces all modes of awareness and sub-awareness—individual, social, biological, and spiritual as they resonate with lives (p. xx). Further, Schneider and colleagues note that "Contemporary humanistic psychology is an integrative psychology that addresses the most pressing issues of our times" and that "Contemporary humanistic psychology brings that which the earlier generation of humanist psychologists also prized—the heart or personal dimension" (p. xxi). Schneider and colleagues add to the definition of an evolving humanistic psychology the propositional question: "What if psychology's next step was a holistic one, a rich mosaic consisting of each of the emerging trends but threaded throughout by the depth, breadth and pathos of intimate human experience?" (p. xx).

In arriving at this contemporary view and definition, Schneider and colleagues (2001) trace the roots of humanism from the 5th century B.C.E Greek classical humanism, a second great wave flourishing during the Renaissance, a third wave in the period of Enlightenment spanning the 17th and 18th centuries, and the latest wave in the 20th century emerging in reaction to the chain of psychologies from the psychoanalytic lineage of Freud through reactive and compensatory approaches of behaviorism. They suggest that the post-modern, even post-structural view emphasizes humanity as a social construction, with fulfillment seen as a culturally relative value. Given this relativity, multicultural consciousness raises similar questions about what is universal to the human condition and what are relative humanistic precepts? What does it mean to be optimally human in other than European and American cultural contexts? What are the reciprocal influences and impacts of inhumanity in its varied forms on humanity? Can both be held in consciousness or coexist to inform each other and "Othering"? Transcultural and transdisciplinary research methodologies ask which elements are common to human existence and how can they be compared across cultures? They build on Jung's archetypal approach to the structure of consciousness, meaning in psyche, and cultural relativity in environmental influences. The life cycle is the common biosociocultural frame for all humans and their societies. I believe they all have the common goals noted as survival, maintenance, and evolution of the human species. Schneider, Bugental, and Pierson (2001)—consistent with Jenkins (2001)—suggest that "There are as many 'humanisms' for some multicultural thinkers as there are races, ethnic identities, and languages. Who can stand above them all and identify global human qualities?" (pp. xix–xxiii). I think a transcendent consciousness can embrace the concept of a Global Culture of cultures in which we now live. The portal to the vision is cultural equivalence (Helms, 1992).

Maslow, Schneider, Jenkins, and others provided a psychological matrix to understand my quest for meaning and consciousness and a culturally compatible worldview grown directly out of lived experience. Maslow's (1943, 1954, 1968) hierarchy of needs displayed in the kemetic Egyptian cultural graphic icon of a pyramid—a numinous symbol integrating psychology with human development, politics, economics, and the interdisciplinary and intersectional perspectives—became a focus in attempting to answer key questions. At the base of Maslow's pyramid are fundamental survival needs and, at its apex, the need for self-actualization: physiological needs, safety needs, need for love and belonging, esteem, self-actualization, and self-transcendence.

Jung (1966) had earlier described this self-actualization in his theory of individuation. Humanistic psychology raised the foundational question that further expanded my understanding: What does it mean to be fully human? The most fundamental and basic four layers of Maslow's pyramid contain what he called "deficiency needs" or "d-needs": esteem, friendship and love, security, and physical needs. If these deficiency needs are not met, with the exception of the most fundamental (physiological) needs, there may be no physical indication but the individual will feel anxious and tense. Maslow's theory suggests that the most basic level of needs must be met before the individual will strongly desire (or focus motivation on) the secondary or higher-level needs (Corsini & Wedding, 2014). He coined the term "metamotivation" to describe the motivation of people who go beyond the scope of basic needs and strive for constant betterment.

The question this raises is whether being satiated by the successive progression from bottom to top of Maslow's pyramid is essential to being fully human in the Western cultural context? Indigenous Native American, African, Latinx, and Asian cultures begin with transcendence of the self in forms of religious or spiritual practices, and the communal organization of our societies. Philosophically, some consider the path to full humanhood grounded in the collective rather than the individual. An example is the African concept of Ubuntu, "I am because we are, we are because I am."

Existential Psychology

Existentialist philosophers Jean Paul Sartre and Gabriel Marcel, who focused on the subjectivity of human experience rather than objective diagnostic categories of psychotherapy, further advanced my exploration of existential psychology and psychotherapy and what defines humanness and humanity. Irvin D. Yalom (1980) outlined the "ultimate concerns" for individuals attempting to live a constructive life: freedom, fear of isolation, search for meaning, and relationship with death. The directness of this approach helped elevate my consciousness. Centered within these four existential dynamics is the individual whose life is based on freedom of choices and on good judgment, leading to the conscious realization of a purposeful and meaningful life. The individual who faces a sense of terror generated by feelings of existential isolation, of being alone in the universe, is responsible for finding meaning or experiences that give existence purpose. They must recognize that death is a companion in life's journey. This existential reality seeks to clarify that what one does between birth and death is a personal choice once the age of reason in the life cycle is reached. In resonance with the multicultural perspective, existential psychology and psychotherapy have a major focus on the recognition and exercise of freedom in relation to living. All human beings, regardless of ethnocultural ancestries and backgrounds, share these dilemmas of existence. They must come to terms with the ultimate concerns for freedom, isolation, meaningfulness—and death. Some turn to religions and spiritual practices to do so.

The theories and values outlined in existential psychology refined my quest and underscored the importance of personal and political freedom, which helped to frame the question to clients in clinical practice: "What do you want to do with or in your life between now and death?" The answer often shifts the focus to personal choice and responsibility for making a life of one's choosing. The question, consciousness, and answers make salient the known truth that individuals have only to live and die and that there is a reciprocal relationship between the two dispositions, with the latter enhancing the former and the former recognizing the existence and limits of the life cycle.

In the context of Western cultural history in the United States, coming to terms with these concerns has been complicated by apartheid, the system of White supremacy, a shadow dynamic of capitalism, and ongoing practices of inhumanity in racism. This is illustrated by the U.S. Supreme Court jurisprudential decisions and examining Congressional legislation on immigration affecting people of color from the multicultural perspective and what is known about approaches to humanistic and existential psychology. This discussion supports the need for a depth humanistic psychology to engage its shadow and the collective shadow of European American cultural history to become more relevant, to deconstruct "Othering," to help others become optimally human, and to develop humane societies. Just as consciousness of life enhances the possibilities of lives vitally lived, so too does conscious engagement with inhumanity enhance the possibilities of becoming more human and humane in the World Culture of cultures. In the United States, this jurisprudence has caused significant complex intergenerational trauma, adversely affecting the freedoms and field of choices for individuals and ethnic group members. The proffered freedoms of existential philosophy and psychology reflect a Eurocentric rather than a multicultural perspective and obscure the shadow elements of European and American cultural hegemony in a global system of capitalism. A relational bridge is needed to bring existential and humanistic psychology forward from its shadow to shed light on multiculturalism and multicultural psychology, and to stimulate authentic phenomenological discourse about the pursuit of freedom in liberation struggles, imposed conditions of economic and political isolation, subordination, and exploitation.

Multicultural Psychology

Comas-Diaz (2014) offers commentary on the multicultural perspective, psychology, and psychotherapies as centered in multiculturalism that emerged as consciousness in theory and clinical practice from the domestic social and political U.S. civil rights movement from the 1950s through the 1980s and today (p. 563). I posit that multiculturalism also emerged from the synchronous influences of the Pan-African Liberation Movement in Africa and the Caribbean, and the African diaspora that includes the United States. This was the same freedom movement within the African diaspora, a collective movement against Western cultural hegemony in the forms of domestic apartheid and international colonialism, practices of domestic and international forms of inhumanity. I underscore that the broader contextual historiography was the African diaspora—that is, the shared geopsychological and sociocultural space occupied by persons with ancestral origins in Africa dispersed across the globe. In the 21st century, the multicultural perspective and psychology promote awareness of worldview, global citizenship, and pursuit of cultural competence as a life-long process. Multiculturalism accommodates integration of ancient ethnocultural history and healing traditions in theory, research, and clinical practice. It fosters equity and equitable relations to "other" and "otherness" among members of the human family. It promotes consciousness, empowerment, change, and transformative dialogue on oppression and privilege (Comas-Diaz, p. 544).

The United Nations Universal Declaration of Human Rights (1948)

Relational themes in humanistic, existential, and multicultural psychologies can be seen in a cross-sectional view at the intersections of the history of Western psychology, and U.S. political economic and jurisprudential institutions in the 1940s and 1950s, through the 1960s and forward. The aspiration and affirmation of these relational themes of freedom, equity, and security are seen in the example of the Universal Declaration of Human Rights (1948). Broad concepts and principles outlined in humanistic and existential psychology are articulated in the Declaration: recognition of freedom; refutation of social, political, and economic isolation; self-determination; meaning, purpose; freedom from anxiety related to health, general well-being, food and water security, and safety from violence and oppression, intensified if not generated by World War II. They were underscored and encoded in the Universal Declaration of Human Rights and were foundational to the U.S. civil rights and Pan-African Liberation movements occurring in the African diaspora during this period of world history.

The theme of humanistic perspectives on multiculturalism can be exemplified and interrogated in one of several agencies of the United Nations, itself an idealized institution that aspires toward an equitable global multicultural worldview serving the common good, even as it is recognized that this intent is compromised in its architecture, by the veto power of the United States and the other major Western nations, Russia, and China. The Universal Declaration of Human Rights was adopted and proclaimed on December 10, 1948 by the General Assembly of the United Nations. The Declaration itself comprised a preamble and 30 specific and related articles, too numerous to consider here (Black, 1979).

In its foundational premise and intent, the Declaration offers guidelines and direction toward human freedoms, the common good of nations and citizens, social security, safety, and conflict resolution within and between nation states. The preamble outlines the scope of basic human needs and rights, and the existential freedoms implied in humanistic–existential psychology and the multiculturalism, among them:

> There is recognition of the inherent dignity and of the equal and inalienable rights of all members of the human family in the foundations of freedom, justice and peace in the world,
>
> Whereas disregard and contempt for human rights have resulted in barbarous acts which have outraged the conscience of mankind, and the advent of a world in which human beings shall enjoy freedom of speech and belief and freedom from fear and want has been proclaimed as the highest aspiration of the common people.
>
> Whereas it is essential, if man is not to be compelled to have recourse, as a last resort, to rebellion against tyranny and oppression, that human rights should be protected by the rule of law,
>
> Whereas it is essential to promote the development of friendly relations between nations,
>
> Whereas the peoples of the United Nations have in the Charter reaffirmed their faith in fundamental human rights, in the dignity and worth of the human person and in the equal rights of men and women and have determined to promote social progress and better standards of life in larger freedom,
>
> Whereas Member States have pledged themselves to achieve, in co-operation with the United Nations, the promotion of universal respect for and observance of human rights and fundamental freedoms,
>
> Whereas a common understanding of these rights and freedoms is of the greatest importance for the full realization of this pledge.
>
> (Kirgis, pp. 777–782)

The General Assembly proclaimed the Universal Declaration of Human Rights as a common standard of achievement for all peoples and all nations, so that every individual and every organ of society would strive by teaching and education to promote respect for these rights and freedoms. Its aim was to secure the recognition and international observance of these rights among peoples of U.N. member states and among peoples of territories under their jurisdiction. This was a step in the right direction against the inhumanity practiced in colonialism.

Humanistic and Multicultural Perspectives on the Shadow of Inhumanity in the U.S. Constitution and U.S. Constitutional Jurisprudence in Retrospect and the Long View Forward

The seven articles of the U.S. Constitution provide the architecture and vision for the United States first held by the European elite landowners and founding fathers. Multiculturalism emerged from the shadow of the U.S. Constitution on the north American landscape in the lived experiences of people of color. Themes of freedom, justice, security, and welfare of the human family were set forth in the preamble to the U.S. Constitution. Upon historical reflection, and based on prior and current jurisprudence and practices, the document articulates an aspiration. Its shadow is illuminated in the cultural history of the United States as the inhumane treatment of populations of color. Selected legislative acts of the U.S. Congress and decisions in U.S. Constitutional Jurisprudence have codified the shadow in historical practices of inhumanity that include domestic apartheid, racism, discrimination, terror, and the violence of murder.

Racism as a psychopathology that causes pathos or suffering continues today in mutable forms that permeate United States history through the agency of the covenant of whiteness, white supremacy, sociocultural elitism and derivative privileges to indentured classes of those with European ancestry or claims to white identities. The American cultural shadow manifests in the ongoing violence against and decimation of Indigenous Native American populations in the dispossession and illegal seizure of their common land as private property, in the captivity and enslavement of Africans to develop massive acres of lands in the South and North of the United States, in the use of cheap Chinese labor to create the transnational railroad, and with the Mexican and Japanese populations in cultivation of the agricultural community.

Ibram Kendi (2016), in *Stamped from the Beginning*, documents the historical arc of racist ideas, practices of racism, and challenges thereto. He offers these insights on the definition of racist ideology and the practices of racism:

> My definition of a racist idea is a simple one: it is any concept that regards one racial group as inferior or superior to another racial group in any way. ... Time and again, powerful and brilliant men and women have produced racist ideas in order to justify the racist policies of their era, in order to redirect the blame for their era's real disparities away from those policies and onto Black people.
>
> (p. 9)

As part of the Covenant of Whiteness and institutionalized practices of inhumanity, each ethnic group was subordinated and oppressed in kind, and deprived of these Constitutional guarantees of freedom, justice, security, and welfare. It is the divisive nature of inhumanity practiced as racism to inflame strife between and among ethnic groups—strife more deleterious than the competition prized in free market capitalism.

The multiculturalism and globalism offer the worldview to be integrated in humanistic–existential psychology. Historically, these theories have failed to cultivate dialecticism and to integrate the structure and acts of inhumanity as they attempt to answer questions of "what it means to be fully human." Real ground for growth and evolution of a depth humanistic–existential psychology is the integration of dialecticism, dialogic conversation, and interrogation of the complexities of what it means to be fully human and fully inhumane in multicultural contexts. The psychopathology of racism is an aspect of this broader inhumanity and fertile ground for such discussion undertaken in this book. Is it not a current inhumane U.S. Government policy to separate Latinx infants and children from their parents and caretakers as they attempt to cross the U.S. border in pursuit of freedom, safety, security, and a better life? Racism as xenophobia militates against humanistic and existential traditions and their lived experience in the multicultural context.

The United States Constitution begins with the proffer,

> We the People of the United States, in Order to form a more perfect Union, establish Justice, insure domestic Tranquility, provide for the common defense, promote the general Welfare, and secure the Blessings of Liberty to ourselves and our Posterity, do ordain and establish this Constitution for the United States of America.

In the shadow of Justice there lies trickery and injustice; in the promise of domestic tranquility there is turmoil, strife, and violence; in the general welfare there is harmful discrimination and hatred; in the blessings of liberty there is incarceration, servitude, and oppression; and in posterity there is the legacy of poverty.

From a multicultural perspective, selected U.S. Supreme Court decisions illustrate practices of inhumanity that contravene the proffer of the U.S. Constitution and the Universal Declaration of Human Rights and challenge principles of humanistic–existential psychology. These include the:

- Indian Removal Act, Native American Trail of Tears (1830)
- Civil Rights Cases: *Dred Scott v. Sanford*, (1857), *Plessey v. Ferguson*, (1896), and *Brown v. Board of Education of Topeka* (Brown I and Brown II) (1954 & 1955)
- Chinese Exclusion Act (1882)
- *Korematsu v. United States* (1944).

Native Americans: The Trail of Tears and Death

The U.S. Indian Removal Act (1830) legalized the appropriation of millions of acres of Native American land. The appropriation was rationalized by the precedents in European property law and the theory of privatization of public land that Native Americans had shared in common. The greatest horror and violence of this action was the "Trail of Tears and Death." Between 1830 and 1850, the Chikasaw, Chocktaw, Creek, Seminole, and Cherokee peoples were forcibly removed from their traditional lands in the southwest United States. The Trail of Tears and Death had specific reference to the relocation of the Cherokee Nation in 1838. European American settlers pressed the federal government to remove Native Americans from the southeast as the encroachment of their lands escalated. The early wealth of America was in the land and in the freedom from the private property laws of feudal systems in Europe, by the elites. President Andrew Jackson was able to drive the Indian Removal Act through the U.S. Congress. It authorized the U.S. government and the state governments of the Union to extinguish Native possession of common lands in the southeast (see Sue & Sue, 2008; Zinn, 1999).

African American U.S. Civil Rights Cases (1857–1954)

Having taken land by force, Congressional enactments, and rule of law, European American elites in the South cultivated wealth through a combination of private property ownership, agriculture, free labor, and the commodification of Africans as property for use and sale. In the North, real property and industrialization produced comparable or greater wealth. The inhumanity in the European American psyche was on display in the 300-year institution of slavery. The violence and violation of the cannons of humanity and religious values were seen in the captivity and enslavement of Africans brought to the New World as sources of free labor and commodities for trade, sale, and purchase. The challenges in the journey to freedom from oppression, physical and mental trauma, alienation, and existential fear and anxiety can be seen in the arc of Congressional legislation and several U.S. Supreme Court decisions: *Dred Scott v. Sanford* (1857, 60 U.S. [19How.] 393); 13th Amendment to the U.S. Constitution (1865); *Plessey v. Ferguson* (1896, 163 U.S. 537); *Sweat v. Painter* (1950, 339 U.S. 629); and *Brown v. Board of Education of Topeka I* (1954, 347 U.S. 483) and *II* (1955, 349 U.S. 294).

The Dred Scott decision rendered Africans captives in America with no legal rights to citizenship. They were chattel property with no redress in the U.S. Judiciary. Later, in 1865, the 13th amendment "abolished slavery and involuntary servitude" with the exception of punishment for criminal conduct. Criminality became the mode of continued enslavement and servitude of African Americans, males in particular (see DuVernay, 2016).

There was the promise of freedom and integration with neither substantive intent nor enforcement. The hunger of capitalism for free labor and excess capital did not abate in the South. The 1896 decision in *Plessey v. Ferguson* gave legal effect to the American system of apartheid and the fiction of "separate but equal." It was not until 1950 in the case of *Sweat v. Painter* that the court debunked the fallacy of "separate but equal" with the admission of the first African American to the University of Texas Law School. In 1954, the decision in *Brown v. Board of Education of Topeka* continued the progress of desegregation in public education and the public space of American society and her cultural institutions. The pursuit of and challenges to these freedoms continue today in the courts and state and federal legislatures with a resurgence of voter suppression, gerrymandering, and large sums of anonymous capital released into the electoral process to leverage outcomes. This was the result of the 2010 *Citizen's United v. Federal Election Commission* decision (Bell, 1980b; Franklin & Moss, 2000).

Chinese Exclusion Act (1882)

During the tenure of President Chester A. Arthur, the Chinese Exclusion Act was the first law implemented to prevent all members of a specific ethnic group from immigrating to the United States. The law excluded skilled and unskilled Chinese laborers from employment in gold mining for ten years under penalty of imprisonment and deportation, although the Chinese had been a cheap labor source for the U.S. transnational railroad. The act was thought by some to legalize racial discrimination, with intent to preserve white superiority and access to scarcer quantities of gold. The Chinese Exclusion Act was repealed in 1943.

Korematsu v. United States, 323, U.S. 214 (1944)

The decision in this case affirmed Executive Order 9066 for internment of Japanese American citizens during World War II, rationalized on the bases of the war with the Japanese Empire and feared invasion of the West Coast. The court decided that the military urgency of circumstances demanded that all citizens of Japanese ancestry be segregated. In May 1942, Japanese Americans were forced to move into relocation camps. Fred Korematsu decided to resist and stayed in his home in San Leandro, California. He had plastic surgery to obscure, if not conceal, his ethnic identity. He was arrested, convicted, and fought the case on grounds that Executive Order 9066 was unconstitutional. On appeal, the 9th Circuit affirmed his conviction, and the U.S. Supreme Court granted certiorari. The case was upheld.

Forty-four years later, apologies and reparations were made to the Japanese families who lost everything during internment. The Federal Civil Liberties Act of 1988, Pub.L, 100–383, granted reparations to 82,219 families who had been interned by the U.S. government during WWII. Race prejudice, war hysteria, and failure of political leadership were reasons for this action.

These cases, viewed from the multicultural perspective, support Kendi's (2016) statement:

> Time and again, powerful and brilliant men and women have produced racist ideas in order to justify the racist policies of their era, in order to redirect the blame for their era's real disparities away from those policies and onto Black people.
>
> (p. 9)

Conclusion

What it means to be optimally human/humane and detrimentally inhuman/ inhumane is the robust question to be raised, discussed and answered in an evolving depth humanistic–existential psychology that integrates dialectics, dialectical analysis, and the transdisciplinary and transcultural/multicultural perspectives in theory, disciplined inquiry, training, and professional practice within core institutions of United States society. How to create optimally humane individuals and a humane society must be considered. Can active imagination be engaged to envision and construct them? Are there existing constructive models of more humane societies upon which to build? A dialectical analysis, of the shadow of humanity, inhumanity, must be engaged and mindfully integrated into the dialog as it operates in the micro systems of United States culture and her social institutions; and in shadowed relational cultural historiographies of her citizens brought to light in multiculturalism. Multiculturalism, in contrast to Eurocentrism, and the multicultural perspective invite a worldview and all human beings into the conversation addressing this question in the 21st century and beyond; breathing life into the proffer of the U.S. Constitution for all of its citizens and the global Declaration of Human Rights.

How are the values of the West and the rest of the world aligned/ misaligned around equity retribution, and distribution of human, economic, and ecological resources (Ferguson, 2011)? The question and answers require integration of transdisciplinary and intersectional perspectives to expand, deepen, and inform humanistic–existential psychology as an agent/agency for survival and evolution of the human species and its sustainable environments. The indigenous multicultural historiographies and wisdom traditions of subordinated populations through varied forms of inhumanity hold promise to support this evolution of consciousness, cultural institutions, communalism, and civilization in this one world. This is one world connected by optic cables lining the oceans of the world and satellites traversing the heavens beaming images of humans and the planet (s) we all inhabit.

Ecology, eco-psychology, and agra-ecology are important topics in the discourse within a contemporary depth humanistic–existential psychology and should be a subject of the dialectical conversations within the evolving field. It seems critical to move beyond the self-interest of individualism embraced by Western philosophical and psychological traditions to cultivate the collective attitudes and values of communalism and planetary consciousness. The earth is our home and there is the need to advocate for a new and equitable Planetary League of Nations, to embrace the sustainability of this single planet inhabited by all—making the Earth, her land, oceans, rivers, and the heavens sacred. This sacred relation to nature is common in the spiritual and religious systems, attitudes, and practices of many human groups in a Global Culture of cultures, living in close connection to nature, as the Indigenous Native Americans once did and many Africans do. They honor the earth and its inter-species inhabitants. Humanity has always been one world, which is better known now with a new consciousness born from 21st century technology. Through advances in technology, the world at a glance can be seen, including the imbalances and other destructive forces of inhumanity in humans and nature. Commentary on technology and its helpful and not so helpful impact on humanity can be addressed in the contemporary discourse within and between depth humanistic–existential and multicultural approaches to psychology.

References

Azibo, D. (1996). *African psychology in historical perspective and related commentary.* Trenton, NJ: African World Press.

Bell, D. (1980a). *Race, racism and American law.* Boston, MA: Little Brown & Company.

Bell, D. (Ed.). (1980b). *Civil rights: Leading cases.* Boston, MA: Little Brown & Company.

Black, H. (1979). *Black's law dictionary.* St. Paul, MN: West Publishing Company.

Comas-Diaz, L. (2014). Multicultural theories of psychotherapy. In D. Wedding, & R. Cosini (Eds.), *Current psychotherapies* (10th ed., pp. 533–564). Belmont, CA: Brooks/Cole Publishers.

Corsini, R., & Wedding, D. (Eds.). (2014). *Current psychotherapies* (10th ed.). Belmont, CA: Brooks/Cole Publishers.

DuVernay, A. (2016). (13th, documentary film). Retrieved from www.avaduvernay.com.

Ferguson, N. (2011). *Civilization: The West and the rest.* New York, NY: Penguin Press.

Franklin, J., & Moss, A. (2000). *From slavery to freedom: A history of African Americans.* New York, NY: Alfred A. Knopf.

Gunther, G. (1980). *Cases and material on Constitutional law* (10th ed.). Mineola, NY: The Foundation Press.

Helms, J. E. (1992). Why is there no study of cultural equivalence in standardized cognitive ability testing? *American Psychologist, 47*(9), 1083–1101.

Jenkins, A. (2001). Humanistic psychology and multiculturalism: A review and reflection. In R. Corsini, & D. Wedding (Eds.) (2014), *Current psychotherapies* (10th ed., pp. 37–48). Belmont, CA: Brooks/Cole Publishers.

Jones, R. (Ed.). (2004). *Black psychology* (4th ed.). Hampton, VA: Cobb & Henry Publisher.

Jung, C. G. (1996). *The practice of psychotherapy* (2nd ed.). Princeton, NJ: Princeton University Press.

Kendi, I. (2016). *Stamped from the beginning, a definitive history of racist ideas in America.* New York, NY: Nations Books.

Maslow, A. (1954). *Motivation and personality.* New York, NY: Harper.

Maslow, A. (1968). *Toward a psychology of being* (Ed.). New York, NY: Van Nostrand Reinhold.

Maslow, A.H. (1943). A theory of human motivation. *Psychological Review, 50*(4), 370–396. Retrieved from http://psychclassics.yorku.ca/Maslow/motivation.htm.

Moss, D. (2001). The roots and genealogy of Humanistic psychology. In K. Schneider, J. Bugental, & J. Pierson (Eds.), *Handbook of humanistic psychology* (pp. 5–20). Thousand Oaks, CA: Sage Publications.

Schneider, K., Bugental, J., & Pierson, J. (Eds.). (2001). *Handbook of humanistic psychology.* Thousand Oaks, CA: Sage Publications.

Sue, D., & Sue, D. (2008). *Counseling the culturally diverse, theory and practice* (5th ed.). New York, NY: John Wiley & Sons.

Yalom, I. D. (1980). *Existential psychotherapy.* New York, NY: Basic Books.

Zinn, H. (1999). *A people's history of the United States 1492–present.* New York, NY: Harper Collins Publisher.

Part II

Multicultural Competencies and Beyond in Humanistic Psychology

6 Multicultural Competencies in Humanistic Psychology

Lisa Vallejos and Zonya Johnson

In a culturally diverse world, cultural competencies are essential for the effective practice of humanistic psychotherapy. It is widely acknowledged that cultural competencies represent foundational skills for all clinicians (American Psychological Association, 2017). Humanistic therapists must successfully address three challenges to acquire these foundational skills. First, they must become acutely aware of their own ethnocultural values, expectations, and biases. This process of self-examination is often emotionally challenging, sometimes exhilarating, for those who have been unaware of their cultural values, but this exploration is an essential component of foundational cultural competencies. Second, clinicians must acquire in-depth knowledge of a variety of ethnocultural groups, and of how the lived experience of these groups varies from their own. As one's knowledge of other groups will always be limited, it is necessary to maintain appropriate cultural humility and have a strategy that facilitates learning about the values of others. Third, the clinician must adopt an ongoing critical stance that acknowledges and deconstructs the values embedded within humanistic psychology and their impact upon those with differing cultural values (see Hoffman, Cleare-Hoffman, & Jackson, 2015). Unacknowledged difference can impede the development of the therapeutic alliance and consequently clinical efficacy.

The American Psychological Association (APA) established initial guidelines on training in multiculturalism in 2002; however, in 2017 the guidelines were expanded to encompass a greater appreciation of the complexity of this topic. The APA published *Multicultural Guidelines: An Ecological Approach to Context, Identity, and Intersectionality*, revising the standards to emphasize the concept of intersectionality as well as the critical importance of understanding one's own cultural identity.

The concept of *intersectionality* (Crenshaw, 1989) spotlights the fact that people hold multiple identities and that these identities cannot be held separately from each other (see also Chapter 17). For instance, as Crenshaw stated, a Black woman has experiences that are informed by being Black and by being a woman. These identities are not separate, and in fact may serve to reinforce one another.[1] APA guidelines encourage clinicians "to recognize and understand that identity and self-definition are fluid and complex and that the interaction between the two is dynamic" (p. 4). Intersectionality reflects the reality that all of an individual's social contexts impact one's identity. It is, consequently, an important consideration for psychologists working in a multicultural context.

Correspondingly, the APA guidelines suggest that therapists become knowledgeable of their own ethnocultural values, expectations, and biases. This emphasis upon cultural self-awareness, and ongoing self-reflection is relatively new in contemporary clinical psychology and training programs have not universally embraced this goal. In fact, many universities fail to require a comprehensive inclusivity track to their programs and some fail to require any diversity courses or trainings at all. Although Sue, Arredondo, and McDavis (1992) note that between the years of 1977 and the early 1980s there was an increase from 1% of universities that had at least one course on multicultural issues to 89%, they also note that there is no way of measuring the efficacy or appropriateness of the courses (p. 477). APA, as part of their accreditation process, suggests,

> As a basic standard of eligibility for accreditation by the American Psychological Association (APA), the institution is expected to provide evidence of "actions that indicate respect for and understanding of cultural differences and individual diversity" (APA, 1995, p. 57). This standard should be reflected in the program's policies, faculty, students, curriculum, and field placements.
>
> (APA, 2/06/2019)

However, it has not clarified what specifically needs to be included in the curriculum.

Should such a curriculum become standardized, it should not only include cultural facts and academic knowledge, but also training on skills in working with diverse and multicultural populations. It should also require deep exploration into attitudes, implicit biases, and the power of systemic/cultural influences on all aspects of life.

How Can Humanistic Psychologists Achieve These Goals?

Until recent years, many psychology training programs had no curricular requirements in multiculturalism. Others may have had one required course into which all relevant cultural issues were presumably channeled. While better than nothing, such "ghettoized" courses could not possibly have an impact on developing a broad-based cultural perspective. Other programs simply included the phrase "cultural considerations" in their syllabi without an explanation of what those considerations might be. Unfortunately, this paucity in training has created quite a gap between the stated goals of multicultural awareness and the achievement of those goals.

Strengthening curricular offerings can be difficult, as faculty often need substantial personal and curricular support to teach in this area. They may be willing yet not feel well equipped or culturally competent themselves. It is important that this be acknowledged without judgment and support should be offered. An additional obstacle to addressing these issues results when institutions claim to place a high value on diversity and multiculturalism, yet the faculty and administration remain predominantly White. They fail to implement effective recruitment processes that would result in a more diverse institution, including diverse students, faculty, and administration. Hoffman (2016) similarly critiqued humanistic psychology in the United States for explicitly stating a value for diversity while failing to actualize this value. The failure to actualize was rooted, in part, to a lack of sustained intentionality to become more diverse. In conclusion, it is necessary that humanistic psychologists address these systemic and pedagogical obstacles to ensure that multiculturalism and diversity goals are achieved.

Impact of Unexamined Cultural Values

Johnson (2001) addressed some of the ongoing challenges to developing cultural competencies in humanistic psychology. She suggested that unacknowledged cultural value differences embedded within humanistic psychology may serve as a deterrent to clients seeking therapy and an obstacle to effective ongoing therapy. One such deterrent, according to Johnson, is the strong individualistic perspective of humanistic psychology. This Euro–American cultural value is reflected in the importance of self-actualization and the way in which this concept has been developed.

However, as Johnson (2001) points out, in many cultures, individualism and a strong focus upon self is not as highly valued as it is in Euro-American cultural groups. Many other cultures focus on a culturally defined collective good rather than pursuing individual goals or self-actualization. The relevant collective may range from a small nuclear family, to a broadly defined extended family, to society at large, but in these cultures the focus is not on the individual. Here, the value is placed on goals that benefit the group rather than the self, and a therapy that aims for individualization, autonomy, and self-determination may be jarring for those members of those groups. This often leads to therapeutic disconnects that are rarely acknowledged or discussed, damaging the development of a therapeutic alliance. In fact, in the absence of an awareness of these values, the therapist may be unaware of the disconnect.

In addition to not prioritizing individual goals, there are cultures where self-actualization is not believed to be possible or desirable (Johnson, 2001). The cultural values reflected in the Western desire to overcome all obstacles, or in the concept of "manifest destiny," may be at odds with the values of other groups. In those cultures, the prevailing value may be upon learning to adjust to the human condition rather than pursuing what to them may seem like a futile goal. These cultural values are often opaque to therapist and client and yet they can still cause significant strain and a failure to connect. The danger here is not whether the value is "adaptive" or not. The danger is in a lack of awareness of this value conflict, which prevents any exploration of its impact and introduces the possibility of unintentional imposition of values. Acknowledgement and discussion of the value differences may be necessary to moving forward.

In seeing themselves as "citizens of the world" (p. 217), Johnson (2001) wrote that humanistic psychologists run the risk of limiting their perspective to the larger issues, and not seeing real and immediate social challenges faced by many marginalized and oppressed clients as well as challenges related to the daily and unavoidable experience of racism, sexism, homophobia, poverty, and the like. Indeed, those who carry cultural privilege have a choice of addressing the larger picture while navigating life, without having to consider the immediate and pervasive impact of race, color, gender identity, and sexual orientation on daily experience. Humanistic psychology's focus on an individual's potential risks falling prey to naïve views that—like naïve views on the American Dream—advocate all people can succeed if they work hard enough. They do not recognize the additional barriers to actualizing one's potential for many individuals from marginalized groups.

Finally, it is important that clients who experience oppression or who are "othered" find a safe environment in their therapy (Johnson, 2001). This requires proactive effort toward awareness of how the biopsychosocial environment—including current and historic oppression, systemic racism, and societal systems such as the legal system, educational system, penal system, and the health care system—may have impacted the client. Awareness of the impact of these factors requires a sophisticated understanding of the psychologist's internalized privilege, racism, and other possible manifestations of implicit bias. Without a keen awareness of these dynamics, the psychologist will miss vital aspects of their clients' lived experience, rendering the therapeutic experience much less effective.

History of Multicultural Counseling

It was not until the latter part of the 20th century that multicultural counseling competencies began to be addressed. It was largely the work of Sue et al. (1992) that began to shine a light on the need for a cultural competencies framework for counseling. As Sue and colleagues noted, it was the work of the Association of Multicultural Counseling and Development (AMCD) at their conference in 1991 that thrust the conversation of multicultural competencies into the spotlight. At this meeting, 31 competencies were developed and the AMCD encouraged the counseling profession to consider adopting them for accreditation purposes. While multiculturalism had been a hot topic for a number of years to that point, there had yet to be one organizing document or call to action. The development of the Multicultural Competencies and Standards was a call to arms that was needed to push the profession into deeper reflection and integration. It is important to note that, prior to this time, clients from various backgrounds and demographics were treated in the same way as their White/European counterparts. There were no studies or inquiries into the efficacy of therapy for diverse clients and the client who did not thrive in these traditional environments was considered to be flawed. For example, diverse clients often were labeled as not verbal enough or not psychologically minded, rather than inquiring as to whether the therapy was a good fit.

Quinn (2012) pointed out that the 2001 report from the U.S. Department of Health and Human Services Surgeon General concluded "definitive multicultural research evidence demonstrating psychotherapy's relevance for minority populations was nonexistent" (p. 203). Quinn goes on to note that "since then, however, counseling research has emerged suggesting that culturally adapted psychotherapy may be effective compared to both unadapted forms and to no treatment" (p. 203).

Multicultural competencies in therapy are important because studies have reflected that even though minorities are only a small portion of the U.S. population, about 84% of psychologists and mental health providers are White (Lin, Stamm, & Christidis, 2018). With the publication of the APA Standards for Practice, the recommendations for competent practice included several suggestions that had been put forth in the previous several decades (APA, 2002). These suggestions brought increasing refinement to the task facing the clinician. As a first step, in keeping with the historical developments in this field, clinicians were encouraged to be culturally aware. This step involved asking psychologists to notice and celebrate diversity and multiculturalism in an environment where diversity was often not even acknowledged. Next, clinicians were encouraged to learn cultural details of the ethnocultural groups that they are likely to work with (i.e., acquiring knowledge). This led to an appeal to avoid being intentionally or unintentionally racist or ethnocentric, which required self-reflection. The last guideline was to use interventions that are appropriate to the cultural group. It was felt that with attention to these guidelines put forth by the APA—awareness, knowledge, self-reflection and appropriate intervention—the clinician could achieve cultural competency.

Recent focus in this field has included the concept of *cultural humility*. This concept embraces a process-oriented approach to cultural competencies that involves a lifelong commitment to self-evaluation and critique (Tervalon & Murray-Garcia, 1998). It highlights that cultural competencies are not a static goal to be achieved but a lifelong process to be engaged in. This concept also focuses attention on the unnecessary power imbalances that exist in relationships and it places a high value upon therapist partnerships with those who advocate for others. Thus, cultural humility incorporates the concept of cultural competencies and advocacy for others, while emphasizing that competencies and humility are an accomplishment that is larger than the individual. This situates the concept within a systemic perspective.

In summary, the traditional path to competencies required that psychologists be culturally aware, and that they notice and celebrate difference. The field requires moving beyond cultural awareness and knowing the cultures of those with whom we work with while using culturally appropriate interventions. Most recently, clinicians are being asked to engage these tasks within a framework of cultural humility.

History of Humanistic Psychology and Multicultural Competencies

Hoffman et al. (2015) noted that even,

> as the field of psychology became more diverse, humanistic psychology continued to be led and represented primarily by white male voices. Additionally, important female voices, such as Charlotte Bühler and Eleanor Criswell, were often under acknowledged and neglected in professional literature.
>
> (p. 42)

They note that in 1999 Eleanor Criswell drafted a statement to include multicultural perspectives that sadly never gained much traction. However, the ball had begun to roll and the original version of *The Handbook of Humanistic Psychology* (2001) contained a chapter critiquing humanistic psychology for not having been successful in addressing multicultural counseling. The handbook included other critiques of humanistic psychology, including the lack of inclusion of women, particularly in leadership and scholarship (Serlin & Criswell, 2001). Other chapters included discussions on cross-cultural counseling and other frameworks. Unfortunately, these efforts failed to make much of an impact in the field of humanistic psychology as a whole.

It was not until 2007 that the movement toward diversity and inclusion started to gain momentum, with many stops and starts. As Hoffman et al. (2015) wrote, at the First Annual Conference for the Society for Humanistic Psychology, most of the presenters were White males and few presentations considered diversity. However, by the second year there were more presentations on these topics, albeit poorly attended. By the third year, the majority of presenters were not White males, and presentations on diversity were more popular and well attended. In 2012–2013, under the leadership of Louis Hoffman during his tenure as the President for the Society of Humanistic Psychology, greater strides were taken to increase diversity and representation. This was reflected in continued progress, resulting in books, chapters, presentations, and task forces specifically created to address multiculturalism and diversity, including the advancement of the Indigenous Psychology Task Forces that began under Louise Sundrarajan's leadership when she was president of the Society for Humanistic Psychology as well as the Presidential Task Force on Diversity that was developed in 2012 by Hoffman. Both Kirk Schneider and Shawn Rubin, in their roles as Editors for the *Journal of Humanistic Psychology*, were intentionally inclusive in their efforts to increase the representation of multicultural experts on the board of editors, and to make efforts to include more content focusing on diversity. Additionally, there have been successful initiatives to make cross-cultural connections, including annual trips to China under the leadership of Louis Hoffman, Mark Yang, and Xuefu Wang. Of note, an article published in 2016 titled, "An Existential–Humanistic Perspective on Black Lives Matter and Contemporary Protest Movements" (Hoffman, Granger, Vallejos, & Moats, 2016), is one of the most downloaded articles in the history of the *Journal for Humanistic Psychology*. All of these signs point to a more engaged and intentionally diverse future for humanistic psychology.

Recently, Donna Rockwell, during her term as the President of the Society for Humanistic Psychology, implemented a Heritage award, titled the Eleanor Criswell Hanna Award Celebrating Women in Humanistic Psychology. Fittingly, the first award recipient was Eleanor Criswell Hanna. Additionally, in 2017, Nathaniel Granger, Jr. was elected as the second African American President for the Society for Humanistic Psychology and he governs the most diverse board in the history of the Society of Humanistic Psychology. While these are important developments, history has shown that it is important to maintain ongoing intentionality in the commitment to diversity or regressions are likely to occur.

Multicultural Counseling Model and/or Practitioner Skills

Sue et al. (1992) established a Multicultural Counseling Model with foundational components that the therapist ought to master in the development of cultural competencies. This model is in keeping with those competencies suggested in the APA Guidelines. These items are knowledge of the client's worldview, therapist awareness of their own assumptions, and learning culturally adapted inventions.

A well-known adage in the therapeutic world is "therapist, know thyself" and this is strikingly important in multicultural counseling. Helms' (1990) White Racial Identity Development model illustrates the importance of considering the question of what it means to be White in the United States. Many therapists have not taken the time to consider the ways in which their reality differs in substantive ways from those who are outside of the cultural norms (White, cis, hetero, male, Christian, middle class). That lack of awareness includes a lack of awareness of unconscious biases and a dismissal of cultural differences, such as a colorblind ideology.

Sue et al. (1992) wrote that "a culturally skilled counselor is one who is actively in the process of becoming more aware of [their] own assumptions about human behavior, values, biases, preconceived notions, personal limitations and so forth" (p. 481). This is important in considering the impact of blind spots on the client's experience.

Various writers have identified their experience in therapy with therapists who lack cultural competencies as having been traumatic. For instance, in a piece titled "Why I Left my White Therapist," the author describes having discussed race with her therapist who then became combative and hostile (Babu, 2017). The piece goes on to say "They (white therapists) pathologize the client. Racism becomes 'paranoia,' or 'hostility.' For black men especially, they translate their experiences into terrible mental health diagnoses that end up putting their lives at further risk." Often, therapists can inadvertently cause harm by perpetuating stereotypes such as, "I'm sure you can cope with this as you're a strong Black woman," "I know Black people are very religious," or "did you grow up in the inner city?" (Constantine, 2007, p. 5). Additionally, therapists lacking these skills can fail to acknowledge the role race plays in oppression that contributes to victim blaming or the myth of meritocracy, which pushes the narrative that "if Black people just worked harder, they could be successful like other people" (p. 5).

Sue et al. (1992) state, "a culturally skilled counselor is one who actively attempts to understand the worldview of [their] culturally different client without negative judgments" (p. 481). Cultural awareness is important so as not to misunderstand clients and their variety of expressions or their way of being in the world. One example can be the community and connectedness found in Latinx families, which can be viewed as enmeshed by those who strictly operate from a Western worldview. This ability to see things through the client's worldview is also important in terms of diagnosis, because what is a cultural norm in some cultures could easily be pathologized through a Western lens. For example, in Mexican families, it is not uncommon to hear people say that they are afflicted by *mal de ojo* (evil eye) and that their afflictions are caused by it. The treatment for *mal de ojo* is to see a "curandero" (healer). A therapist without cultural context could easily see this person as mentally ill and misdiagnose or misunderstand their experience.

Finally, the culturally competent counselor is "in the process of actively developing and practicing appropriate, relevant, and sensitive intervention strategies and skills in working with his or her culturally different clients" (Sue et al., 1992, p. 481). This is particularly relevant with understanding cultural expression. Hoffman and Cleare-Hoffman (2011) note that there are various ways in which particular cultures express emotion, with Latinx and African American cultures being more expressive, which can lead to them being identified as "angry, out of control or too emotional" (p. 262). They typically are labelled such by people from Euro-American cultures that value greater restriction upon emotional expression. They go on to note,

> Chinese people typically express their emotion in more subtle forms. For individuals who are not familiar with the Chinese ways of expressing emotions, these subtle forms are often not recognized, leading to the stereotype that Chinese do not experience or express emotions.
>
> (p. 263)

In these cases, a therapist rooted in cultural competencies would not immediately label the individuals as such but would take measures to increase awareness of the cultural context and adapt their interventions appropriately.

It can be argued that therapists who encourage their clients to operate within the status quo contribute to the problem if there is not a shared understanding of the conflicting values in play (Nadal, 2017). Consequently, another important therapist competency involves understanding when and how adjustment to existing systems might be maladaptive. Whether involving the use of medication, adaptive and/or coping behaviors, or learning to adjust to society, therapists often encourage people to try to adjust to their circumstance when adjusting to an oppressive environment. This generally is not beneficial and may, in fact, be harmful or even immoral (Nichols & Vallejos, 2018). According to Utsey, Chae, Brown, and Kelly (2002), there are race-related issues that are present in clients of minority backgrounds that do not represent evidence of pathology and mental illness but rather adaptive responses to ongoing racial stressors.

Clinical Vignette

Bobby was a 26-year-old African American male who presented for therapy for "anger issues." The therapist was a woman of Latinx background. The young man was on the brink of losing yet another job due to angry outbursts and came to therapy for help. He described his latest outburst at work being related to a co-worker committing racial microaggressions on a regular basis. During therapy, the therapist asked Bobby if he'd considered how being a Black man in the United States may have affected his experience at work. This started an exploration in which Bobby developed a deeper understanding of his life and experiences. It led him to finding a quote by James Baldwin that reads "To be a Negro in this country and to be relatively conscious is to be in a rage almost all the time" (Baldwin et al., 1961, p. 205). Finally, he felt he had a voice and an understanding for why he had been so angry for so long. This led him down a path of learning how to advocate for himself, and to understand that being angry was a normal response to being aggrieved. While it did not immediately change his anger, it helped Bobby to contextualize and to begin to find different coping mechanisms.

Had this client been seen in another environment, he might have been misdiagnosed or pathologized when really what he needed was a way to give voice to his anger and to learn to advocate for himself in more productive and generative ways. This is how a culturally responsive framework can help to fulfill the vision of Rollo May (1981): "the purpose of psychotherapy is to set people free" (p. 19).

Toward a Liberation Framework

We maintain that it is impossible to move forward with a culturally competent humanistic psychology without therapists developing what is known as a *critical consciousness*. Critical consciousness is a pedagogy developed by Paulo Freire (1970) in his book *Pedagogy of the Oppressed*. This book proposes a new way of thinking that encourages examining one's social and political position as well as their way of seeing the world. It encourages people to move from being subjects of their social position toward acting on their social position. This means that instead of being passively acted upon by their society, they find ways to act on their situation. This may include becoming engaged in civics, creating protest art, becoming more vocal, or generating activities that can help channel energies into productive venues. While these activities may not always change the external situation, they may help the person feel more engaged and empowered in their situation, leading to decreased levels of hopelessness and powerlessness. Hoffman et al. (2016) similarly note that engaging in activism can be a powerful source of community and communal healing. Lewis and Lee (2009) propose that educators should "directly and consistently educate students to critically discuss sexism, homophobia, racism, classism, and cultural respect" in every discipline, but especially psychology (p. 50).

Freire's work would later lead into a framework known as *Liberation Psychology*, which is relatively unknown in humanistic psychology, despite falling under its umbrella. Liberation psychology has many components, but a central theme involves challenging psychology's role of upholding the status quo instead of challenging its inherent suppositions that support Western perspectives, Eurocentrism, and institutional racism. Often, therapies for people of color include encouraging adaptation to pathological conditions. Ignacio Martin-Baro, another trailblazer in Liberation Psychology, believed that psychology must consider whether the client's behavior and thought reflected an abnormal response, or whether it reflected a normal response to an abnormal situation (Watkins and Shulman, 2008). Smith, Chambers, and

Bratani (2009) wrote that it is important to address "oppression not only as a contextual factor but also as a direct, specific cause of emotional and physical trauma" (p. 160). A liberation framework helps individuals understand that they can "deconstruct what is normalized, raise consciousness on how to combat oppression, and (re)conceptualize themselves as members of a collective" (Nadal, 2017, p. 943).

Martin-Baro (as cited in Watkins & Shulman, 2008) proposed new ways of approaching psychology to create circumstances of liberation that would be an appropriate "next step" for humanistic psychology. He suggests that psychological wellness should be viewed in the context of social, economic, and political environments as well; psychology needs a new epistemology wherein the therapist is no longer the expert, but a collaborator, a witness, and a "holder of faith" (Watkins & Shulman, 2008, p. 26) for people who have been silenced in their effort to find their voices. Finally, psychology needs a new praxis that is, according to Watkins & Shulman (2008), "to transform and humanize repressive or failing human institutions. All of the people who participate in them must also be transformed and humanized through participatory dialogue and creative imagination about alternatives" (p. 27).

Conclusion

It is important to remember our past and to honor it in going forward. While historically humanistic psychology has not been in the forefront of developing multicultural perspectives, there is an emerging solid commitment to create a culturally responsive, multicultural competencies framework. With the increased efforts toward multicultural perspectives as well as continued leadership in this direction, humanistic psychology has continued to be a leader in developing standards for the lifelong quest to develop cultural competencies within a framework of cultural humility. The goal is for humanistic psychology to continue to provide leadership in the journey toward social justice, and the creation of a psychology that endeavors to be of service to, and an effective tool of, the liberation of people of all backgrounds.

- Future trends in humanistic psychology ought to consider implementing a liberation perspective to incorporate a holistic view of how oppression impacts marginalized individuals and groups.
- Humanistic psychology may benefit from research studies that examine the benefit of adapted humanistic approaches with multicultural clients. One critique of humanistic psychology is that there has not been enough empirically based research focused upon multiculturalism, and, as such, future humanistic practitioners will benefit from such research. An ongoing critique of humanistic psychology is the lack of empirical research available to support clinical and theoretical positions; thus, the profession would benefit from studies that address this concern.

- Humanistic psychology has adapted and grown in terms of multi-cultural competencies but there is still much more work to be done. Humanistic psychology must continue to be intentional about bringing in diverse individuals into the field, but it is also important to go beyond increased numbers to fully integrate these diverse voices into discussions and positions of leadership.
- Humanistic clinicians must be aware that multicultural competencies and cultural humility are part of an ongoing process of self-reflection and growth. To be culturally competent requires an ongoing effort to continually increase one's awareness of diversity and effectiveness in working with diverse groups.

Note

1 It is important to note that the term Intersectional, as defined by Crenshaw, was specifically related to the experience of Black women. As with many things, including the Me Too movement, other groups have appropriated this term and its application has become increasingly broad.

References

American Psychological Association. (2002). Report of the APA task force on the implementation of multicultural guidelines. Retrieved from www.apa.org/about/policy/multicultural-report.pdf

American Psychological Association. (2006). Guidelines and principles for accreditation of programs in professional psychology (G&P). Retrieved from www.apa.org/ed/accreditation/about/policies/guiding-principles.pdf

American Psychological Association. (2017). *Multicultural guidelines: An ecological approach to context, identity, and intersectionality.* Retrieved from www.apa.org/about/policy/multicultural-guidelines.pdf

American Psychological Association. (2019). Diversity and accreditation. Retrieved from www.apa.org/pi/oema/resources/brochures/accreditation

Babu, C. (2017). *Why I left my White therapist.* Retrieved from https://tonic.vice.com/en_us/article/d7pa5j/why-i-left-my-white-therapist

Baldwin, J., Capouya, E., Hansberry, L., Lentoff, N., Hughes L., & Kazin, A. (1961). The Negro in American culture. *CrossCurrents, 11*(3), 205–224. Retrieved from www.jstor.org/stable/24456864

Constantine, M. (2007). Racial microaggressions against African American clients in cross-racial counseling relationships. *Journal of Counseling Psychology, 54*(1), 1–16.

Crenshaw, K. (1989). Demarginalizing the intersection of race and sex: A Black feminist critique of antidiscrimination doctrine, feminist theory and antiracist politics. *University of Chicago Legal Forum, 1989*(1), 139–167.

Freire, P. (1970). *Pedagogy of the oppressed.* New York, NY: Continuum.

Helms, J. E. (1990/1993). Toward a model of White racial identity development. In J. E. Helms (Ed.), *Black and White racial identity* (pp. 49–66). New York, NY: Greenwood/Praeger.

Hoffman, L. (2016). Multiculturalism and humanistic psychology: From neglect to epistemological and ontological diversity. *The Humanistic Psychologist, 44*, 56–71.

Hoffman, L., & Cleare-Hoffman, H. (2011). Existential therapy and emotions: Lessons from cross-cultural exchange. *The Humanistic Psychologist, 39*(3), 261–267.

Hoffman, L., Cleare-Hoffman, H., & Jackson, T. (2015). Humanistic psychology and multiculturalism: History, current status, and advancements. In K. J. Schneider, J. F. T. Bugental, & J. F. Pierson (Eds.), *The handbook of humanistic psychology* (2nd ed., pp. 41–55). Thousand Oaks, CA: Sage Publications.

Hoffman, L., Granger, N. Jr., Vallejos, L., & Moats, M. (2016). An existential–humanistic perspective on Black Lives Matter and contemporary protest movements. *Journal of Humanistic Psychology, 56*, 595–611.

Johnson, Z. (2001). Cultural competencies and humanistic psychology. *The Humanistic Psychologist, 29*, 204–222.

Lewis, M., & Lee, A. (2009). Critical consciousness in introductory psychology: A historically black university context. *Pedagogy and the Human Sciences, 1*(1), 50–60.

Lin, L., Stamm, K., & Christidis, P. (2018). How diverse is the psychology workforce?. *Monitor on Psychology, 49*(2), 19.

May, R. (1981). *Freedom and destiny*. New York, NY: Norton & Company.

Nadal, K. (2017). "Let's get in formation": On becoming a psychologist-activist in the 21st century. *American Psychologist, 72*(9), 935–945.

Nichols, J., & Vallejos, L. (2018). *Pain is not pathology*. Presentation at the Society of Humanistic Psychology Annual Conference, Boulder, CO.

Quinn, A. (2012). A person-centered approach to multicultural counseling competence. *Journal of Humanistic Psychology, 52*(2), 202–251.

Serlin, I. D., & Criswell, E. (2001). Humanistic psychology and women: A critical-historical perspective. In K. J. Schneider, J. F. T. Bugental, & J. F. Pierson (Eds.), *The handbook of humanistic psychology* (2nd ed., pp. 29–36). Thousand Oaks, CA: Sage Publications.

Smith, L., Chambers, D-A., & Bratani, L. (2009). When oppression is the Pathogen: The participatory development of socially just mental health practice. *American Journal of Orthopsychiatry, 79*(2), 159–168.

Sue, D. W., Arredondo, P., & McDavis, J. R. (1992). Multicultural counseling competencies and standards: A call to the profession. *Journal of Counseling & Development, 70*, 477–486.

Tervalon, M., & Murray-Garcia, J. (1998). Cultural humility versus cultural competence: A critical distinction in defining physician training outcomes in multicultural education. *Journal of Health Care for the Poor and Underserved, 9*, 117–125.

Utsey, S., Chae, M., Brown, C., & Kelly, D. (2002). Effect of ethnic group membership on ethnic identity, race-related stress, and quality of life. *Cultural Diversity & Ethnic Minority Psychology, 8*, 366–377.

Watkins, M., & Shulman, H. (2008). *Toward psychologies of liberation*. New York, NY: Palgrave MacMillan.

7 Microaggressions and Humanistic Psychology

Nathaniel Granger, Jr.

There is little literature focused on specific issues of the effects of micro-aggressions from a humanistic perspective. There is, however, increasingly a significant body of empirical research on the impact of microaggressions on various marginalized groups. Chester Pierce first coined the term racial microaggressions in 1978, referring to the everyday subtle and often automatic *put-downs* and insults directed toward Black Americans (Pierce, Carew, Pierce-Gonzalez, & Willis, 1978). While Pierce's theory focused solely on racial microaggressions, microaggressions can be expressed toward any marginalized group. These actions can be gender-based, sexual orientation-based, class-based, or disability-based (Sue, Capodilupo, & Holder, 2008).

Sue (2010) expounded on the definition as "Brief and commonplace daily verbal, behavioral, and environmental indignities, whether intentional or unintentional, that communicates hostile, derogatory, or negative racial, gender, sexual orientation, and religious slights and insults to the target person or group" (p. 5). Perpetrators are often unaware of having engaged in an exchange that demeans the recipient of the communication or action. Often referred to as *the new racism* (Cleare-Hoffman, Granger, & Hoffman, 2010), microaggressions are intentional or unintentional ways of communicating indignities through verbal, behavioral, or environmental mediums directed toward people from particular cultural groups (Sue, 2010). Frequently, microaggressions are rather ambiguous, leaving it difficult to determine whether a slight was intended and making it easy to deny that a microaggression even occurred. Common responses to microaggressions include feelings of confusion and anger, often followed by feelings of inferiority. The internal struggle is exacerbated when it seems obvious that the perpetrator had no ill intent in conveying the denigrating message. Society is replete with these microaggressions that more often than not go unnoticed and yet often have a lasting impact on the recipient.

When microaggressions remain hidden, and unspoken, or are excused as innocuous slights with minimal harm, this enables individuals to continue behaviors that insult, demean, alienate, and oppress marginalized groups

(Sue, 2010). For this to change, it is critical that mental health professionals as well as a majority of the general public recognize microaggressions and seek to ameliorate their effects. Hence, facilitation in *making the invisible visible* when it comes to microaggressions becomes the substratum on which much of the research outcomes are predicated. The term itself has gained popularity in the past decade; however, due to the ambiguous and ubiquitous nature of the term, divisions between and within groups are perpetuated as a result of a lack of understanding the many nuances associated with microaggressions and the universality of this deleterious human condition. The distinction between microaggressions and other alleged social ills must be clearly delineated in order to ameliorate the impact of microaggressions and enumerate the role of the clinician, particularly in existential–humanistic psychology.

Microaggressions can be categorized under three types: *microassaults, microinsults,* and *microinvalidations.*

- Microassaults are described as "conscious, deliberate, and either subtle or explicit racial, gender, or sexual-orientation biased attitudes, beliefs, or behaviors that are communicated to marginalized groups through environmental cues, verbalizations, or behaviors" (Sue, 2010, p. 28).
- "Microinsults are characterized by interpersonal or environmental communications that convey stereotypes, rudeness, and insensitivity that demeans a person's racial, gender, or sexual orientation, heritage, or identity. Microinsults represent subtle snubs, frequently outside the conscious awareness of the perpetrator, but convey an oftentimes hidden insulting message to the recipient" (Sue, 2010, p. 31).
- "Microinvalidations are characterized by communications or environmental cues that exclude, negate, or nullify the psychological thoughts, feelings, or experiential reality of certain groups, such as people of color, women, and LGBTs. In many ways, microinvalidations may potentially represent the most damaging form of the three microaggressions because they directly and insidiously deny the racial, gender, or sexual-orientation reality of these groups. The power to impose reality upon marginalized groups represents the ultimate form of oppression" (Sue, 2010, p. 37).

Providing evidence that microaggressions are not restricted to racial microaggressions, Sarno and Wright (2013) note, "Homonegative microaggressions are small verbal, behavioral, or environmental slights, intentional or unintentional, that communicate hostile or derogatory messages toward sexual minorities" (p. 63). Albeit, there is a plethora of evidence to indicate that perceptions of discrimination based on sexual orientation negatively impacts the mental health of lesbian, gay, bisexual, transgender, and nonbinary individuals (LGBT+) individuals. Discrimination and harassment are still very pronounced realities for members of the LGBT+

community: it was found in one study that 33.5% of LGB participants experienced perceived discrimination in their lifetimes (Kessler, Mickelson, & Williams, 1999).

The polarized, Black–White/straight–gay/right–wrong way of thinking is a primary culprit to microaggressive behaviors. Schneider (2013) notes that polarization "has appeared as bigotry, bullying, tyranny, vengefulness, and arrogance; and it has also manifested as narrowness, rigidity, pedantry, and obsession" (p. 19). He attributes the polarized mind as arising as a defense to one's existential place in the world and a feeling of *cosmic insignificance* that becomes heightened in times of individual or collective trauma. The individual with a polarized mind (Schneider, 2013) may feel an especially strong need to cling to his or her perspectives, ideologies, and psychological constructs in order to avoid feeling helpless, powerless, or small.

Critics have accused researchers of exaggerating the detrimental impact of microaggressions (Schacht, 2008; Thomas, 2008). However, microaggressions are constant and continuing experiences of marginalized groups. Microaggressions assail the self-esteem of recipients, produce anger and frustration, deplete psychic energy, lower feelings of subjective well-being and worthiness, produce physical health problems, shorten life expectancy, and deny minority populations equal access and opportunity in education, employment, and health care (Brondolo, Kelly, Coakley, Gordon, Thompson, & Levy, 2005; Clark, Anderson, Clark, & Williams, 1999; Franklin, 2000; Noh & Kaspar, 2003; Smedley & Smedley, 2005; Solórzano, Ceja, & Yosso, 2000; Sue, Capodilupo, & Holder, 2008; Wei, Ku, Russell, Mallinckrodt, & Liao, 2008; Williams, Neighbors, & Jackson, 2003; Yoo & Lee, 2008). Any one microaggression alone may be minimally impactful, but when they occur continuously throughout a lifespan, their cumulative nature can have major detrimental consequences (Holmes & Holmes, 1970; Meyer, 1995; Utsey, Giesbrecht, Hook, & Stanard, 2008; Utsey & Ponterotto, 1996). Many Whites, for example, fail to realize that from the moment of birth people of color are subjected to multiple racial microaggressions from the media, peers, neighbors, friends, teachers, and even in the educational process and/or curriculum itself. These insults and indignities are so pervasive that they are often unrecognized. Consequently, White individuals are often unaware of the cumulative harm that people of color experience from being routinely subjected to various racial microaggressions (Sue, 2010).

Under the umbrella of "good intent" are subtle forms of racial bias, referred to as *color-blind racism* (Bonilla-Silva, 2006). This refers to the conception among White individuals that considerations of race are presently no longer relevant in people's lives in the United States. Bonilla-Silva describe contemporary color-blind racism as the prevailing racial ideology of the post-civil rights era expressed in everyday beliefs, attitudes, and behaviors that are considered acceptable, and even commendable, by many

White individuals who use them and a noble goal for many Whites who are socialized to think that seeing race is inherently wrong. Because of how deeply these attitudes are embedded within society, many White people with good intentions consider themselves nonracist despite holding and expressing these problematic beliefs (Sue, 2003). Color-blind racism often contributes to occurrence of racial microaggressions (Pierce, Carew, Pierce-Gonzalez, & Willis, 1978). Color-blind racial attitudes have been negatively correlated with multicultural competency (Chao, 2006). Similarly, color-blind attitudes have been correlated with negative attitudes about affirmative action (Awad, Cokley, & Ravitch, 2005), a tendency to deny the existence of structural and ideological racism (Bonilla-Silva, 2002), and minimization of the role race contributes to perceived racist events, and avoiding discussions of racial differences to appear nonbiased (Apfelbaum, Sommers, & Norton, 2008; Bonilla-Silva, 2002).

Individuals from marginalized groups often are asked to "calm down," "discuss topics rationally," "not be so sensitive," or "let things go" when confronted with microaggressions. While individuals offering this advice may have or perceive themselves as having good intentions, they are not aware that this represents further oppression through asking them to conform to how others want them to communicate while encouraging them to leave behind their own cultural way of being. Good intentioned therapists, too, can easily fall into the pattern of asking their clients who have experienced microaggressions or other forms of racism to calm down or let go of the associated pain. Therapists with multicultural competence instead honor the cultural differences and ways of being even when causing the therapist discomfort (Cleare-Hoffman, Granger, & Hoffman, 2010).

Historical Implications

Members of the dominant or privileged cultural group are the typical perpetrators of microaggressions. While the term *microaggression* is a contemporary concept, they are rooted in and cannot be understood apart from history. One example of the historical implication of slavery on the mindset of African Americans in reference to education is captured in the poetic work of Granger's poem "'Dat 'Dere Book," (Granger, 2012), which goes back in time to a period where knowledge and literacy were seen as a threat to the prosperous institution of slavery. The current struggle for knowledge, education, and justice within the African American community, or why schooling and access to integrated schools was denied, was at the heart of the Civil Rights Movement:

> Whatchu doin?! Put 'dat book down!
> You's gone git us alls in trouble!
> Who learned you how to read anyway?

Miss Paulie?!
You tell Miss Paulie don't she ever learn you how to read no mo'
You's gone git us alls in trouble!
Master said da biggest sin for a negro
Is the sin of learnin'
Master said a negro ain't s'posed to be learned
Master said negroes s'posed to be trained
Just like 'dat scrong mule out back
And like 'dat mare over there
Likes all the other animals on this here plantation.
Master said it's right 'dere in the Good Book.
You's gone git us alls in trouble!
You's be better off sirein' the master's handmaid
Than to git caught readin' from 'dat 'dere book.
My daddy couldn't read
My mammy couldn't read
I's can't read
And I's be damned if I's 'low
One of mine's to read from 'dat 'dere book.
If 'da master don't kill you
I'll kill you myself,
So, help me God!
You's gone git us alls in trouble!
You's gone git us alls in trouble!

For the African American, DeGruy Leary (2005) advocated that many generations since slavery are suffering from *Post Traumatic Slave Syndrome* (PTSS). PTSS is the consequence of multi-generational trauma with continued oppression and the absence of opportunity to heal or access the benefits available in society. Even when people have not directly experienced the event, they can be traumatized by it, and this trauma can continue through being passed on to future generations. This trauma has occurred not just through physical assaults, but also in deep psychological ways connected to centuries of abuse (DeGruy-Leary, Wade, & Wyatt, 2005), and this condition is perpetuated by microaggressions (Granger, 2011). Multi-generational trauma is not unique to African Americans. Native Americans, LGBT+ individuals, and women, amongst others, have also experienced pervasive cultural trauma that has left an impact transcending the time period in which the systemic oppression occurred.

Moving Forward

Due to the widespread misunderstandings pertaining to the experience of individuals from different cultural groups, including microaggressions, it is evident that sustained attention to improving cross-cultural attention to cultural understanding and empathy is needed (see also Chapter 9). Changes at the individual and systemic level are needed. At the individual level, it is important that the changes are congruent with one's personal identity and worldview to avoid the development of dissonance (Granger, 2011). For example, if one engages in changes intended to increase acceptance yet continues to be rejected due to others judging attributions or affiliations related to one's cultural group, such encounters promote disillusionment and suffering while preventing genuine acceptance.

At the systemic level, it is important to remember that racism can be understood as actions, attitudes, institutional structures, or social policies that subordinate, oppress, or otherwise disadvantage individuals from marginalized groups (Jones, 1997; Ponterotto, Utsey, & Pedersen, 2006). This can include individuals and families from these groups being relegated to inferior housing, education, employment, and health services (Sue, 2003). Although more overt forms of racism (hate crimes, physical assaults, and racial epithets) and blatant discriminatory acts have decreased overall, some have maintained that this has morphed into subtler and institutional forms of the same fundamental issue that drove earlier, more explicit racism (DeVos & Banaji, 2005; Dovidio, Gaertner, Kawakami, & Hodson, 2002; Nelson, 2006; Sue, Capodilupo, Nadal, & Torino, 2008). Stated differently, racism has transformed into something that is often invisible, subtle, and more indirect, operating outside of many people's awareness. This contemporary form has been encapsulated in what is referred to as symbolic racism (Sears, 1988), modern racism (McConahay, 1986), implicit racism (Banaji, Hardin, & Rothman, 1993), and aversive racism (Dovidio & Gaertner, 1996). It is important to note, too, that more overt forms of racism, which had decreased for some time, are once again on the rise. Since 2015, hate crime and hate incidents have increased (McCarthy, 2018).

Aversive racism is a concept closely related to racial microaggressions. Dovidio and Gaertner (1996) describe this form of racism as an avoidance of interaction with other cultural groups, which then protects them from recognizing racist attitudes and beliefs. Furthermore, they maintain that a majority of White individuals view themselves as moral and decent human beings that would not intentionally discriminate against others. However, evidence of racism remains pervasive in the United States as well as many other countries. Consistent with microaggressions, aversive racism occurs outside of conscious awareness and intention (Sue, Capodilupo, & Holder, 2008; Sue, Capodilupo, Torino, Bucceri, Holder, Nadal, & Esquilin, 2007). In this way, aversive racism can serve to hide individuals from recognizing their microaggressions. As long as microaggressions remain hidden and unrecognized, individuals will continue to cause harm to marginalized groups. Sue, Lin, Torino, Capodilupo, and Rivera (2009), for example, found that microaggressions often are the impetus for difficult conversations about race in the classroom. According to Sue et al. (2009), when this occurs, White professors and students alike often experience confusion and uncurtaining about what is occurring. Apfelbaum, Sommers, and Norton (2008) further note that, in order to avoid being seen as racist, these White professors and students often become focused on clarifying what they perceive as innocent misunderstandings.

Without awareness and critical consciousness, fear of clarifying the meaning associated with tension-filled conversations and avoidance of understanding maintains invisibility of these offenses (Goodman, 1995; Henry, Cobb-Roberts, Dorn, Exum, Keller, & Shircliffe, 2007), which can lead to what Sue (2015) calls a "conspiracy of silence." Therefore, making the invisible visible is an essential component of combating the prevalence of microaggression and racism in contemporary times. This requires difficult and courageous conversations. It takes courage for individuals from marginalized groups and allies to initiate these conversations, and it also takes courage for individuals from the privileged group to remain open and engaged in these conversations despite defensive reactions. Making the invisible visible is demonstrated in the following example of a microaggressive scenario:

> An African American male,[1] while exiting an elevator as the lone rider, finds himself confronted with six or seven White people as the elevator doors opened and he tried to exit at his floor. As he wiggled past the whites that had just rushed into the elevator, he made it to the exit. Upon exiting, he turned back, standing in the threshold of the elevator, stuck his hand up to hold the elevator door open precluding its movement, and says, "Excuse me. Please help me understand, but isn't it common courtesy to allow those exiting an elevator to exit first before entering in?" The large White male at the back of elevator turned red and clutched his fist. After a very intense minute, they all apologized upon the invisibility of their microaggressive behavior being made visible by the lone African American taking courage in a non-threatening manner to address the microaggressive behavior to his White counterparts.

As long as microaggressions remain hidden, invisible, unspoken about, and excused as innocent slights with minimal harm, individuals will continue to insult, demean, alienate, and oppress marginalized groups. When the invisibility of microaggressions is made visible, communications are facilitated and a seat allowed at the table of brotherhood. Exposing microaggressions was never intended to shut down communications but to foster dialogue between people from different walks.

Humanistic Contributions to Understanding and Addressing Microaggressions

There is limited acknowledgement of microaggressions in the humanistic and existential psychology literature to date. However, this is beginning to change and humanistic psychology has the potential to make important contributions to theory, research, and applications relevant to microaggressions. Hoffman, Cleare-Hoffman, and Jackson (2014) noted that humanistic psychology must first address its own struggles with multiculturalism before it can become an authentic voice speaking out against prejudice and discrimination. As part of this, they identified three common humanistic microaggressions: (1) diversity as an unnecessary condition, (2) individualistic bias, and (3) invitations, patronization, and embracing. These microaggressions can be recognized in the humanistic scholarship and practice and warrants a swift attentiveness if there will be any resolve within and without the clinical setting.

Despite these microaggressive tendencies in humanistic psychology, there are also constructive ways humanistic psychology can contribute to the microaggression literature and practice. Oft-times, microaggressions are rather ambiguous, leaving it difficult to determine whether a slight was intended, thus making it easy to deny that a microaggression even occurred. Although humanistic psychology's stance has historically been one of valuing diversity, its trivializing of microaggressions is manifest in the propensity for humanistic psychology to regard diversity as an unnecessary condition or to not recognize microaggressions as a major contextual factor in therapeutic outcomes. Common responses to microaggressions include feelings of confusion and anger, often followed by feelings of inferiority, leading one to feel disenfranchised and marginalized. The internal struggle is exacerbated when it seems obvious that the perpetrator had no ill-intent in conveying the denigrating message and, conversely, the heightened response to advocate and or protest when the ill-intent is obvious. To marginalize, consequently, is the process of relegating or confining to a lower or outer limit or edge, as of social standing (Granger, 2013). Hence, marginalization is the process within a society where a group within the larger society becomes or is made marginal: "the marginalization of the underclass" or "the marginalization of literature." Since marginalization is often defined as the process of making a group or class of people less important or relegated to a secondary position (e.g., when one class of people is grouped together as second class citizens), it is important to illuminate the implications of marginalization at the opposite end of the spectrum—outer limit or edge—patronization.

No two humans are alike and individualistic biases are a part of the human condition as much as there are cultures. As it is in humanistic psychology, be it within the scholarship and/or practice, the field is replete with microaggressions that frequently go unnoticed or addressed yet they have a lasting impact on the clinician and client alike. Additionally, existential–humanistic therapies in their zealousness to accept and embrace humanity, make concerted efforts to advocate and identify with others, and inadvertently, at times, perpetuate microaggressions and the problem of marginalization by patronization (Granger, 2013). The client is made to feel good in the moment with all the sugary praise but fails to establish a genuine rapport with their clinician. On the other hand, clinicians of color are subjected to a barrage of microaggressions from White clients who mean well but present with preconceived notions of what members of the marginalized group are like. This is often played out by excessive praise, often with statements such as, "I heard a lot of great things about you but I didn't expect you to be Black" or "You're a lot *different* from any therapist I have seen before." The multicultural-competent therapist who is knowledgeable of the many nuances associated with race relations is not immune to the emotional turmoil resulting from microaggressions but recognizes the client's patronizing is usually a need to identify with the therapist. The most damaging form of patronization is perhaps that of excessive praise to select members of marginalized groups. This not only is inauthentic, but it undermines the individual and group they are associated with and contributes to their experience of alienation. This consequently leads to shame, embarrassment, and more often than not disconnectedness from one's group, which in turn perpetuates the familiar emotion of feeling invisible within and without one's given group. As the clinician of color, there is that struggle with cultural alienation and "invisibility"; however, it allows the clinician to constructively utilize the discomfort of the moment to educate the client on what he or she didn't know about the clinician's culture and simultaneously welcome the client's story about their culture, thus humanizing both self and the client and fostering a healthy dialogue.

Clinical Applications

As humanistic clinicians, it is important to entertain the question of how mental health professionals adaptively respond to racial microaggressions in their daily professional lives. This issue has key practical implications on the professional development and mentoring of mental health professionals in contemporary training and practice settings where standards of cultural competence are expected (Hernández, Carranza, & Almeida, 2010). It would serve the clinician well to recognize the implications of microaggressions on diverse clients as well as the impact of microaggressions on self, particularly the clinician of color. In one study, Hernandez, Carranza, and Almeida indicated that participants followed processes by which they identified their thoughts, feelings, and responses to a perceived racial microaggression. The researchers postulate that this process involves multiple steps and decision points. At times, each individual must respond to her or his personal need for self-care and choose how and when to respond to a microaggression individually, collectively, and/or for the protection of others. Participants noted that they must balance their knowledge that racism exists while taking distance from a situation that they may deem as racist or potentially racist. They remind themselves not to interpret every situation as racial. If a situation occurs that is ambiguous enough to require pondering whether it was a microaggression or not, a decision is made as to whether it is worth it to invest energy in pursuing its understanding and possibly responding. However, if appraisal deems it necessary to respond, a decision is made to reflect on the situation alone or with others (Hernández, Carranza, & Almeida, 2010). Drawing from Sue (2010), four applications from clinical practice can be identified:

- Making the "invisible" visible. As long as microaggressions remain hidden, invisible, unspoken about, and excused as innocent slights with minimal harm, individuals will continue to insult, demean, alienate, and oppress marginalized groups.
- Establishing expertise and trust. As Sue (2010) states, "Acquiring knowledge and understanding of the worldviews of diverse groups and clients are all important in providing culturally relevant services" (p. 278).
- Providing appropriate services to diverse populations. Helping professionals must begin the process of developing culturally appropriate and effective intervention strategies in working with clients different from them. This includes developing skills that involve interventions aimed at organizational structures, policies, practices, and regulations within institutions, if they are to become culturally competent.
- It is important that clinicians become aware of their values, biases, and assumptions about human behavior (see also Chapter 6).

Summary

As multicultural and social justice initiatives are advanced in the mental health professions, improvements in training and service settings can be accomplished by expanding the understanding of microaggressions. A key dimension in this endeavor involves addressing White privilege, its misuse and abuse (Hernández, Carranza, & Almeida, 2010). It can be argued that this is what makes possible and sustains overt and subtle racism (Almeida, Dolan-Del Vecchio, & Parker, 2007). However, as posited by Moats in the previous chapter, "Privilege is a starting point, not an end." In conclusion, operating within the mental health field should be predicated on multicultural awareness and approached phenomenologically as not to ascribe the worldviews of the clinician upon the client and vice versa. No one is free from the impact of microaggressions—all are victims in one way or another through a social conditioning process that has imbued all humans with biases, fears, and stereotypes about others. In conclusion, some important lessons from the chapter include:

- Recognizing that microaggressions are insidious in nature and, although they present as harmless, prove to have a detrimental impact on the psychological wellbeing of the recipient.

- An awareness of one's personal biases, fears, and stereotypes is paramount in obliterating the perpetuation of microaggressions.
- Understanding that microaggressions originate from privilege is crucial. In the clinician's aspirations for multicultural competencies, it is important to include in that quest an understanding of White privilege.
- Anticipating difficult dialogical exchanges, however, making the obscurity of microaggressions discernable, should always facilitate increased dialogue, instead of shutting it down.
- Microaggressions are factors that can gravely affect clinical outcomes. The clinician of color, though in the position of power in the clinical setting, can be the victim of microaggressions from White clients and must be able to recover quickly so as to maintain the therapeutic relationship.

Note

1 The African American male is the author and the scenario is his experiential reality.

References

Almeida, R., Dolan-Del Vecchio, K., & Parker, L. (2007). Foundation concepts for social justice-based therapy: Critical consciousness, accountability, and empowerment. In E. Aldarondo (Ed.), *Advancing social justice through clinical practice* (pp. 175–206). Mahwah, NJ: Lawrence Erlbaum Associates.

Apfelbaum, E. P., Sommers, S. R., & Norton, M. I. (2008). Seeing race and seeming racist? Evaluating strategic color-blindness in social interaction. *Journal of Personality and Social Psychology, 99,* 918–932.

Awad, G. H., Cokley, K., & Ravitch, J. (2005). Attitudes toward affirmative action: A comparison of color-blind versus modern racist attitudes. *Journal of Applied Social Psychology, 35*(7), 1384–1399.

Banaji, M. R., Hardin, C., & Rothman, A. J. (1993). Implicit stereotyping in person judgment. *Journal of Personality and Social Psychology, 65*(2), 272–281.

Bonilla-Silva, E. (2002). The linguistics of color-blind racism: How to talk nasty about Blacks without sounding racist. *Critical Sociology, 28*(1–2), 42–64.

Bonilla-Silva, E. (2006). *Racism without racists: Color-blind racism and the persistence of racial inequality in the United States.* Lanham, MD: Rowman & Littlefield.

Brondolo, E., Kelly, K. P., Coakley, V., Gordon, T., Thompson, S., & Levy, E. (2005). The perceived ethnic discrimination questionnaire: Development and preliminary validation of a community version. *Journal of Applied Social Psychology, 35,* 335–365.

Chao, R. K. (2006). The prevalence and consequences of adolescents' language brokering for their immigrant parents. In M. H. Bornstein, & L. R. Cote (Eds.), *Acculturation and parent–child relationships: Measurement and development* (pp. 271–296). Mahwah, NJ: Lawrence Erlbaum Associates.

Clark, R., Anderson, N. B., Clark, V. R., & Williams, D. R. (1999). Racism as a stressor for African Americans: A biopsychosocial model. *American Psychologist, 54*(10), 805–816.

Cleare-Hoffman, H. P., Granger, N., & Hoffman, L. (2010). Microaggressions: The new racism. *Journal of Psychological Issues in Organizational Culture, 1,* 85–90.

DeGruy-Leary, J., Wade, B., & Wyatt, G. E. (2005). *Our legacy: Breaking the chains.* Retrieved from: www.joydegruy.com/assets/docs/BreakingChains.pdf.

DeGruy Leary, J. (2005). *Post traumatic slave syndrome: America's legacy of enduring injury and healing.* Milwaukie, OR: Uptone Press.

DeVos, T., & Banaji, M. R. (2005). American = White? *Journal of Personality and Social Psychology, 88,* 447–466.

Dovidio, J. F., & Gaertner, S. L. (1996). Affirmative action, unintentional racial biases, and intergroup relations. *Journal of Social Issues, 52*(4), 51–75.

Dovidio, J. F., Gaertner, S. L., Kawakami, K., & Hodson, G. (2002). Why can't we just get along? Interpersonal biases and interracial distrust. *Cultural Diversity & Ethnic Minority Psychology, 8,* 88–102.

Franklin, J. H. (2000). *From slavery to freedom* (8th ed.). Boston, MA: McGraw Hill.

Garrow, D. (1987). Martin Luther King, Jr.'s 'I Have A Dream' speech. In D. Nasaw (Ed.), *The course of United States history* (Vol. 2, pp. 351–361). Chicago, IL: Dorsey Press.

Goodman, D. J. (1995). Difficult dialogues: Enhancing discussions about diversity. *College Teaching, 43,* 47–52.

Granger, N., Jr. (2011). *Perceptions of racial microaggressions among African American males in higher education: A heuristic inquiry.* Ann Arbor, MI: ProQuest LLC.

Granger, N., Jr. (2012). 'Dat 'dere book. In L. Hoffman & N. Granger, Jr. (Eds.), *Stay awhile: Poetic narratives on multiculturalism and diversity* (p. 23). Colorado Springs, CO: University Professors Press.

Granger, N. (2013, April 5). Marginalization: The pendulum swings both ways. *The New Existentialists.* Retrieved from Saybrook University website: www.saybrook. edu/newexistentialists/posts/04-05-13.

Henry, W., Cobb-Roberts, D., Dorn, S., Exum, H. A., Keller, H., & Shircliffe, B. (2007). When the dialogue becomes too difficult: A case study of resistance and backlash. *College Student Affairs Journal, 26,* 160–168.

Hernández, P., Carranza, M., & Almeida, R. (2010). Mental health professionals' adaptive responses to racial microaggressions: An exploratory study. *Professional Psychology: Research and Practice, 41*(3), 202–209.

Hoffman, L., Cleare-Hoffman, H. P., & Jackson, T. (2014). Humanistic psychology and multiculturalism: History, current status, and advancements. In K. J. Schneider, J. F. Pierson & J. F. T. Bugental (Eds.), *The handbook of humanistic psychology: Theory, research, and practice* (2nd ed., pp. 41–55). Thousand Oaks, CA: Sage Publications.

Holmes, T. S., & Holmes, T. H. (1970). Short-term intrusion into the life style routine. *Journal of Psychosomatic Research, 14,* 121–132.

Jones, J. M. (1997). *Prejudice and racism* (2nd ed.). Washington, DC:McGraw-Hill.

Kessler, R. C., Mickelson, K. D., & Williams, D. R. (1999). The prevalence, distribution, and mental health correlates of perceived discrimination in the United States. *Journal of Health and Social Behavior, 40,* 208–230.

McCarthy, N. (2018, Nov. 14). FBI: Hate crimes have increased for the third straight year. Forbes. Retrieved from: www.forbes.com/sites/niallmccarthy/

2018/11/14/fbi-hate-crimes-have-increased-for-the-third-year-straight-info
graphic/#6434fd641701.

McConahay, J. B. (1986). Modern racism, ambivalence, and the modern racism
scale. In J. F. Dovidio & S. L. Gaertner (Eds.), *Prejudice, discrimination, and racism*
(pp. 91–125). San Diego, CA: Academic Press.

Meyer, I. H. (1995). Minority stress and mental health in gay men. *Journal of Health
and Social Behavior, 3*, 38–56.

Nelson, C. A. (2006). Of eggshells and thin-skulls: A consideration of racism-related
mental illness impacting Black women. *International Journal of Law and Psychiatry,
29*(2), 112–136.

Noh, S., & Kaspar, V. (2003). Perceived discrimination and depression: Moderating
effects of coping, acculturation, and ethnic support. *American Journal of Public
Health, 93*, 232–238.

Pierce, C., Carew, J., Pierce-Gonzalez, D., & Willis, D. (1978). An experiment in
racism: TV commercials. In C. Pierce (Ed.), *Television and education* (pp. 62–88).
Beverly Hills, CA: Sage Publications.

Ponterotto, J. G., Utsey, S., & Pedersen, P. B. (2006). *Preventing prejudice: A guide for
counselors and educators.* Thousand Oaks, CA. Sage.

Robbins, B. D. (2016). The heart of humanistic psychology: Human dignity
disclosed through a hermeneutic of love. *Journal of Humanistic Psychology, 56*,
223–237.

Sarno, E., & Wright, A. J. (2013). Homonegative microaggressions and identity in
bisexual men and women. *Journal of Bisexuality, 13*, 63–81.

Schacht, T. E. (2008). A broader view of racial microaggression in psychotherapy. *American Psychologist, 63*(4), 273.

Schneider, K. J. (2013). *The polarized mind: Why it's killing us and what we can do about
it.* Colorado Springs, CO: University Professors Press.

Sears, D. O. (1988). Symbolic racism. In P. A. Katz & D. A. Taylor (Eds.),
Eliminating racism: Profiles in controversy (pp. 53–84). Boston, MA: Springer.

Smedley, A., & Smedley, B. D. (2005). Race as biology is fiction, racism as a social
problem is real. *American Psychologist, 60*, 16–26.

Solórzano, D., Ceja, M., & Yosso, T. (2000). Critical race theory, racial microaggressions, and campus racial climate: The experiences of African American college
students. *The Journal of Negro Education, 69*(1/2), 60–73.

Sue, D. W. (2003). *Overcoming our racism: The journey to liberation.* San Francisco, CA:
Jossey-Boss.

Sue, D. W. (2010). *Microaggressions in everyday life: Race, gender, and sexual orientation.*
Hoboken, NJ: John Wiley & Sons.

Sue, D. W. (2015). *Race talk and the conspiracy of silence: Understanding and facilitating
difficult dialogues on race.* Hoboken, NJ: John Wiley & Sons.

Sue, D. W., Capodilupo, C. M., & Holder, A. M. B. (2008). Racial microaggressions in the life experience of Black Americans. *Professional Psychology: Research and
Practice, 39*(3), 329–336.

Sue, D. W., Capodilupo, C. M., Nadal, K. L., & Torino, G. C. (2008). Racial
microaggressions and the power to define reality. *American Psychologist, 63*(4),
277–279.

Sue, D. W., Capodilupo, C. M., Torino, G. C., Bucceri, J. M., Holder, A. M. B.,
Nadal, K. L., & Esquilin, M. (2007). Racial microaggressions in everyday life:
Implications for clinical practice. *American Psychologist, 62*(4), 271–286..

Sue, D. W., Lin, A. I., Torino, G. C., Capodilupo, C. M., & Rivera, D. P. (2009). Racial microaggressions and difficult dialogues in the classroom. *Cultural Diversity and Ethnic Minority Psychology, 15,* 183–190

Thomas, K. R. (2008). Macrononsense in multiculturalism. *American Psychologist, 63,* 274–275.

Utsey, S. O., Giesbrecht, N., Hook, J., & Stanard, P. M. (2008). Cultural, socio-familial, and psychological resources that inhibit psychological distress in African Americans exposed to stressful life events and race-related stress. *Journal of Counseling Psychology, 55,* 49–62.

Utsey, S. O., & Ponterotto, J. G. (1996). Development and validation of the Index of Race-Related Stress (IRRS). *Journal of Counseling Psychology, 43,* 490–502.

Wei, M., Ku, T-Y., Russell, D. W., Mallinckrodt, B., & Liao, K. Y- H. (2008). Moderating effects of three coping strategies and self-esteem on perceived discrimination and depressive symptoms: A minority stress model for Asian international students. *Journal of Counseling Psychology, 55,* 451–561.

Williams, D. R., Neighbors, H. W., & Jackson, J. S. (2003). Racial/ethnic discrimination and health: Findings from community studies. *American Journal of Public Health, 93*(2), 200–208.

Yoo, H. C., & Lee, R. M. (2008). Does ethnic identity buffer or exacerbate the effects of frequent racial discrimination on situational well-being of Asian Americans? *Journal of Counseling Psychology, 55,* 63–74.

8 White Privilege

A Multifaceted Responsibility

Michael Moats

The United States has a history of bravery and tenacity, and is viewed as a place of opportunities. However, those stories have shadows that are not inclusive of many that do not fit within the White male paradigm, and those shadows have blood, bruises, and invisible wounds. Some of these wounds are still being perpetuated today—some overtly and some unconsciously. White privilege is a detrimental reality that still is often unrecognized by, or invisible to, much of White America. With power came privilege, and the Euro-invasion of North America began imposing what was *right* through *might*, including separating people by race, religion, and gender. The *might-is-right* paradigm favored the White, Christian male. As a White, Christian, cisgender male, I am afforded advantages, benefits, and freedoms that my brothers and sisters of color have not, and thirty years ago no one could have convinced me that this truth had any validity. However, there were too many examples that challenged my enculturated beliefs to continue denying it. It was a process of discomfort, disbelief, amazement, sadness, shame, and worthwhile growth. It allowed me to *see* people for the first time in a new way.

Recognizing the enculturated training that privilege brings is vital in understanding unconscious resistance to change, as well as humanizing the privileged; however, White America cannot hide in this unconsciousness. Race tensions and discussions are too prevalent and too important to avoid. As Cornell West (1994) noted, "The paradox of race in America is that our common destiny is more pronounced and imperiled when our divisions are deeper" (p. 8).

Each person has a responsibility to engage with people who are different from their own cultural background within one's current level of understanding. Having experienced a vision change as it relates to privilege, I attest that ignorance is real and not necessarily being used as an excuse. However, it is imperative to be purposeful in openly listening to paradigm challenges, to look beyond oneself to broader realities, and to look at things with different lenses. Miller (2003) noted that, "no drug is so powerful as the drug of self. No rut in the mind is so deep as the one that says I am the world, the world belongs to me, all people are characters in my play" (p. 182). One can embrace not knowing in a way that promotes inquiry, growth, and productive discomfort. As Theopia Jackson stated, "breathe in through the discomfort and out to the possibilities" (2015).

This chapter has more of a personal tone than academic because, while theory encourages one to think, relationship can change the world. It also focuses on race privilege versus the intersectionality of different privileges, although it is important to recognize the multiple forms of privilege. This chapter is not about bashing or shaming, but attempts to offer a broad overview of White privilege while encouraging self-reflection.

> I doubt the past can be apologized for in any case, because it is beyond the reach of forgiveness. The past can only be understood and integrated into the present—its effects on the present recognized and incorporated into a daily practice of repair that cannot have an ending any more than the past has an ending.
>
> (Malcomson, 2000, p. 507)

Defining White Privilege

White privilege is diversely understood; however, it can be defined as "the unearned advantages afforded to people who are assumed, based largely on complexion and related physical features, to be of European ancestry" (Smith, Crosthwaite, & Clark, 2014, p. 1), but also includes being free from negative experiences. White people can perpetuate this privilege without the conscious knowledge of its presence, including through *colorblindness*, in which people deny seeing a person's race. To not see a person's race is a naïve approach at best and signifies not seeing the whole person. Race does not have to be the first recognition or delineation, but to negate it is to negate the person, their story, and the combined history of their lineage.

Most definitions of White privilege speak to the unearned privileges that a person has solely based on race without earning them. Some equate White privilege to racial privilege; whereas others will add additional privileges such as gender (Brody, Fuller, Gosetti, Moscato, Nagel, Pace, & Schmuck, 2005), religion (Blumenfeld, Joshi, & Fairchild, 2009), sexual preference (Sue, 2010), ability (Pease, 2013), and class (Moss, 2003). One reward of privilege that is implicitly described but often not explicitly stated is inclusiveness, or the feeling of belonging. The feeling of being negated, invisible, or less than is the psychological equivalent to being isolated or neglected. There is an abundance of research on the power of neglect in attachment theory (Cicchetti, 2005; Myers, 2011), literature on aging (del Carmen & LoFaso, 2014; World Health Organization, 2008), and research on the detrimental effects of isolation in confinement (Abramsky & Fellner, 2003; Rasmussen, 2017). Yet, the less obvious or less dramatic daily messages of neglect that many people of color endure is ignored or disregarded. Privileged individuals sometimes are either blind to these messages or choose to dismiss them as insignificant or rationally justifiable. As Martin Luther King, Jr. (1968) stated, "The white majority, unprepared and unwilling to accept radical structural change, is resisting and producing chaos while complaining that if there were no chaos orderly change would come" (p. 180). Tillich (2000) shares, "The dangers connected with the change, the unknown character of the things to come, the darkness of the future makes the average man a fanatical defender of the established order" (p. 66).

Since Peggy McIntosh (1989) began popularizing the phrase *White privilege*, it has been a point of enlightenment, debate, a tool, a weapon, a perceived excuse, and a source for understanding or for hate-spewing, depending on one's willingness to understand and remain open to the concept. Suffice it to say, it is a controversial topic. For example, Boatright-Horowitz and Soeung (2009) provided evidence that addressing White privilege in the classroom tended to lead to poorer course evaluations. The notion of White privilege was not new in cultures of color, and the exposure of this disparity was prevalent in the writings of W. E. B. Dubois (2014), James Baldwin (1998), Baldwin and Standley (1996), and Martin Luther King, Jr. (King & Washington, 1991), as well as later in prominent writers such as bell hooks (1995, 2006), Michael Yellow Bird (2005), Cornell West (1994), and Derald Wing Sue (2010, 2015). These early non-White works of literature were not as widely read and accepted partially because they challenged the power paradigm and were written by a non-White author. Out-group information often is rejected much quicker in an effort to support homeostasis.

What It Is Not

Privilege is a starting point, not an end. The term is often mislabeled as an excuse or a barrier, instead of an unfair starting point and process hindrance. Privilege is often erroneously discredited by outliers, such as claims that Barack Obama's presidency disprove the reality of privilege. It is not that a person of color has to start at the back or is unable to move to the front, but there is an empirically supported truth that shows an unfair advantage heavily favors the White population, in particular the White male (Sue, 2010).

A Black friend/colleague and I have joked about how, based on where and how we grew up, that we were destined to never be friends. To the contrary, through our conversations, arguments, biases, and respect, we have found that we have more commonalities than differences. We were both raised poor, in prejudice settings, with lesser educated support systems, around people that abused substances, and with people that had strong spiritual convictions. There were a lot of bridges of connection, and many commonalities of being unprivileged. However, where I once would have discredited privilege because of some of these examples, I no longer dismiss the significance and impact of these differences and the privileges I *do have* that gave me advantages and access. Unfortunately, society has often made this a discussion of all or nothing, dismissing privilege through identifying other forms of privilege one does not have.

My friend is a fellow doctor held in high regards in our predominantly White professional circle; yet, he is still seen by some as *the Black psychologist*, a focus on pigment that I never have had to endure. His achievements are recognized by many on the merit and effort he has given, but not by all. Some chalk it up to tokenism—another emotional slash privilege defends me from. I do not feel shame for this; however, I feel responsible to challenge the faulty beliefs and assumptions, regardless of what it may cost me in comfort or favor from individuals in this group. I can do this without ever being quickly labelled as the angry White man— a privilege I have from being White.

Privilege also does not explain everything about a White person and does not reduce them to a single quality. Privilege plays a part in all of it, but does not explain all of it; likewise, examples of success in the Black population does not disprove the existence of White privilege. It is important to caution against the propensity to minimize the power of privilege, as well as its ability to be weaponized through overgeneralization. Individuals are more than privilege, and privilege is about more than individuals. It is about a systemic paradigm and power that creates an unfair playing field, and it is vital that *we* continue to have discussions on privilege and learn from one another (Maxwell, Nagda, & Thompson, 2011).

A transformational change can occur when one lets go of the old-school power paradigm in favor of change and advocacy. However, there can be a misguided parallel power shift in which the well-intended advocate switches from power and blindness to blind desire. This can be seen with well-intended allies unconsciously perpetuating one's privilege by holding the reins of being the *White Knight* going in to battle to save the marginalized. As many women have tried to tell men for centuries that they do not need them to jump in and fix things, marginalized groups do not need White heroes; Whites need to be companions that help create community, as King dreamed, which means pulling the tables together as an invitation to all and not telling other Whites they are not worthy to eat at this new shared space. I have listened to the in-group, White advocates trying to dominate one another on who is doing it right or who is doing it better, as well as how more enlightened they are in their journey. Miller (2014) states, "Sometimes relationships feel like we're trying to emotionally cuddle with each other at the same time we're tearing each other down" (p. 97).

Patterson, Grenny, McMillan, and Switzler (2012) suggest stepping out of the embattlement of *the how* to come back to *the why*. Quoting Martin Luther King while shaming those who are trying, but are not doing it right, is not helpful. King had a gift of calling people out, holding a mirror in front of them, and calling for their accountability, but he did so with love. Intertwined was a consistent message of the desire for inclusiveness for all.

If we were to gather all the cultural criticism and critical theory on the subject of white supremacy, whiteness, race, and racism, in this huge body of work, we would find little or no focus on love. Yet all our deconstructive explanatory theory is meaningless if it is not rooted in the recognition that the most fundamental challenge to domination is the choice to love.

(hooks, 2013, p. 199)

There was a time in my life that I would have used that quote to shift responsibility away from myself and focused on the expressed frustration and pain of people of marginalized groups. However, it is important to hear the words of love from hooks within the healthy tension of her counter point, "This notion that folks in positions of powerlessness are somehow able to transcend exploitation, oppression, or simply unjust circumstances and offer love to those who exert power over them—is a fantasy" (hooks, 2013, p. 43). This is a call for all people to work together with recognition that with privilege comes a heavier share of the load.

One argument that attempts to discredit White privilege is the counter argument of Black privilege, or more often declared as reverse racism (Allan, 2015). The *feeling* behind the belief of reverse racism is a real experience. However, racism is about systemic power that can be expressed individually or institutionally, and systemically the White population is not being oppressed. Attempts to rectify the imbalance of privilege and oppression do not always work out in a fair manner because it will come at a cost to the power paradigm. It cannot always work out in a fair manner because the system is unfair, which points to the need for a systems change.

If my humanity is interdependent with other people's humanity (Battle, 1997), then what is best for me and my family also considers what is best for my community, for my neighbors, and for my brothers and sisters of color that are a part of all of these. Similarly, (De Beauvoir, 1948/1976) maintained that one's own freedom in necessarily tied to the freedom of others. What is best for me and my family is to continue to become aware and teach my children to be aware of their privilege and to use that privilege in a responsible manner that honors the greater view of community and relationship beyond the self. To honor all people includes empathy for the White individual that feels cheated out of a job or an admission to a school because there is still a cost to him or her; it is part of the conversation that is often dismissed. Having empathy for this loss is actually a bridge for shared experience, albeit not equal. *The not equal needs to be emphasized, particularly given the history of inequality,* or the possible bridge can readily become a wall. The son of the man who planned the 1993 World Trade Center bombing highlights this difficult interdependence:

Empathy, peace, nonviolence—they may seem like quaint tools in the world of terror that my father helped create, but, as many have written, using nonviolence to resolve conflicts doesn't mean being passive. It doesn't mean embracing victimhood, or letting aggressors run riot. It doesn't even mean giving up the fight, not exactly. What it means is humanizing your opponents, recognizing the needs and fears you share with them, and working toward reconciliation rather than revenge.

(Ebrahim, 2014, p. 88)

Privilege, and the related concept of *White fragility*, are real but should not be used as weapons. Conversely, if the privileged are truly listening and responding appropriately for change, there may not be a desire for weaponization, protest, or riot, which often are acts of frustration (Hoffman, Granger, Vallejos, & Moats, 2016). Think of your own relationships in which you are desperately trying to be heard and to feel validated as well as your response when it does not happen.

Clinical Implications

There has been historical distrust by marginalized groups with the helping professions for good reasons. From the misuse of research data to the abuse of participants of marginalized groups, trust has appropriately not been earned (Guthrie, 2004). The Tuskegee Study of Untreated Syphilis in the Negro Male, a study that abusively withheld treatment to infected participants without giving Black participants complete knowledge necessary for informed consent, as well as projecting the study to last six months and continuing for forty years, was stopped in 1972 only after a new article prompted a review of the study.

Even less overtly misguided research has been shaped with unconscious biases. Guthrie (2004) uses the phrase "scientific racism" (p. 104) to describe how misuse of research utilized the authority of science to systemically create so-called facts, such as falsely claiming the lesser intelligence of Black people, which was then used to end "compensatory education programs" (p. 106). Historically, Black individuals are more likely to be diagnosed with Antisocial Personality Disorder without taking context into consideration. Less eye contact is often judged as hiding something, anxiety, or disrespect, instead of considering culture and the meaning of not looking at an elder or an authority figure (i.e., therapist/doctor) as a sign of respect or adaptive anxiety. D'Andrea (2003) advocates that a disproportionate number of clinicians of color, White clinicians with inadequate competencies in working with diverse groups, the use of culturally biased assessments, and the use of theories that "reflect a monocultural and ethnocentric view of mental health" perpetuate the distrust (p. 18). The insertion of U.S. clinicians into international disasters and the perceived right to use this as a personal research lab without recognizing the unintended side effect that remains after the departure in a couple of weeks further reflects the entitlement of privileged Western clinicians (Ren, 2008). Whether talking about international or domestic therapeutic work, U.S. clinicians and scholars tend to impose their ideals, ethics, and biases, instead of listening to the language of the culture (Ren, 2009), which is an aspect of privilege.

Practitioners are responsible to continuously self-evaluate, seek counsel, and be accountable (see Chapter 6). Therapists cannot ask clients to go where they refuse to go, especially considering history. This demands uncomfortably seeking blind spots and challenging paradigms beginning in one's everyday personal life. For instance, I can try to relate to those that are marginalized through some of my experiences of being unprivileged, but those experiences are limited.

One of the best experiences I have found is to be exposed to what it is like to be somewhere where I am the minority (Moats, Claypool, & Saxon, 2011). This does not equate to what people of color experience in the world of White supremacy, but the feeling of being different, not belonging, and being looked at like an oddity gave me some insight into a different experience that I do not *have* to feel if I do not want, due to my privilege. A person does not have to travel across the world or even the U.S. to look for opportunities to experience growth and change. Stepping into something different or uncomfortable allows one to see with new eyes, sometimes the truths of disparity. Recognizing disparity at the micro, meso, and macro levels (Goodman, Liang, Helms, Latta, Sparks, & Weintraub, 2004) and learning to responsibly use privilege for positive change is vital for personal growth and facilitating change in one's community. Unfortunately, this discomfort is sometimes displayed as well-intentioned White advocates using social justice as a weapon, which may help that person feel more distant from one's privilege, instead of harnessing it as a tool for positive change and bridge for connection. To do nothing or to remain silent is not an appropriate option either, as is reflected in the common activist saying, *silence is violence.*

When one is serving as a mental health professional, the responsibility to be aware of the impact and implications of White privilege is heightened. The therapy room is an example of space that allows two people to come together. It is not about the absence of bias as much as it is about the recognition and suspension of bias in an effort to actively listen, understand, and be of service to the other person. In doing so, it is also an opportunity to challenge one's own biases and to grow through the interaction; however, what the clinician gains is not the priority and should not be at the expense of the client's time. Early in my career I had a supervisor, Geneva Reynaga-Abiko, share the importance of opening the discussion of potential barriers that marginalized clients may feel, in the context of privilege, during therapeutic interactions. I knew the value of discussing the relationship in therapy, but due to *my* privilege I had not thought about it in the context of privilege. This lesson was quickly validated during the clinical interview of an educational evaluation with a Latina in her early twenties. I prefaced that I would like to ask a couple of questions that may be uncomfortable but important.

"How does it feel to work with an older, White male in this setting?" I asked.

"It's fine," she responded, yet her body language suggested something different.

"Can I share something with you? Your words said one thing, but it seemed like your body disagreed and had something else to say. I may be wrong, but I want to assure you that you do not have to protect my ego. I really would like to know. *Is there* something else you would like to say?"

She paused, slightly sighed, took a deep breath and exclaimed, "White people just don't get it!"

I started laughing and said, "I would generally have to agree with you, but please tell me more about how you have experienced this so that I can have a better understanding."

One aspect of privilege is that White people do not have to get it; they are protected from experiences many people of color are thrown into regularly. We were able to process her experience and concerns, and build a relationship that allowed something greater than providing a service. She released some of her guardedness, which opened up an opportunity for trust that resulted in her revealing a trauma and eating disorder history that would have otherwise not been shared. We were able to go beyond the standard protocol and find her assistance to work with what she had kept secret.

Although this encounter was valuable and changed the way I address what is not being said in the room, it easily could have turned into an assumptive expectation of difficulty or barrier when working with persons of color. Through assumption, what is trying to be eliminated is sometimes perpetuated, and in an effort to be aware of and to responsibly use one's privilege, unfortunately, assumption is a privilege that will be at the expense of the client.

A question similar to the one I asked the young Latina was asked of an elderly Black gentleman. He responded, "I've seen plenty of racism, but I have also lived a life of integration. I don't have a problem with any of that. If I see something, I'll tell you about it." I believed him. Had I assumed an imposed response it would have damaged our relationship. When I used an analogy of being in the ocean during a storm and having to swim, he said, "Brother, you're gonna have to find a new scenario. That ain't no Black man's sport." I had to laugh, and I respected his message, as well as his delivery.

The relationship made this encounter possible and was a cornerstone of our work (see Cleare-Hoffman, Hoffman, & Wilson, 2013). The ability to be transparent with one another does not start in the therapy room. Had it not been for dialogue, teachings, and examples from individuals of diverse gender, race, sexuality, and spirituality that could see beyond my beliefs and privilege and into my humanity, I would have most likely defended what had, unknowingly at the time, kept me feeling safe. Seeing the humanity of others and staying with my uncomfortableness allowed me to challenge the thinking and biases that surrounded me earlier in my life and use privilege more responsibly.

> The interplay of individuality and unity is not one of uniformity and unanimity imposed from above but rather of conflict among diverse groupings that reach a dynamic consensus subject to questioning and criticism. As with a soloist in a jazz quartet, quintet or band, individuality is promoted in order to sustain and increase the *creative* tension with the group—a tension that yields higher levels of performance to achieve the aim of the collective project. This kind of critical democratic sensibility flies in the face of any policing of borders and boundaries of "blackness," maleness," "femaleness," or "whiteness."
>
> (West, 1994, pp. 150–151)

Cultivating relationship demonstrates respect while empowering honesty and progress in addressing privilege and other forms of racial tension. This requires tolerance. Tolerance is not intended as *tolerating other people*, but rather *tolerating the discomfort* necessary for understanding and change. Even if one does not accept the other person's perspective, it is vital to empathize and work to understand them (see Chapter 9). Watson and Peterson (2015) state, "The problem of race in America is within us. It's not 'out there.' It's inside here" (p. 81). Even social change often requires that individuals look internally. Often the best tool to learning and better utilizing privilege is acceptance. Acceptance does not equate to agreeing or even understanding, but it does allow room for more than a predetermined paradigm.

Future Directions

King (1968) spoke of *maladjustment* that the field of psychology gave the world, and noted, "There are some things concerning which we must always be maladjusted if we are to be people of good will" (p. 185). However, White clinicians often misinterpret instances of healthy maladjustment for simply maladjustment. Without exposure to experiences outside of the White paradigm, the clinician's lens can be clouded. Exposure comes from better understanding the historical effects of slavery and the civil rights movement, recognition of how immigrants and other cultural groups are misrepresented, current institutional oppression, and every day experiences of racism and impacts of privilege. Additionally, it is vital that White clinicians recognize one's own duality as the advocate and the perpetrator of privilege, in life and in the therapy room. This is where King was calling out to psychology to focus their growth on seeing beyond and stepping from the safety of the privileged paradigm to better serve all people. The field has worked toward making progress, but they have also missed their mark. Too often humanistic psychology focuses on creating change without recognizing unintended consequences that are both real and negative instead of building relationship and creating change through relationship. For example, overcompensating for privilege at times may create an issue where there was not an issue to begin with.

One of the most prominent downfalls to growth is to not seek it, which again can be a form of privilege in which one does not feel the need to grow relevant issues that do not negatively impact them. One is limited by only seeking knowledge within one's own culture and it can be valuable to engage in multiple ways of expanding one's cultural awareness and sensitivity. To increase one's knowledge, discomfort, perspective, and growth, it is important to read authors that are different than the person in the mirror, particularly those that tell of the experience of not having privilege. Read works of academic nature as well as literature. Better yet, engage a community that is different than one's own (Moats, Claypool, & Saxon, 2011; Perrin, 2012). "Without adequate concrete knowledge of and contact with the non-white 'Other,' white theorists may move in discursive theoretical directions that are threatening and potentially disruptive of that critical practice which would support radical liberation struggle" (hooks, 1995, p. 120). It is also important to the field of psychology to expand its perspectives, research, and understandings by greater integration (Hoffman, Cleare-Hoffman, & Jackson, 2014). Rollo May (1975) said that if one wants to learn about human behavior they need not go to the psychology department, rather they should go to the arts department. In the context of the diverse nature of creativity, it could be highly beneficial to have additional research involving diverse perspectives, such as looking at overcompensation by therapists in addressing diversity. One approach to this could utilize a Yalom-esque study, pairing therapists and clients of different races with each making journal entries after each session as to perception of content, feeling heard/understood, perceived successes/barriers, and perspectives on the therapeutic relationship as therapy progresses. Although these are unique and subjective experiences, it is possible to see generalized patterns, pitfalls, and resources within the varied therapist/client groups. If you read this suggestion and registered it as having only White therapists with clients of diverse backgrounds, ask yourself why.

Humanistic psychology offers some unique opportunities to the discussion of privilege. Through humanistic psychology's emphasis on empathetic understanding, holding the humanity of all people, and recognizing all people as basically good with the potential to do harm, it offers a different paradigm through which to consider privilege. It emphasizes understanding the subjective experience of those with and without privilege, and working toward change through understanding and acceptance along with courageous, honest conversations that push people beyond their comfort zone.

Contributions from This Chapter

- It is important for therapists, particularly White therapists, to recognize the reality of White privilege and other forms of privilege, and to learn to use it responsibly to advocate for positive change regarding racial and cultural disparities, prejudice, and discrimination.
- It is important to guard the value of concepts such as White privilege and White fragility to maximize their impact in dialogue concerning disparity and barriers to change, and avoid them being reduced to divisive concepts.
- It is important for practitioners to purposefully read works, attend conferences, and engage with professionals from different cultural backgrounds and identities.
- It would be beneficial to engage in future research concerning overcompensation in therapeutic relationships involving diversity of client and therapist.
- It is important to question one's own actions and need for the feeling of significance through advocacy, yet that may also consequently perpetuate racial divide.

References

Abramsky, S., & Fellner, J. (2003). *Ill-equipped: U.S. prisons and offenders with mental illness*. New York, NY: Human Rights Watch.

Allan, J. (2015, November 28). Ben Shapiro destroys the concept of White privilege [Video file]. Retrieved December 20, 2018, from www.youtube.com/watch?v=rrxZRuL65wQ.

Baldwin, J. (1998). *Collected essays*. New York, NY: Literary Classics of the United States.

Baldwin, J., & Standley, F. (1996). *Conversations with James Baldwin*. Jackson, MS: University of Mississippi.

Battle, M. (1997). *Reconciliation: The Ubuntu theology of Desmond Tutu*. Cleveland, OH: The Pilgrim Press.

Blumenfeld, W., Joshi, K., & Fairchild, E. (2009). *Investigating Christian privilege and religious oppression in the United States*. Rotterdam: Sense.

Boatright-Horowitz, S. L., & Soeung, S. (2009). Teaching White privilege to White students can mean saying good-bye to positive student evaluations. *American Psychologist, 64*, 574–575.

Brody, C., Fuller, K., Gosetti, P., Moscato, S., Nagel, N., Pace, G., & Schmuck, P. (2005). *Gender consciousness and privilege*. London: Taylor & Francis.

Cicchetti, D. (2005). *Child maltreatment: Theory and research on the causes and consequences of child abuse and neglect*. Cambridge, UK: Cambridge University Press.

Cleare-Hoffman, H., Hoffman, L., & Wilson, S. (2013). Existential therapy, culture, and therapist factors in evidence-based practice. *PsycEXTRA Dataset.*

D'Andrea, M. (2003). Expanding our understanding of White racism and resistance to change in the fields of counseling and psychology. In J. S. Mio & G. Iwamasa (Eds.), *Culturally diverse mental health: The challenges of research and resistance* (pp. 17–37). Philadelphia, PA: Brunner/Routledge.

De Beauvoir, S. (1976). *The ethics of ambiguity.* New York, NY: Citadel Press (Original work published in 1948).

del Carmen, T., & LoFaso, V. M. (2014). Elder neglect. In L. M. Gibbs & L. Mosqueda (Eds.), *Medical implications of elder abuse and neglect* (1st ed., Vol. 30, Clinics in Geriatric Medicine, pp. 769–777). Philadelphia, PA: Elsevier.

Dubois, W. (2014). *The souls of black folk.* New York, NY: Simon & Schuster.

Ebrahim, Z. (2014). *The terrorist's son: A story of choice.* New York, NY: TEDBooks.

Goodman, L. A., Liang, B., Helms, J. E., Latta, R. E., Sparks, E., & Weintraub, S. R. (2004). Training counseling psychologists as social justice agents: Feminist and multicultural principles in action. *The Counseling Psychologist, 32,* 793–837.

Guthrie, R. V. (2004). *Even the rat was white: A historical view of psychology.* Boston, MA: Allyn & Bacon.

Hoffman, L., Cleare-Hoffman, H. P., & Jackson, T. (2014). Humanistic psychology and multiculturalism: History, current status, and advancements. In K. J. Schneider, J. F. Pierson & J. F. T. Bugental (Eds.), *The handbook of humanistic psychology: Theory, research, and practice* (2nd ed., pp. 41–55). Thousand Oaks, CA: Sage.

Hoffman, L., Granger, N., Vallejos, L., & Moats, M. (2016). An existential–humanistic perspective on Black Lives Matter and contemporary protest movements. *Journal of Humanistic Psychology, 56*(6), 595–611.

hooks, b. (1995). Postmodern blackness. In W. T. Anderson (Ed.), *The truth about the truth: De-confusing and re-constructing the postmodern world* (pp. 117–124). New York, NY: G. P. Putnam's Sons.

hooks, b. (2006). *Killing rage.* New York, NY: Henry Holt & Company.

hooks, b. (2013). *Writing beyond race: Living theory and practice.* New York, NY: Routledge.

Jackson, T. (2015). *Humanistic psychology, your house is on fire: There is no rest for the weary.* Keynote presented at the 8th Annual Society for Humanistic Psychology Conference, Chicago, IL.

King, M. L., Jr. (1968). The role of the behavioral scientist in the civil rights movement. *American Psychologist, 23*(3), 180–186.

King, M. L., & Washington, J. (1991). *A testament of hope.* San Francisco, CA: HarperSanFrancisco.

McIntosh, P. (1989). White privilege: Unpacking the invisible knapsack. *Peace and Freedom,* (July/August), 10–12.

Malcomson, S. L. (2000). *One drop of blood: The American misadventure of race.* New York, NY: Farrar Straus Giroux.

Maxwell, K. E., Nagda, B. A., & Thompson, M. C. (2011). *Facilitating intergroup dialogues bridging differences, catalyzing change.* Sterling, VA: Stylus.

May, R. (1975). *The courage to create.* New York, NY: W. W. Norton & Company.

Miller, D. (2003). *Blue like jazz: Nonreligious thoughts on Christian spirituality.* Nashville, TN: Thomas Nelson.

Miller, D. (2014). *Scary close: Dropping the act and finding true intimacy.* Nashville, TN: Nelson Books.

Moats, M., Claypool, T., & Saxon, E. (2011). Therapist development through international dialogue: Students' perspectives on personal and professional life changing interactions in China. *The Humanistic Psychologist, 39*(3), 276–282.

Moss, K. (2003). *The color of class: Poor whites and the paradox of privilege.* Philadelphia, PA: University of Pennsylvania Press.

Myers, J. E. (2011). *The APSAC handbook on child maltreatment.* Los Angeles, CA: Sage.

Patterson, K., Grenny, J., McMillan, R., & Switzler, A. (Eds.) (2012). *Crucial conversations: Tools for talking when stakes are high.* New York, NY: McGraw Hill.

Pease, B. (2013). *Undoing privilege: Unearned advantage in a divided world.* London: Zed Books.

Perrin, P. B. (2012). Humanistic psychology's social justice philosophy. *Journal of Humanistic Psychology, 53*(1), 52–69.

Rasmussen, J. (2017). *Man in isolation and confinement.* New York, NY: Routledge.

Ren, Z. (2008). *Psychology is dog shit.* Presented at the Existential Psychology Forum, Chengdu, China.

Ren, Z. (2009). On being a volunteer at the Sichuan earthquake disaster area (translated version). *Hong Kong Journal of Psychiatry, 19*(3), 123–125. Retrieved from Academic Search Complete database.

Smith, A., Crosthwaite, J., & Clark, C. (2014). White privilege. In S. Thompson (Ed.), *Encyclopedia of diversity and social justice.* Lanham, MD: Rowman & Littlefield. Retrieved from https://search-credoreference-com.contentproxy.phoenix.edu/content/entry/rowmandasj/white_privilege/0.

Sue, D. (2015). *Race talk and the conspiracy of silence.* Hoboken, NJ: Wiley.

Sue, D. W. (2010). *Microaggressions in everyday life: Race, gender, and sexual orientation.* Hoboken, NJ: Wiley.

Tillich, P. (2000). *The courage to be* (2nd ed.). New Haven, CT: Yale University Press.

Watson, B., & Peterson, K. (2015). *Under our skin: Getting real about race – and getting free from the fears and frustrations that divide us.* Carol Stream, IL: Tyndale Momentum.

West, C. (1994). *Race matters.* New York, NY: Vintage.

World Health Organization. (2008). *A global response to elder abuse and neglect: Building primary health care capacity to deal with the problem worldwide: Main report.* Geneva, Switzerland: Author.

Yellow Bird, M., & Wilson, W. A. (2005). *For indigenous eyes only: A decolonization handbook.* Santa Fe, NM: School of American Research Press.

9 Culture and Empathy in Humanistic Psychology

Louis Hoffman

Empathy is a cornerstone of humanistic psychotherapy and is increasingly identified as a cornerstone of psychotherapy in general (Bohart, Elliott, Greenberg, & Watson, 2002; Bohart & Greenberg, 1997; Elliott, Bohart, Watson, & Murphy, 2018; Wickramasekera, 2007). What is meant by empathy is not agreed upon across the field of professional psychology. As Grogan (2013) notes, much of humanistic psychology has been incorporated into other approaches to therapy, often without any acknowledgment given to humanistic psychology. Once incorporated, these humanistic approaches frequently are changed through attempts to operationalize them or by cutting the depth of understanding. While this has, at times, served to advance and develop concepts that originated in humanistic psychology, often, as in the case of empathy, the therapeutic approaches have been simplified or reduced when incorporated into other approaches.

Empathy becomes more complex when examined in a cultural context that embraces different conceptions of the self. This requires some advancement beyond the original conceptions of empathy as advocated for by Rogers (1959). In this chapter, I advocate for a broader, more inclusive understanding of empathy drawing, in particular, from the writings of O'Hara (1997). Additionally, I consider barriers to empathy and empathetic failures that often occur in culturally diverse contexts.

Understanding Empathy

Although not the first to discuss empathy in the context of psychotherapy, Carl Rogers introduced empathy as a core aspect of the psychotherapy process. According to Rogers (1959),

> The state of empathy, or being empathetic, is to perceive the internal frame of reference of another with accuracy, and with the emotional components and meanings which pertain thereto, as if one were the other person, but without ever losing the "as if" condition. Thus it means to sense the hurt or the pleasure of another as [they] sense it, and to perceive the causes thereof as [they] perceive them, but without ever

losing the recognition that it is as if I were hurt or pleased, etc. If this "as if" quality is lost, then the state is one of identification.

(pp. 210–211)

In this quote, Rogers clarifies that empathy includes cognitive, emotional, and relational components that facilitate understanding. However, the therapeutic value of empathy goes beyond increasing understanding of the other person and can be curative in itself.

Bohart and Greenberg (1997) note that empathy can facilitate three categories of therapeutic functions: (1) empathetic rapport, (2) experience-near understanding of the client's world, and (3) communicative attunement. Empathetic rapport may be the most common contemporary understanding of empathy, but also the one most divergent from Rogers's conception. Empathy, here, is understood as a basic kindness and acceptance of the client that serves the primary function of helping develop a good therapeutic alliance.

The second category, experience-near understanding of the client's world, focuses on empathy as a path to cognitive and/or emotional understanding, although the emphasis is more commonly on the cognitive aspects (Bohart & Greenberg, 1997). This understanding of empathy is more prevalent in psychoanalytic perspectives, and focuses more on what the therapist is able to do with empathy (i.e., understand). The final category, communicative empathy, is the most consistent with humanistic and existential–humanistic therapy, and it recognizes the innate healing potential of empathy (Bohart & Greenberg, 1997). Empathy is understood as a relational process experienced by the therapist and client.

Pedersen, Crethar, and Carlson (2008) distinguish between various different conceptions of empathy. In particular, they note the difference between "empathy as cognitive skill or ability and empathy as an emotion or dimension of personality" (p. 9). The latter, again, is closer to Rogers's perspective. For Rogers's (1980), empathy can be conceived of as *a way of being*. This recognizes empathy as something deeper than an emotion or aspect of personality, although it may be connected with these. Empathy, rather, is a human potential that people possess that can be cultivated, nurtured, and developed.

In part, these distinctions reflect divergence in which empathy is understood primarily as a cognitive experience or skill versus being seen as an emotional experience, way of being, or way of engaging others. Some therapists conceive of empathy as a means to a therapeutic end (Bohart & Greenberg, 1997; Jenkins, 1997). Through helping build the therapeutic alliance or deepening the therapist's understanding of the client, empathy contributes to a context in which positive therapy outcomes are more likely to occur. However, in this conception, empathy is not directly impacting change but rather preparing the road to change. From a humanistic perspective, empathy serves various roles. It does help establish the therapeutic alliance and contributes to the therapist understanding the client, but empathy also is healing in and of itself.

Building upon these differentiations of empathy, Hoffman (2019) emphasizes the difference between empathy as a technique and empathy as a way of being. When using it as a technique, it is often reduced to prescribed or planned interactions with a client. As Bohart and Greenberg (1997) note, empathy is sometimes understood merely as being reflective or sympathetic statements. While these may be useful, they are not empathy. To illustrate this difference, when teaching about empathy I often ask students how they feel when someone uses empathy as a technique with them (Hoffman, 2019). Next, I ask how it feels when they experience someone being empathetic. I have used this questioning while teaching in four different countries and various contexts, yet the response is fairly consistent. When empathy has been used as a technique, the students typically identify responses of feeling dismissed and objectified, and their emotional reaction is often sadness, loneliness, and anger. When experiencing someone as being empathetic, they report feeling cared for and supported, and often describe this experience as healing.

Empathy, however, is not without detractors. Bloom (2016) is one of the more vocal critics advocating that empathy and emotions often contribute to poor decisions and can lead to great harm. Instead, he advocates for *rational compassion*. Bloom's criticisms are consistent with the rational and reductionist biases common in Western culture and psychology that often include a general distrust of emotions. While I would agree with Bloom that empathy can be misused and should not be blindly trusted, the same could be said of other ways of knowing and ways of being, including rationality.

Research on Empathy

A challenge to researching empathy and interpreting the results of this research is the varying understandings of empathy and disagreements about how to measure it (Bohart & Greenberg, 1997). Yet, overall, there is support for the efficacy of empathy (Bohart et al., 2002; Bohart & Greenberg, 1997; Elliott et al., 2018). A limitation in the meta-analyses and reviews of research on empathy is that they often do not distinguish between different types of empathy.

Empathy is often understood as one of the most important aspects of the therapeutic alliance, which is identified as one of the "common factors" of therapy (Wampold & Imel, 2015). After client factors (i.e., motivation for change, personal strengths, etc.), Wampold and Imel, in their comprehensive review of the outcome literature and meta-analyses, identified the therapy relationship as the most important predictor of positive therapeutic outcomes. Empathy, then, has direct and indirect contributions to positive therapy outcomes.

Developing Empathy

A common debate in the field of psychotherapy is whether therapists are born empathetic or can become more empathetic. Teding van Berkhout and Malouff (2016) conducted a meta-analysis of research on empathy training. Their results supported the position that empathy can be developed. The studies focusing on mental health students and professionals tended to be more effective than studies with other adults, teenagers, and children.

Furman (2005) advocated that writing exercises and poetry can assist in developing empathy. He utilized a variety of exercises, including reflective, imaginative, and focusing exercises, to promote the capacity for empathy. Similarly, Hoffman and Granger (2015) advocated that poetry helps individuals develop an emotional capacity for empathy. They suggested strategies such as writing poetry in the voice of another person, which could be a client, a friend or family member, or someone in a movie or novel.

Wickramasekera (2007) found cognitive and affective empathy had a positive correlation with absorption. Absorption is defined as a highly focused state in which one's attention is concentrated on a particular experience. A risk with absorption, especially in the interpersonal context, is that one can become lost in the experience, which signifies losing the "as if" quality Roger's (1959) discussed, thus becoming identification. Wickramasekera's research suggests that activities promoting focused attention may be beneficial for empathy, particularly if the individual is able to direct this within an interpersonal context.

Orah Krug (2009; see also Schneider & Krug, 2017) advocates for presence as a core feature of existential–humanistic therapy that can be an important basis for psychotherapy in general. Presence, however, is a complex term and there is not agreement upon how it should be understood even within existential–humanistic therapy. As Krug (2009) notes, presence can be focused on intrapersonal experience, such as in the work of James F. T. Bugental, or interpersonally focused, such as in the work of Irvin D. Yalom. It may be ideal to incorporate both intrapersonal and interpersonal processes in the development of presence. Presence can be understood as entailing a capacity that includes focused attention in the here-and-now on the intrapersonal processes as well as the interpersonal and intersubjective aspects of the relationship. Although more intentionally focused on another person, this has similarities to Wickramasekera's (2007) absorption. The cultivation of presence, then, may also help one develop a capacity for empathy.

Various psychological difficulties may present a barrier to the cultivation and experience of empathy. For example, Wickramasekera (2007) found that repressive coping, or tendencies toward repression, was negatively correlated with affective empathy. Individuals with repressive tendencies tend to be less aware of their own emotions, and as Wickramasekera found, are likely to be less aware of the emotions of others as well. If psychological difficulties may be a barrier to empathy, then it follows that psychological growth may be beneficial for developing the capacity for empathy. As a therapist and supervisor, I have observed empathetic abilities of clients, students, and supervisees naturally developing through the course of therapy or supervision even without intention being directed to this development.

Individuals desiring to develop the capacity for empathy may engage in various activities to promote emotional awareness, focused attention, and here-and-now awareness. Mindfulness exercises, engagement with the expressive arts as a consumer or artist, and one's own psychotherapy and/ or supervision all may be beneficial in the development of one's capacity for empathy.

Empathy and Culture

What constitutes culture and how it should be defined is not agreed upon in the professional literature. For the purpose of this chapter, I understand culture as referring to values, beliefs, attitudes, and behaviors that tend to be shared by a group (Tanaka-Matsumi, 2001). In this section, I draw upon a number of examples connected with racial and ethnic groups; however, I do not intend to suggest that culture is limited to racial and ethnic groups.

The primary premise of this chapter is built upon the assumption that accurate and genuine empathy is more challenging across cultural differences. In this section, I will consider two challenges to empathy in diverse cultural contexts. First, traditional conceptions of empathy focusing on the individual in a more egocentric conception may need to be revised to understand the individual in relationship, including instances where identity is rooted in culture or group identity (Comas-Diaz, 2016; O'Hara, 1997; Pedersen et al., 2008). Second, when working across cultural differences, empathy failures are more common (Jenkins, 1997), which suggests a need to help therapists address common barriers to accurate and effective empathy with clients from different cultural backgrounds. The former challenge is rooted in limitations connected with a particular understanding of self and identity that reflects a Euro-American bias. The latter challenge reflects a more pragmatic failure in implementing empathy with individuals whose experience as well as their beliefs and values are divergent from one's own.

Expanding Conceptions of Empathy

O'Hara (1997) noted that Rogers began to rethink the limitation of his earlier conceptions of empathy following cross-cultural experiences, including a trip to Brazil. Also participating in this trip, O'Hara noted that herself, Rogers, and others from the United States became aware of more developed empathetic abilities in Brazilians with whom they were engaging. Empathy played a more central role in their communication, relationship, and decision-making process, and it was a more natural way of being for them. This conception of empathy was broader and more inclusive than many other Western conceptions that focused on individual, subjective experience without consideration of the relational aspects of identity and one's sense of self, such as identity rooted within the cultural group. As O'Hara and Lyon (2014) demonstrate, consideration of culture should have implications for epistemology, the view of well-being, and how relationships are understood.

O'Hara (1997) and Pedersen et al. (2008) note that traditional conceptions of empathy in psychotherapy emerged within the individualist mindset of Western psychology that recognized the person as an independent individual. As Jenkins (1997) notes,

> One of the hallmarks of American racism has been the assumption that the Euro-American cultural vision represented the "reality." Other cultural perspectives were seen as distortions. People of color coming to mental health institutions have expected to be greeted from this perspective.
>
> (p. 336)

Psychology has not escaped the biases of European and United States culture and, in accordance, that which is not individualistic has often been pathologized in Western mental health. This has been a barrier to understanding people who do not conform to Western norms, including the more individualized conception of self, and has contributed to the distrust many people of color have with the mental health system.

Hoffman, Stewart, Warren, and Meek (2009) advocated that different conceptions of the self are more beneficial for different people. Individualistic versus collectivist or socio-centric views of self are one example of this; however, it is important to note that there are different ways to be individualistic, collectivistic, and socio-centric. There are different conceptions of what constitutes "the self" in various cultures as well as variations across the psychological schools of thought. Hoffman and colleagues are concerned about the imposition of values upon clients through identifying particular conceptions of the self as being the standard for mental health. As noted by O'Hara (1997; O'Hara & Lyon, 2014), in the West, this is the individualist view of the self. However, in some cultures, the self is understood as part of a larger whole and cannot be understood apart from this context, which could be understood as one form of collectivism. Western psychology tends to pathologize this with labels such as enmeshment, dependency, or a lack of individuation. What may promote a well-being in one culture may contribute to harm in another culture.

Emergent from similar concerns about empathy being rooted in individual subjective experience, Pedersen and colleagues (2008) advocated for *Inclusive Cultural Empathy* (ICE). They argue that in Western psychology anything outside of focus on an individual's subjective experience is seen as a distraction or distortion. ICE advocates that empathy needs to recognize various cultural factors that are part of the individual's identity, such as ethnicity, age, gender, and status (social, educational, economic). Comas-Diaz (2016) similarly emphasizes the importance of considering culture with empathy. She defines *cultural empathy* as "A process of perspective taking by using a cultural and contextual framework as a guide for understanding the client from the outside" (p. 163).

O'Hara's (1997) alternative to traditional conceptions of empathy is *relational empathy*. She notes, "When looked at through a sociocentric lens, empathy provides a means of knowing relationships not only egocentrically in terms of its particulars, but also holistically as wholes that are more than the sum of their parts" (pp. 306–307). This recognizes that empathy must take into account individual subjective experience as well as the recognition that the person is part of a larger whole that entails other relationships. Empathy occurs within relationships or a relational context, which incorporates the conception of empathy identified in the quote by Rogers at the beginning of the chapter but goes beyond to be inclusive of a broader whole embedded in a relational context. This, too, allows for empathy that recognizes and embraces others who may maintain a different conception of the self not consistent with the more egocentric Western views.

Ways to Develop Empathy in Cultural Contexts

Increasing one's ability to experience genuine and effective empathy in diverse settings requires that one do their own work (i.e., work on one's own psychological issues and limitations, including addressing one's biases; see also Chapter 6). To have bias (that is, subjective experience) is part of the human condition, and this bias/subjective experience is influenced by cultural differences. The denial of biases, or cultural influences (e.g. colorblind racism), increases the chances that these biases will find expression outside of one's conscious awareness and increases the possibility of causing unintentional harm (Monk, Winslade, & Sinclair, 2008; Sue, 2010; see also Chapter 7). Thus, doing one's own work relevant to biases is a foundation for empathy.

Hoffman and Granger (2015) advocated that poetry and sharing of narratives may be effective in promoting deeper understanding across cultural differences. Conversations about political or cultural issues are increasingly subject to polarization, which Schneider (2013) refers to as the "elevation of one point of view to the utter exclusion of competing points of view" (p. 1). These conversations quickly become intractable, often reinforcing biases. The sharing of poetry and stories shifts the focus from the objective stance often sought in debate to a subjective focus on each person's experience. This focus on subjective experience is more conducive to empathy.

While striving for universal, objective truths often polarizes and creates division, seeking knowledge about human differences without judgment promotes understanding. Although it is not realistic for therapists to have knowledge about all cultures, particularly when considering the intersectionality of various cultures or aspects of identity that often exist within individuals, being familiar with a range of cultural variations relevant to an individual's personal, social, and political differences helps a therapist improve their ability to recognize difference otherwise hidden. The lack of awareness of potential differences blinds people from recognizing them.

It is important to discuss three limitations pertaining to knowledge, particularly when considering in multicultural contexts. First, it is vital to always recognize that even when one is knowledgeable about cultural differences, this does not mean their knowledge is complete or accurate, nor does it make the therapist competent to work with individuals from that culture. As Comas-Diaz (2016) notes,

> Culturally competent clinicians subscribe to a position of 'knowing they do not know.' In other words, instead of knowing facts, multicultural clinicians focus on understanding significant processes that occur during therapeutic encounters (Comas-Diaz, 2016). Such a therapeutic stance, also known as cultural humility, enhances the development of a positive therapeutic alliance.
>
> (p. 164)

In other words, cultural humility is an essential aspect of empathy with culturally diverse individuals. Second, while knowledge can help see differences, it can also serve to promote prejudices, especially when within group differences and intersectionality are not considered. Third, while empathy can help understand others, it is important to recognize empathy is not always accurate and can be subject to various types of distortion. For example, I often encourage people to write poetry or stories in the voice of someone else as a way of deepening empathy; however, there are risks with this. It is important not to mistake the insights one attains through empathy as a shared truth—relationally or socially—particularly when this is applied across cultural differences. When writing in the voice of someone from a different cultural background, this is likely to include some limitations and inaccuracies that must be recognized and acknowledged. Additionally, caution should be used when sharing these to avoid colonizing the experience of someone from a different cultural background. Here again, cultural humility is essential.

In summary, improving one's empathy with people from different cultural backgrounds can be done through various approaches, some of which were discussed in this section. Improving one's self-awareness, particularly relevant to being in relationship with people from other cultures; increasing knowledge about cultural differences; and engaging in the arts and story-telling or narratives with people from different cultural backgrounds are important ways to help develop better empathetic abilities cross cultural differences.

Clinical Applications

Empathy is a powerful force of healing and understanding (Bohart et al., 2002; Elliott et al., 2018). The utility of empathy goes far beyond the therapy room. If empathy and understanding replaced the polarized debates common in society today, there is little doubt that this would facilitate much social and individual healing while decreasing the unnecessary harm caused by these divisions. However, in this section, I focus on empathy in the therapy room.

In humanistic psychotherapy, empathy is more than a technique or foundation for establishing a good therapeutic alliance; it is healing in and of itself (Bohart et al., 2002; Elliott et al., 2018; Hoffman, 2019). Yet, empathy is something that therapists must continue to work at and cultivate. Being competent in engaging empathetically with clients who share a similar cultural background does not necessarily mean that the therapist is competent in engaging empathetically with clients from diverse backgrounds different than their own. Various biases and prejudices, as well as a lack of cultural awareness, can create barriers to the provision of empathy.

Cultural knowledge is a complex issue in relation to empathy. While knowledge empowers the possibility of empathy through an improved frame of reference to see and understand another person's experience, it also can serve to restrict one's understanding of another person. Therapists must consistently take into account within group differences and the complexity added by the intersectionality of various aspects of identity and difference (Monk et al., 2008; see Chapter 17). It is important that the knowledge of difference includes and honors different conceptions of the self and identity, including those that fall outside of the Western conceptions of individualism pervasive in much of psychology as well as reified, narrow conceptions of collectivism.

Therapists must not assume that empathy is accurate or provides a correct understanding of the other person's experience, particularly with clients from a different cultural background. While empathy may inform the therapist of possibilities as to what the client is experiencing, it is important to verify this with the client and recognize that empathy, too, can be subject to distortions. Therapists must continually work to check and refine their empathetic capacity.

The development of the capacity for empathy also can be healing for clients; however, not always. For example, it can be harmful to encourage clients toward developing empathy with people who have harmed them.

For clients emerged in conflict with people from different cultural groups, recognizing their biases and developing empathy may help them to engage with people from different backgrounds with less conflict and pain.

Case Illustration

Bryah[1] is a 32-year-old biracial client. Her mother is of Latinx and Native American ancestry, but identified more closely with the Latinx side of her family. Her father's family is Black, the descendants of people who were enslaved in the United States. Bryah is close with both of her parents and their families but has identified primarily as Black through her adult life. She has been in therapy several times previously. In the first session, she stated, "I'm giving therapy one more chance" after several bad experiences, which she attributed to cultural differences, including with two therapists that advertised themselves as having multicultural expertise. Although a White male, I was recommended by a Latinx friend of hers.

In the first session, Bryah discussed issues of loneliness and conflict with her boyfriend, who was a Black male. I suspected there was much Bryah was not sharing in the first session but did not pursue this yet. Bryah did not discuss anything connected with ethnicity in her first session except to mention her boyfriend was Black. In the second session, I asked Bryah what it was like having a White male therapist. A long pause in which I noticed Bryah's anxiety followed. She said, "It is uncomfortable. I don't trust you and don't know if I can." Recognizing her attempts to protect herself, I noted to myself to reflect upon this after the session. Although briefly pulled out of my empathetic stance, as I made the note to myself, I was able to refocus and connect with her discomfort, "It is not easy to trust White people—even your therapist."

Bryah later revealed that when she shared her replies to my questions, she was beginning to prepare herself to not return, but she sensed something different in my response. She began to feel some tears emerge, but tightly held them back. She shared a negative experience with a previous White therapist. As I listened and remained empathetic, she began sharing other bad experiences. I felt a few twinges of fear and defensiveness, especially as Bryah touched upon her anger. Each time, I noted this and shifted my focus back to maintaining an empathetic presence in which I was resonating with her feelings. After the session, as I was reflecting upon what transpired, I recognized that I focused on her sadness, not her anger, in my empathetic responses. This concerned me.

In session three, I tried to be attentive to anger, but Bryah stayed with the sadness. Halfway through the session, I stated,

> Last session, there were a lot of different emotions that emerged. As I was thinking about this during the week, I realized I focused on responding to the emotions that I was more comfortable with: your

sadness and loneliness. I did not acknowledge your anger. I am sorry for this. I want you to know that I am committed to honoring all of your emotions.

Bryah began softly crying. She then discussed her fears of being labeled an "angry Black woman," and that talking about her boyfriend's anger may cause me to think of him as a "Thug." As Bryah noticed her voice becoming louder, she became afraid and was quickly attentive to me.

T: "Something shifted there ..."
B: "I shouldn't have told you all those things."
T: "It's scary to trust me. That's okay."
B: "No, it's not. It's not okay to me."
T: "Tell me more about that."
B: "I don't want you to think bad about us."
T: "Us?"
B: "Me, Reggie, about all of us ... all of us who are not White."
T: "Bryah, you can ask about my response at any time and I will give you an honest answer. Right now, what I feel is a deeper connection to you. I feel sadness at what you've experienced, and I feel anger, too, at what has happened to you."

This exchange helped Bryah begin trusting, but it remained a gradual process. Bryah had many negative experiences with White people in power roles, including previous therapists. Given this, it could be maintained that it is dangerous, potentially harmful, to trust me too quickly. Even after a solid therapeutic alliance and trust were established, Bryah questioned this at times. I recognized that I sometimes felt defensive, not of myself, but of White people, when Bryah became upset and generalized in her language. Each time this happened, I noted this and then shifted back to focusing on Bryah's experience. When reflecting on these reactions after the session, I identified aspects of my own work that needed more attention.

In later sessions, Bryah discussed her struggles with identity. She confronted me for what she perceived was pushing her toward individuating from her family, which she viewed as culturally insensitive. I accepted the critique and acknowledged this probably was coming from my cultural background. Genuinely appreciating the feedback, I invited her to continue letting me know anytime she was concerned about this. Although Bryah's assumptions about relationships and identity were different than my own, I directed my empathy toward recognizing that her identity was essentially connected with her family and culture while remaining aware of my limitations in fully understanding this. After Bryah's confrontation, she began to explore what it meant to be multiracial, which helped her begin to integrate different aspects of her cultural identity, including those previously neglected, such as her Native American ancestry.

Reflections on Bryah's Therapy

At the outset of therapy, I would have been considered by most as a culturally competent, and maybe even culturally proficient, therapist. Part of this competency was rooted in a recognition of my limitations, the need to continue ongoing personal reflection about implicit biases, commitment to continued growth toward cultural proficiency, and openness to feedback, even when uncomfortable. I recognized, too, the potential for personal biases and sensitivities to negatively impact empathy and worked to remain aware of this possibility. For Bryah, several factors helped her to be able to experience my empathy and develop trust. First, she could see my empathy through nonverbal responses. Second, Bryah recognized that I was fairly knowledgeable about her culture, but also did not make assumptions about her based on this information.

Summary

- Empathy as a way of being or an aspect of presence is an important part of the healing process in therapy, especially in humanistic and existential–humanistic therapy.
- Therapists can develop their empathetic capacity, including their empathetic capacity with people from different cultural backgrounds.
- Doing one's own work pertaining to cultural biases, developing knowledge about cultural differences, and engaging with narratives and the arts relevant to cultural differences and intersectionality can help therapists develop their empathetic capacities.
- It is important not to mistake empathy with truth, particularly when working with clients from different cultural backgrounds.
- The development of empathy is also an important resource for resolving and healing social and political conflicts.

Note

1 Bryah is a fictional character. The story is inspired by real interactions with multiple clients. Any resemblance to an actual person is coincidental.

References

Bloom, P. (2016). *Against empathy: The case for rational compassion.* New York, NY: HarperCollins.

Bohart, A. C., Elliott, R., Greenberg, L. S., & Watson, J. C. (2002). Empathy. In J. C. Norcross (Ed.), *Psychotherapy relationships that work: Therapist contributions and responsiveness to patients* (pp. 89–108). New York, NY: Oxford University Press.

Bohart, A. C., & Greenberg, L. S. (1997). Empathy and psychotherapy: An introductory overview. In A. C. Bohart & L. S. Greenberg (Eds.), *Empathy reconsidered: New directions in psychotherapy* (pp. 3–31). Washington, DC: American Psychological Association.

Comas-Diaz, L. (2016). Multicultural therapy. In H. S. Friedman (Ed.), *Encyclopedia of mental health* (2nd ed., pp. 163–168). Waltham, MA: Academic Press.

Elliott, R., Bohart, A. C., Watson, J. C., & Murphy, D. (2018). Therapist empathy and client outcome: An updated meta-analysis. *Psychotherapy, 55*, 399–410.

Furman, R. (2005). Using poetry and written exercised to teach empathy. *Journal of Poetry Therapy, 18*(2), 103–110.

Grogan, J. (2013). *Encountering America: Humanistic psychology, sixties culture, and the shaping of the modern self.* New York, NY: Harper Perennial.

Hoffman, L. (2019). Introduction to existential–humanistic psychotherapy in a cross-cultural context: An East–West dialogue. In L. Hoffman, M. Yang, F. J. Kaklauskas & A. Chan (Eds.), *Existential psychology East–West* (pp. 1–71). Colorado Springs, CO: University of the Rockies Press.

Hoffman, L., & Granger, N., Jr. (2015). Introduction. In L. Hoffman & N. Granger, Jr. (Eds.), *Stay awhile: Poetic narratives on multiculturalism and diversity* (pp. 7–17). Colorado Springs, CO: University Professors Press.

Hoffman, L., Stewart, S., Warren, D., & Meek, L. (2009). Toward a sustainable myth of self: An existential response to the postmodern condition. *Journal of Humanistic Psychology, 49*, 135–173.

Jenkins, A. H. (1997). The empathic context in psychotherapy with people of color. In A. C. Bohart & L. S. Greenberg (Eds.), *Empathy reconsidered: New directions in psychotherapy* (pp. 321–341). Washington, DC: American Psychological Association.

Krug, O. T. (2009). James Bugental and Irvin Yalom: Two masters of existential therapy cultivate presence in the therapeutic encounter. *Journal of Humanistic Psychology, 49*, 329–354.

Monk, G., Winslade, J., & Sinclair, S. (2008). *New horizons in multicultural counseling.* Thousand Oaks, CA: Sage.

O'Hara, M. (1997). Relational empathy: Beyond modernism egocentricism to postmodern holistic contextualism. In A. C. Bohart & L. S. Greenberg (Eds.), *Empathy reconsidered: New directions in psychotherapy* (pp. 295–319). Washington, DC: American Psychological Association.

O'Hara, M., & Lyon, A. (2014). Well-being and well-becoming: Reauthorizing the subject in incoherent times. In T. J. Hämäläinen & J. Michaelson (Eds.), *New horizons in management. Well-being and beyond: Broadening the public and policy discourse* (pp. 98–122). Northampton, MA: Edward Elgar Publishing.

Pedersen, P. B., Crethar, H. C., & Carlson, J. (2008). *Inclusive cultural empathy: Making relationships central in counseling and psychotherapy.* Washington, DC: American Psychological Association.

Rogers, C. R. (1959). A theory of therapy, personality, and interpersonal relationships, as developed in the client-centered framework. In S. Koch (Ed.), *Psychology: A study of science* (Vol. 3 Formulations of the persona and the social context, pp. 184–256). New York, NY: McGraw-Hill.

Rogers, C. R. (1980). *A way of being.* Boston, MA: Houghton Mifflin.

Schneider, K. J. (2013). *The polarized mind: Why it's killing us and what we can do about it.* Colorado Springs, CO: University Professors Press.

Schneider, K. J., & Krug, O. T. (2017). *Existential–humanistic therapy* (2nd ed.). Washington, DC: American Psychological Association.

Sue, D. W. (2010). *Microaggressions in everyday life: Race, gender, and sexual orientation.* Hoboken, NJ: John Wiley & Sons.

Tanaka-Matsumi, J. (2001). Abnormal psychology and culture. In D. Matsumoto (Ed.), *The handbook of culture and psychology* (pp. 265–286). New York, NY: Oxford University Press.

Teding van Berkhout, E., & Malouff, J. M. (2016). The efficacy of empathy training: A meta-analysis of randomized controlled trials. *Journal of Counseling Psychology, 63*(1), 32–41.

Wampold, B. E., & Imel, Z. E. (2015). *The great psychotherapy debate: The evidence for what makes psychotherapy work* (2nd ed.). New York, NY: Routledge.

Wickramasekera, I. E., II. (2007). Empathetic features of absorption and incongruence. *American Journal of Clinical Hypnosis, 50*(1), 59–69.

10 Cultural Myths, Rituals, and Festivals[1]

Heatherlyn Cleare-Hoffman, Louis Hoffman, and Jane Perlstein

Cultural rituals and festivals served to promote communal and individual well-being, including healing from various challenges and tragedies, long before the advent of psychotherapy. In contemporary culture, rituals and festivals continue to benefit psychological well-being, even when not intentionally engaged for these purposes. Often, rituals and festivals have been coopted and transformed by popular culture in a manner that limits their healing potential. In this chapter, we focus primarily on cultural festivals, which frequently incorporate rituals and mythic functions, and their healing potential for individuals and cultural groups.

Myth, Rituals, and Festivals

Myth, ritual, and festival are closely related, often with significant overlap. Rollo May (1991) described myths as "a way of making sense in a senseless world. Myths are narrative patterns that give significance to our existence" (p. 15). Myths, often misunderstood in contemporary society, are not falsities, but rather the nature of myths is that they cannot be proven to be true. Myth, therefore, can be understood as a way to organize meaning. Meaning is a complex construct, and there is not agreement upon the definition or understanding of meaning, even within existential psychology (Vos, Cooper, Hill, Neimeyer, Schneider, & Wong, 2017). Hoffman (2019) distinguishes sustaining meaning as a type of meaning that helps cope with and transform suffering while also promoting well-being.

Rituals have been more extensively considered in the psychological literature than festivals. According to Achterberg, Dombrowne, and Krippner (2007), "The term *ritual* can be conceptualized as a prescribed, stylized, step-by-step goal-directed performance of a mythological theme" (p. 264). Cultural rituals are developed to meet a particular need of individuals or the community. Cultural festivals are communal activities typically designed to bring people together with a singular purpose that typically reflects values and meanings important to the community. As compared with rituals, the communal aspect of festivals is more prominent. Festivals frequently contain a collection of activities and may incorporate multiple rituals.

One potential difference between rituals and festivals is the way in which they contribute to individual well-being. Rituals often are intended to have a more direct positive impact upon the individual or individuals performing them. At times, this is through connecting individuals with the community. Festivals, however, primarily function to benefit the community or culture, and the individual benefits are secondary. We are not suggesting a rigid distinction here; many rituals have been designed for community benefits as well. Furthermore, the modernization and Westernization of rituals has shifted the focus and purpose of many rituals in a more individualistic manner. For example, Idowu (1992), focusing on religion, notes that African religion tends to be more communal, whereas Western religion focuses increasingly on the individual. Rituals in the West gravitate toward being more individualistic even though the same ritual may be more communal in other countries.

Our usage of myth, ritual, and festival is closely related. In fact, there may be times where a singular activity can be seen as being a myth, ritual, and festival concurrently. However, there are differences. In particular, myths are more detached from activity, and often serve to bring a meaning framework to stories or activities. Thus, cultural rituals and festivals can often be interpreted through their mythic meaning and function. The distinction between cultural rituals and festivals is subtler, with cultural festivals typically being broader and comprised of multiple rituals.

The Healing Potential of Myth, Ritual, and Festivals

It is difficult to directly assess the healing potential of myth. A primary role of myth is to provide meaning, including serving an integrative function of helping make sense of one's experiences. Meaning is increasingly supported in the research literature as being able to transform suffering and promote well-being (Hoffman, Vallejos, Cleare-Hoffman, & Rubin, 2015; Vos, 2018).

Achterberg and colleagues (2007) note that rituals promote healing through various means, including reconnecting with one's community, facilitating hope, "providing a roadmap for the unseen, unknown, uncharted territory ahead" (p. 282), and promoting coping strategies. Ritual is the basis of many healing ceremonies and traditional healing practices. Even when not developed with the intent of healing, rituals frequently promote well-being. For example, Palmer (2010) examined how an Ethiopian coffee (Buna) ceremony impacted the psychological and social well-being of displaced Ethiopians. The results supported that engaging in this ceremony provided social and psychological benefits.

There is not as much research on festivals as compared to rituals, and much of the research that has been conducted focuses on the economic and cultural implications of festivals. Getz's (2010) interdisciplinary review of literature on festivals identified numerous benefits that festivals bring to community, including both fostering and reinforcing positive community identity and feelings of belonging and interconnectedness, as well as the potential benefit of authentic experience and celebration. Similarly, Yolal, Gursoy, Uysal, Kim, and Karacaoglu (2016) suggest that individual subjective well-being benefits of festivals may be mediated through the community benefits. In other words, when festivals have a positive impact on the community, this also promotes benefits for individual well-being. Looking at a particular festival, Idowu (1992) found social and psychological benefits for Africans participating in the Oshun Festival; however, he acknowledged some limitations in the benefits as the needs of Africans change over time.

The Loss of Meaning in Myth, Ritual, and Festival

Rollo May (1991) believed that the loss of myth was one of the great threats to contemporary society. In addition to providing meaning, myth also can bring people together and to unite a culture. If myth, rituals, and festivals serve to unite people, then the loss of these can be seen as part of the destruction of a culture. Wade Nobles (2006) states,

> when the symbols, rituals, and rites of a culture lose their legitimacy and power to compel thought and action, disruption occurs within the cultural orientation and reflects itself as a pathology in the psychology of the people belonging to that culture.
>
> (p. 187)

This can be seen as related to what Achterberg and colleagues (2007) call *soul loss*: "Perhaps the most widespread diagnosis on the planet is soul loss …, which usually implies dissociation from vital aspects of oneself or alienation from one's family, friends, and community" (p. 280). The displacement of individuals or groups, whether the displacement is by choice or forced, can result in estrangement from one's sources of meaning and support. The implications are particularly nefarious when the groups are not welcomed or appreciated.

For displaced cultures, myths serve a vital role in preserving culture as well as promoting psychological and communal well-being. Irobi (2007) notes that the arts, including song, dance, and drama, carried collective memory prior to modernism. Through connection with one's history and cultural legacy, the memories embodied in myth, ritual, festival benefit both the individual and the community, and disconnection from them can cause harm. This is one of the harms inherent in assimilation, particularly when it involves disconnection from one's history and culture. According to Nobles (2006), "The de-legitimization/defamation of African culture, in fact, has been the principal instrument in the negative transformation of the African-American family institution" (p. 205). Displaced and migrant cultures frequently are encouraged to exchange their myths, rituals, and festivals for those of the dominant culture. This, however, can have destructive outcomes, including loss of sustaining meaning, identity, and community.

The Capitalization of Cultural Festivals and Rituals

According to the World Tourism Organization (2015), tourism is one of the fastest growing sectors in the global economy, and has become especially essential for many developing economies. As noted by Sosale (2013), globalization and new media technologies have made inroads into areas of the private sphere, entering traditional practices and community life and enabling aspects of local traditions to be captured digitally. They then are disseminated through the internet and brought into the public and commercial spheres to be commodified. Cultural tourism has become especially prominent in development literature, particularly for small island nations that have historically relied on tourism (Hendrickson, Lugay, Mulder, Alvarez, & Pérez Caldentey, 2012). As described by Yolal and colleagues (2016), most research today on festivals focuses primarily on their economic impact and potential, and Getz (2010) notes in his literature review that there had been "a marked trend towards treating festivals as commodities" and "tools of tourism and economic development" (p. 5).

The allure of economic growth in developing countries increases the pressure towards using culture as material capital, not only in the private sphere, but also for national governments and for individuals (Sosale, 2013). In many smaller countries that rely on tourism, it has been the government that has taken the lead in promoting tourism and the process of commodifying local culture as a means of furthering economic growth (Misiewicz, 2015; Watts & Ferro, 2012). Driven by these forces, cultures across the world have seen a rapid increase in the promotion of cultural tourism, increasingly bringing about the commercialization of local cultural festivals and traditions (Alamillo, 2003; Fernandes, 2014; Ho, 2000; Kaul, 2009; Misiewicz, 2015; Sosale, 2013; Su, 2011; Whitford, 2008; Whitford & Dunn, 2014).

Under conditions of economic duress, the economic benefits of tourism can appear as the best option for survival, including the survival of cultural traditions that can rely on funding from tourism (Getz, 2010). The process of commercialization is often furthered by locals, exercising their own agency in translating their cultural heritage into entrepreneurial expression designed to exploit the resources of tourists (Su, 2011; Turner, 2010). As Fernandes (2014) describes in his review, communities are often optimistic about the growth that cultural tourism can bring, and promote this growth process with motivation to not only bring income, but also in the larger scheme, satisfy "social and psychological needs, and to improve the community's well-being" (p. 33).

However, Fernandes (2014) argues that host communities often over-look the costs and impacts of cultural tourism and overestimate potential gains. Cultural festivals and rituals typically originate from deep, mean-ingful sources within a culture. When they become commercialized, transformed into large parties, or adapted to accommodate the interests and preferences of those outside of the group in which it originated, then the festivals can lose their meaning as well as many of the other social and psychological benefits they have provided to the community. As described by Kaul (2009) as well as Hall and Tucker (2004), tourism can intensify the process of commercialization in a way that heightens inequalities and reinforces postcolonial dynamics both intra and internationally.

As will be discussed in more detail in the illustration below, many of these dynamics can be seen with Junkanoo, a Bahamian cultural festival, which Cleare-Hoffman (2011, 2019) noted was gradually separated from its historical significance over time. The history and meaning of Junkanoo was no longer taught in most schools and many Bahamians no longer under-stood the rich, meaningful context of the event. When Junkanoo is reduced to a celebration or party, it is limited in its ability to unite the culture and provide psychological and social benefits to the Bahamian people.

Myth, Ritual, and Festivals as a Way of Understanding Culture

Irobi (2007) notes that meaning and culture can be carried in the body (i.e., embodiment) as well as through language. For individuals who are part of the African diaspora, including those who were forced to give up their language and belief system, their bodies became a primary source for maintaining the connection with their history. Irobi notes,

> Western postpositivistic history, particularly the valorization of the printed word and cryptographic literacy over other forms of commu-nication, seems to have drastically affected the way Western scholars understand and value the power of the body as a site of multiple discourses for sculpting history, memory, identity, and culture.
>
> (p. 900)

Rituals and festivals often require an action to participate in them, which can be seen as an invitation to embodiment. Consistent with Irobi's idea of meaning and culture being carried in the body, rituals and festivals can be seen as engaging with a form of embodied memory. This memory relies upon a symbolic way of knowing that does not necessarily rely upon language or even cognitive knowledge.

When attending to the embodied and meaning levels, rituals and festivals reveal core components of a culture. In other words, through these activities, it is possible to better understand the values and worldview of a particular culture. In the next section, we will consider how the Bahamian festival of Junkanoo reveals the values of inherent in Bahamian culture. Additionally, we examine how Junkanoo can serve to promote individual and cultural well-being for Bahamians living in the Bahamas as well as those who have dispersed throughout the world.

Illustration: Junkanoo, a Bahamian Cultural Festival

Cleare-Hoffman (2019) advocated that Junkanoo, which is a Bahamian culture festival with many ritualistic features, could be considered a Bahamian cultural myth (see also Cleare-Hoffman, 2011; Cleare-Hoffman & Hoffman, 2013). It is believed to have originated from West African festivals, possibly the annual yam festival of the Yoruba tribe in Nigeria (Sands, 2003). Another popular theory was that Junkanoo was named after John Canoe, who was variously thought to be a slave rebel or an influential African merchant, among other legends. Junkanoo in its early forms served as a way of preserving cultural memories from Africa. The Bahamian slaves were forced to abandon their spiritual traditions, language, and customs once arriving in the new country, but through the music, dance, and costumes of Junkanoo aspects of these memoires were preserved (Sands, 2008). During slavery and later forms of oppression prior to Bahamian independence, Junkanoo could be seen as a form of social protest (Saunders, 2003); however, it was allowed by the slave owners, perhaps partially because they did not understand the deeper meanings of the festival and partially because it served as a release of tension that, in their minds, prevented uprisings.

After slavery in the Bahamas ended in 1834, Junkanoo continued. Over time, the celebration gradually changed, and for many Bahamians became somewhat removed from its historical context. Contemporary Junkanoo has become much more elaborate and even commercialized. Competition was introduced into Junkanoo where different groups, such as the Saxons, the Valley Boys, and the Music Makers, vied for various prizes. While only Bahamians participate in the performance, many tourists come to watch. The tourism aspect of Junkanoo helps financially sustain Junkanoo and benefits the Bahamian tourism industry, which is one of the Bahamas' two most important industries (Misiewicz, 2015).

Contemporary Junkanoo begins at 2:00 am on Boxing Day (December, 26) and then again New Year's Day. Bahamians gather on Bay Street as various music groups perform for the crowd through music, dance, and colorful, elaborate costumes and floats. The first thing the crowd hears is the cowbells and drums. The drumbeat is viscerally felt in one's body as the tension builds with anticipation for one's favorite group. The various groups march through the street, occasionally stopping to treat the spectators to a special performance. Each year there is a theme that reflects various meanings, which could be political, religious, or current events. For example, after his death there was a celebration of Sir Lynden Oscar Pindling, who is considered the founding father of the Bahamas after leading them to independence in 1973 and serving as its first Black Prime Minister. Dedicating Junkanoo to him helped Bahamians grieve the loss of this important figure in addition to celebrating his life and achievements.

Identification of Bahamian Values in Junkanoo

Junkanoo served as a way of integration the African values embodied in music, dance, and costume with the Christianity that was forced upon them (Sands, 2003). While inspired by African rituals and festivals, Junkanoo has come to represent a unique Bahamian festival that integrates various aspects of Bahamian cultural identity. It has become an important part of Bahamian heritage over the years while also helping to define what Bahamian culture is.

Facilitating Change

According to Sands (2008), "Bahamian Junkanoo, therefore, continues to be a dynamic force for positive progressive and peaceful change in Bahamian society" (p. 67). Junkanoo began as a way to celebrate and unify the various African cultures brought to the Bahamas through the slave trade, and has taken on many different focuses since this time. Through the years, it has transformed from a means by which Black Bahamians resisted slavery and oppression to a celebration of Bahamian heritage. Presently, it is fully integrated into the Bahamian culture and can be seen in art, music, and food (Bethel, 2003).

Sustained Meaning through Adversity

From the time of the first African slaves through Independence from Britain in 1973 and to today, Junkanoo has highlighted and celebrated the Bahamian spirit. For example, Cleare-Hoffman (2019) maintained that historically Junkanoo was a radical embracing of freedom in the face of oppression. The spirit of Junkanoo is now entwined and indistinguishable from the Bahamian spirit and continues to engender a sense of pride, bringing the Bahamian people together as it did in the beginning. Although the spectacle of Junkanoo has also grown to include a prominent part of the Bahamian economy, the average Bahamian still recognizes its importance to the history of the Bahamas. Cleare-Hoffman (2011, 2019) has advocated that recognition of the history and legacy of Junkanoo may help strengthen connection with sustaining meaning for many Bahamians today and for Bahamians in years to come.

Community Identity

Although Bahamian culture has been influenced by Western individualistic values, the culture of the Bahamas represents a form of collectivism. One's family and facets of Bahamian culture are important aspects of most Bahamians' identity. Junkanoo is a powerful community event that unites Bahamians across their differences. With the introduction of competition, many Bahamians have a strong connection with the group that they follow (Saxons, the Valley Boys, Roots and the Music Makers, as well as other groups). While this fierce loyalty may cause disagreement, the Bahamian cultural pride that is entwined with Junkanoo is never lost. Through uniting Bahamian cultural pride with group competition, Junkanoo helps integrate different aspects of one's identity.

Conclusion

For some Bahamians, Junkanoo has lost its conscious meaning, while for others it retains a deep, sustaining meaning. Even when the conscious awareness of the history and significance is lost, there remain powerful communal aspects of Junkanoo, which may reflect its embodied memory, embedded in the costumes, music, and dance. It serves to unite and inspire Bahamians still living in the Bahamas as well as those who have dispersed to other locations around the globe. Junkanoo continues to be a powerful, embodied symbol of Bahamian resiliency.

Clinical Implications

While cultural myths, rituals, and festivals may appear too abstract to be relevant to clinical practice, there are a number of ways therapists can utilize this material. Cultural myths, rituals, and festivals can be a way to explore one's connection with one's culture, or the lack of connection. For individuals experiencing isolation, particularly if this has cultural components to it, encouraging them to explore the cultural myths, rituals, and festivals associated with their cultural identity or identities can be a powerful way of developing meaning, interpersonal connection, and community.

Cultural myths, rituals, and festivals allow therapists who do not share the cultural heritages of their client to better understand the client's culture and values. Through encouraging the client to share about their connection and meaning associated with these activities, the therapist can come to better understand their client. For instance, a Bahamian client sharing about Junkanoo can help the therapist understand their values of community and freedom.

Through recognizing the broader value of cultural myths, rituals, and festivals, therapists can be informed in their social engagement. One theme of this book is that humanistic therapists ought to be socially engaged beyond the therapy office. Therapists can be socially engaged through supporting cultural events that are meaningful to members of that cultural group. Participating in cultural rituals and festivals, when it is appropriate to do so, can help therapists become more culturally aware and competent. When participating, it is important to be sensitive to cultural rules or guidelines for participation by one outside of the cultural group. It may be considered inappropriate to participate, or inappropriate to participate without an invitation. We are not suggesting participating in cultural rituals or festivals with clients, particularly without careful reflection on the relevant ethical issues. Rather, we are suggesting general engagement with various cultural festivals and celebrations to broaden one's cultural awareness, understanding, and experience. For example, smaller versions of the Jamaican Independence Day celebration, Chinese New Year, and other important cultural festivals and celebrations occur in various communities in the United States. It may be part of developing a therapist's cultural competency to attend events such as these to gain a more embodied understanding of these different cultures and cultural expressions.

Not all cultural myths, rituals, and festivals are rooted in history. New ones emerge regularly. For example, it could be maintained that communal responses to tragedy and activism represent or embody elements of a cultural ritual and festival, and may even incorporate aspects of cultural rituals and festivals. For example, for many people in historically oppressed groups, coming together in a vigil or protest after the loss of a member of their community to a hate incident or hate crime can be a powerful form of healing. Hoffman, Granger, Vallejos, and Moats (2016) discussed how Black Lives Matter, and the contemporary protest movements can be an important part of the healing process for many in the African American community. The protests provide an opportunity to grieve together, create meaning, and support each other while also promoting positive social change.

Summary

- Myth, which can include cultural rituals and festivals, is central to the existential–humanistic understanding of meaning.
- Encouraging people to examine their cultural myths, rituals, and festivals can be a way of helping them discover meaning and create community.
- Therapists may consider observing or participating in cultural rituals and festivals as a way of increasing their embodied understanding of cultural differences and improving their cultural competency.

Note

1 We would like to thank and acknowledge Stefka Cleare for her feedback and suggestions on the development of this chapter.

References

Achterberg, J., Dombrowne, C., & Krippner, S. (2007). The role of rituals in psychotherapy. In I. D. Serlin (Ed.), *Whole person healthcare* (Vol. 2: Psychology, Spirituality, & Health, pp. 261–288). Westport, CT: Praeger.

Alamillo, J. M. (2003). *Contesting cinco de Mayo: Cultural politics and commercialization of the postwar fiesta. Smithsonian Center for Latino Initiatives.* Retrieved from: http:// latino.si.edu/researchandmuseums/presentations/pdfs/alamillo_presentation.pdf

Bethel, N. (2003). Junkanoo in the Bahamas: A tale of identity. In College of the Bahamas (Ed.), *Junkanoo and religion: Christianity and cultural identity in the Bahamas* (pp. 118–130). Nassau, Bahamas: The College of the Bahamas.

Cleare-Hoffman, H. P. (2011, November). *An existential analysis of Junkanoo.* Poster session accepted to present at the Caribbean Regional Conference of Psychology, Nassau, Bahamas.

Cleare-Hoffman, H. P. (2019). Junkanoo: A Bahamian cultural myth. In L. Hoffman, M. Yang, F. J. Kaklauskas, & A. Chan (Eds.), *Existential psychology East–West* (Rev. & Expanded ed., pp. 381–389). Colorado Springs, CO: University Professors Press.

Cleare-Hoffman, H. P., & Hoffman, L. (2013, August). *The meaning and history of Junkanoo for Bahamian culture.* Poster presented at the 121st Annual Convention of the American Psychological Association, Honolulu, HI.

Fernandes, C. (2014). The impact of cultural tourism on host communities. In R. Raj, K. Griffin, & N. D. Morpeth (Eds.), *Cultural tourism* (pp. 26–36). Cambridge, MA: CAB International.

Getz, D. (2010). The nature and scope of festival studies. *International Journal of Event Management Research, 5*(1), 1–47.

Hall, M. C., & Tucker, H. (2004). *Tourism and postcolonialism: Contested discourses, identities and representations.* New York, NY: Routledge.

Hendrickson, M., Lugay, B., Mulder, N., Alvarez, M., & Pérez Caldentey, E. (2012). Creative industries in the Caribbean: A new road for diversification and export growth. United Nations ECLAC studies and perspectives series. *The Caribbean, 19,* 1–69.

Ho, C. G. (2000). Popular culture and the aestheticization of politics: Hegemonic struggle and postcolonial nationalism in Trinidad carnival. *Transforming Anthropology, 9*(1), 3–18.

Hoffman, L. (2019). Gordo's ghost: An introduction to existential–humanistic perspectives on myth. In L. Hoffman, M. Yang, F. J. Kaklauskas, & A. Chan (Eds.), *Existential psychology East–West* (Rev. & Expanded ed., pp. 273–288). Colorado Springs, CO: University Professors Press.

Hoffman, L., Granger, N. Jr., Vallejos, L., & Moats, M. (2016). An existential-humanistic perspective on Black Lives Matter and contemporary protest movements. *Journal of Humanistic Psychology, 56,* 595–611.

Hoffman, L., Vallejos, L., Cleare-Hoffman, H. P., & Rubin, S. (2015). Emotion, relationship, and meaning as core existential practice: Evidence-based foundations. *Journal of Contemporary Psychotherapy, 45,* 11–20.

Idowu, A. I. (1992). The Oshun festival: An African traditional religious healing process. *Counseling & Values, 36,* 192–201.

Irobi, E. (2007). What they came with: Carnival and the persistence of African performance aesthetics in the diaspora. *Journal of Black Studies, 37,* 896–913.

Kaul, A. R. (2009). *Turning the tune: Traditional music, tourism, and social change in an Irish village*. New York, NY: Berghahn Books.

May, R. (1991). *The cry for myth*. New York, NY: Norton.

Misiewicz, G. (2015). "The rapture is really coming": On tourism and the creation of the Bahamas Junkanoo Carnival (Master's thesis). Retrieved from Google Scholar.

Nobles, W. W. (2006). *Seeking the Sakhu: Foundational writings for an African psychology*. Chicago, IL: Third World Press.

Palmer, D. (2010). Beyond *Buna* and popcorn: Using personal narratives to explore the relationship between the Ethiopian coffee (*Buna*) ceremony and mental and social well-being among Ethiopian forced migrants in London, UK. *Advances in Mental Health, 9*, 263–276.

Sands, K. C. (2003). Junkanoo in historical perspective. In College of the Bahamas (Ed.), *Junkanoo and religion: Christianity and cultural identity in the Bahamas* (pp. 10–19). Nassau, Bahamas: The College of the Bahamas.

Sands, K. C. (2008). *Early Bahamian slave spirituality: The genesis of Bahamian cultural identity*. Nassau, Bahamas: The Nassau Guardian.

Saunders, G. (2003). *Bahamian society after emancipation*. Kingston, Jamaica: Ian Randle Publishers.

Sosale, S. (2013). Making media commodities from cultural practices: Implications for developing regions. *Journal of Developing Societies, 29*(1), 47–60.

Su, X. (2011). Commodification and the selling of ethnic music to tourists. *Geoforum, 42*(4), 496–505.

Turner, J. A. (2010). Cultural performances in the Guangxi tourism commons: A study of music, place, and ethnicity in Southern China. Doctoral dissertation, Indiana University.

Vos, J. (2018). *Meaning in life: An evidence-based handbook for practitioners*. London, UK: Palgrave Macmillan.

Vos, J., Cooper, M., Hill, C. E., Neimeyer, R. A., Schneider, K. J., & Wong, P. T. (2017). Five perspectives on the meaning of meaning in the context of clinical practices. *Journal of Constructivist Psychology, 32*(1), 48–62.

Watts, M. W., & Ferro, S. L. (2012). The coexistence of folk and popular culture as vehicles of social and historical activism: Transformation of the Bumba-meu-boi in northeast Brazil. *The Journal of Popular Culture, 45*(4), 883–901.

Whitford, M. (2008). Oaxaca's indigenous Guelaguetza festival: Not all that glistens is gold. *Event Management, 12*(3–4), 143–161.

Whitford, M., & Dunn, A. (2014). Papua New Guinea's indigenous cultural festivals: Cultural tragedy or triumph? *Event Management, 18*(3), 265–283.

World Tourism Organization (UNWTO). (2015). Why tourism? Accessed March 4, 2015. Retrieved from: www2.unwto.org/content/why-tourism

Yolal, M., Gursoy, D., Uysal, M., Kim, H., & Karacaoglu, S. (2016). Impacts of festivals and events on residents' well-being. *Annals of Tourism Research, 61*, 1–18.

11 No Time Like the Present

Embracing Psychological, Social, and Ecological Justice

David St. John

Donald Trump is President of the United States of America. It has been well over two years, and I still feel a sense of disbelief at this statement. I know it's true—I witness the effects every day. Yet, like many people, I still feel a great sense of disconnection from it. Better said, a disassociation, which suggests a trauma—and it certainly is traumatic. An egotistical, proto-fascist, racist, sexist oligarch is in charge of the most technologically powerful country that has ever existed in the history of humanity. At a time of unprecedented global crises, Trump's toxic influence reverberates around the world. The suffering is real, and it is experienced daily by millions of people—especially the socially vulnerable.

From a psychological perspective, how else could this feeling of derealization be understood than through the prism of trauma? Disassociation is one of a handful of psychological defenses people have against experiences that are too overwhelming and too painful to experience. The ability to detach from one's own experience—emotionally, cognitively, bodily—is an evolutionary survival technique.

People dissociate from not only the threats from the outside world, but threats from within. Unwanted feelings, desires, and memories can be submerged into the dark waters of the mind, and held under for moments, months, or even years. This is the nature of the self—people are what they forget as much as what they remember. The tight conscious self working hard to keep the unwanted at bay, pushing it down; further and darker and wetter and colder. But it always returns. That's the key to the analytic truth. Usually, once safe, those feelings of pain and terror can be felt, expressed, and processed. That which was disintegrated by trauma can be reintegrated. Sometimes, though, the forgotten is not reintegrated, and, instead, floats somewhere between the repressed and the remembered. Always present in the absence, it's a dark shadow just under the sparkle of the surface.

If it is true that individuals can disconnect from such enormous aspects of themselves as individuals, then it is true of groups as well. Entire families or communities may exile unwanted aspects of themselves. Institutions push out those parts of reality they can't bear to see. Entire nations oppress—I mean repress—aspects of themselves that they choose not to acknowledge. As noted by Zinn (2003), "The history of any country … conceals fierce conflicts of interest (sometimes exploding, most often repressed) between conquerors and conquered, masters and slaves, capitalists and workers, dominators and dominated in race and sex" (p. 10).

America, from its revolutionary inception, has been in perpetual psychological conflict. On the one hand, ideals of liberty, justice, and democracy are boasted. On the other, legally dehumanized Persons of Color, disempowered women, and disenfranchised poor and working class stand mute. This disassociation—between freedom and oppression—is foundational to the nation's identity. Like the individual who hides those unwanted aspects of themselves from themselves, so too has the United States. But at a great cost, as illuminated by the renowned American writer, James Baldwin: "History is not the past, it is the present. We carry our history with us—we are our history. If we pretend otherwise, we are literally criminals" (Baldwin & Peck, 2017).

The White Whale

On November 8th, 2016, Trump was elected president. The next day, Chauncey Devega (2016) wrote: "Trump may not be the president the American people need but he most certainly is the one they deserve." In this one act and sentence, centuries of usually disassociated American history comes pushing through the surface of disbelief. A white whale of corruption exploding into the air, its body twisting, then crashing into waves of shock. After eight years of neoliberal normalcy, helmed by an exceedingly intelligent, honest, and moderate president, the barely hidden criminal conflict of oppression and freedom surged into consciousness.

For hundreds of years, the United States proudly proclaimed the values of democracy, freedom, and justice as the core to its identity. Yet, Trump, an authoritarian aficionada, who enacts his ethics of egoism in daily tweets, is President. He is the perfect symbol of a United States rarely acknowledged by those in positions of authority: bigoted, self-centered, dishonest, and cruel. The naïve national belief that racism and other forms of marginalization were gone, vanished. The high water marks of the election of our first Black president, and the expected election of our first female president, evaporated.

Trump ascended at a time of unprecedented ecological disaster. His rise to power welcomed racist marches, the celebration of sexual assault, and intensified financial incursions on the poor and working class. As noted by Klein (2019), many people around the world face an "imminent ecological unraveling, gaping economic inequality (including the racial and gender wealth divide), and surging white supremacy." The daily news invites people to click on another set of traumas, in the form of flash floods, forest fires, cyclones, neo-Nazi rampages, White Nationalist terror plots, infringements on trans and gay folks, gerrymandered political corruption, and bloating credit card and student loan debt—yet all the while corporate profits grow. The sheer magnitude of human suffering, both directly and vicariously, is astounding. The anxiety and depression, along with the addictions used to cope with them, continue to rise in a perverse correlation with stock earnings (Helliwell, Layard, & Sachs, 2019).

The implications for psychology from the triadic ecological, social, and psychological threats seems obvious. As an organization of professionals, the American Psychological Association (APA) proclaims a duty "to promote the advancement, communication, and application of psychological science and knowledge to benefit society and improve lives" (APA, 2019). But when looking for leadership from the APA in this unprecedented time of trouble, that feeling of disassociation overtakes me again. An organization so steeped in antiquated scientific detachment, and in a glorification of value-free objectivity is surely part of the problem. A profession that insists that its "object" of study—people—are equally detached from their human and natural environments, in the name of "prediction and control," is why the species is so lost.

It is important to be clear here: there is no doubt that the human species, the nation, and the profession are unequivocally lost. However momentarily soothing it is to pretend this is not the case, this will only make matters worse. That there is a potential ecological collapse that will hurt marginalized people first, but everyone sooner rather than later, is an undeniable fact. I refuse to give a citation for it, because it *should go without saying*. It is an outright delusion to pretend otherwise.

It is necessary to find a way forward, as quickly as possible, as time is of the essence (Carbon Countdown Clock, 2019). But in order to figure out which way to go, it is essential to remember the history of how the human species arrived at the present moment. When lost, context is crucial. As the current state is of being lost at this point, and there is limited time, it is necessary to get as much height on the historical background as possible, and move as quickly through the history of the current predicament as possible. Imagine a streamlined satellite traveling—roughly and approximately—through time, attempting to track how *objectively justified ethical detachment* has led to the potentially disastrous moment in space and time. I apologize in advance for the methodological bumps and other scholarly plunges such a brief, high flying jolt of a ride entail.

Ancient Domestic Disconnection

For hundreds of thousands of years, anatomically modern human beings wandered around Africa (Rifkin, 2009). In family-based tribes of roughly twenty or thirty people, they followed the food. Sixty thousand years ago, some hunted and gathered out of Africa to the Middle East; later, further into Europe, Asia, and Australia, and then 15,000 years ago, to North and South America. Across the planet, early modern humans were immersed in the natural environment. People were born, grew up, lived, and died in the wilderness (Shepard, 1992).

Roughly 10,000 years ago, early ancestors of contemporary humans abruptly changed their behavior. In Mesopotamia—modern day Iraq—humans established the first civilizations. People became civilized, in the sense that they began living in cities. This was a gradual process in human time: from wandering, to mostly permanent camp grounds, to small villages, to spreading metropolises. But from a longer view—certainly from a geological view—it was sudden. Through the selection, segregation, and micromanagement of wild grains, and the domination of certain wild animals, humans settled down to cultivate, protect, and enjoy the fruits of their labor.

Why did the Agricultural Revolution begin 10,000 years ago? It seems, in part, it was a combination of being in the specific geographical space—that is, in a place that had plants and animals that were actually capable of being controlled—and a specific time—just after the last ice age—that allowed these people to survive without constant travelling (Diamond, 1999). This was a risky move, but one that paid off. As people became better farmers and herders, they began to create a surplus of food. This *profit* of nourishment allowed some people to focus their attention on things other than figuring out how to fill their bellies. While the vast majority of people were needed for farming, a small few were able to focus on the construction of buildings, astronomy, mathematics, writing, religion and, most importantly, ruling.

Pre-civilized hunter-gatherer cultures tended to be more *egalitarian*, the nodes of command shifting to different people, depending on what the situation required (Lerner, 1986). Power was decentralized and contextualized, not absolute. The "civilized" people took a different route. As cities required the vast numbers of people to live and work together consistently, people were herded through an *authoritarian* model of governance. This hierarchical structure, enforced through psychosocial coercion and physical brutality, revolved around supposed revelations from the gods through priests, or through the kings themselves. The ruler had authority because they were either a literal god, or because the gods ordained their rule.

Slavery, and the exploitation of entire groups of peoples, became the norm. What now is called classism was clearly defined in the ancient stratification of power. Pyramids—first built in Mesopotamia, but found in most early civilizations—are an excellent symbol of the "civilized" social structure. At the wide bottom were the vast majority of people—slaves, workers, and farmers. At the narrow top, there were the small number of military commanders, priests, and kings that ruled them. After hundreds of thousands of years of dynamic, egalitarian leadership, the male-dominated hierarchy—the patriarchy—was born (Lerner, 1986).

The human and environmental impact of this shift—from hunter-gatherers surrounded by nature, to citified humans walled off from nature —cannot be exaggerated. It is one of the most significant changes in human evolution. This detachment from nature—physically, but psychologically as well—drastically changed people.

Western Royal Blood

Although humans have been speculating about their place in the cosmos for as long as they have existed, it was through the committing of philosophical thought onto papyrus—3,000 years ago in Ancient Greece —that the Western world is believed to have been born. When peering back to the beginning, it's the toga-robed philosopher-kings and armor-plated warrior-scribes the West likes to see looking back. With the rise and then fall of Greece and Rome, to the beginning of city-states of Medieval Europe a thousand years ago, many important ideas traveled through the written word. Architectural designs, technical descriptions of the trades, military conquest, strategies and stories, religious practices, and primordial legends were scratched out on parchment, then paper (McNeill, 1991). Most significantly, the great move from polytheism to monotheism was written about extensively. Christian mythology mixing with Greek rationality created a new perspective—scholastic philosophy, echoes of which can still be heard every Sunday. The articles of faith—considered divine truth by the Catholic Church—were at the core of the lessons taught in the first universities. The understanding of the world and wilderness, of humanity and civilization, were heavily influenced by these assumptions for at least a thousand years (Komesaroff, 1993; McNeill, 1991).

What were in those lessons? The legitimacy of an authoritarian hierarchy, but with a Catholic twist: God above, speaking to the pope, who commands the cardinals, bishops, and priests, who lead the lowly practitioners. From this great chain of being, the royal lineages of the Middle Ages gained their power to coerce and exploit the everyday peasants too (Winks, Brighton, Christopher, & Wolff, 1992). As in Mesopotamia 7,000 years previous, the will of the divine perverted into the rule of servitude was still going strong. The serf, beholden to priests and lords alike, toiled in the fields to provide the wealth to both royalty and the church. While still mostly surrounded by it, the nature that the people interacted with every day was systematically segregated and controlled—like the people themselves. All were exploited for the profit consumed by the privileged.

After time, the empire of the Roman Church began to fade (Cahill, 1996). The ideas that began to circulate became too much for the church to hold back. Along with the printing press, the fall of the Byzantine empire created a flood of ideas. The Reformation of European Christianity was beginning. The pressure of new ways of understanding and acting in the world shattered the dam built by the Church Fathers. Europe was adrift on a sea of books (Boorstin, 1983).

Scientific Objectivity

Within the wet pages of new thought came a new world. Poetics of the Ancient Greeks infused the languages of the universities with new life (Porter, 1996). Human reason alone—breaking from the chains of both the dogmas and ethics of faith—was set free. Throughout the Renaissance that began 600 years ago, objective science—the study of the world with nothing but one's senses—took hold (Hammerstein, 1996). The world of God was split and pushed back into heaven; the world left was one to be dissected and studied through the objective quantification of the new science (Bochner, 1973).

Objectivity is the foundational belief of science. It purports that true knowledge can only be observed when a person's ethical values, historical and cultural background, philosophical assumptions, and feelings have been removed, leaving pure, unbiased observation. To be explicit, the term objectivity is being used here to refer to the psychological process of personal detachment that the scientist uses, not the external aspects of the scientific method, such as measurement, or data collection. From this definition, the objective person is able to, rather magically, detach themselves from themselves, and see the world how it "really" is. As Komesaroff (1993) stated:

> The theory of nature is assumed to be inherently and inexorably "objectivist"—that is, subjective and intersubjective contributions to conceptual constitution are excluded from it, along with any cultural variability to which meaning or truth of theoretical forms might be supposed.
>
> (p. 120)

Ethics and morals—those ideals used to guide human behavior—were purposefully discarded. According to Leach (1974): "Value-free scientific objectivity emerged as the ideal ... [which] demands the scientist's value scheme to be logically divorced from scientific standards of explanatory validity" (p. 467).

Although the empirical philosophy of science began in the 1300s, it did not enter into mainstream Western thought until the late 19th, and early 20th, centuries. With the establishment of the logical positivist movement in the 1930s, known as the Vienna Circle (Lavine, 1984), science became as dogmatic as the Church it had supplanted. Their expressed goal was to rid the world of soft subjectivity, and replace it with a hard, empirical mentality. Through this amoral objectivity, the world became one of isolated segments and fractions. All things—living or otherwise—were separated and categorized into small and smaller parts (Capra, 1996). Literally dragged into laboratories, each species—each variable—is detached and isolated from its place in nature, and its connection with other life. At the heart of the new science—and perhaps its true power— was the psychological erasure of ethical thought.

Colonialized Scientific Racism

The strength of the Protestant Reformation combined with the Scientific Revolution created a surge of new power throughout Europe. The nation-states of Spain, France, Portugal, Holland, and Britain moved violently outward into the world. So began the colonization of lands never seen by Europeans before: the "dark" continent of Africa, the "mysteries" of Asia, the "Eden" of the Americas (Boorstin, 1983). Along with a militarized Christianity, the budding new concepts of science— with amoral detachment at its center—spread alongside the viruses that were carried into the new world. The power of science, expressed in its technologies of warfare, medicine, and agriculture, ultimately converted even the most "irrational" of pagan disbelievers (Diamond, 1999).

The British did not embrace the new Eden of North America, and its inhabitants, as kin to be nurtured or protected (Milton, 2000). They were treated as resources to be subjugated, extracted, and sold. Tobacco, cotton and sugar, cultivated by the institution of slavery, fueled the colonial master's craving for control. The products of slavery would produce so much money and power that not even the dogmatic values of Christianity, nor the beautiful ideals enshrined in the U.S. constitution, could stop it at first. The capitalism of Adams and Locke, formulated alongside the burgeoning new nation, found its capital and its work force existing in the same entity—the slaves themselves. From the start, America was putting profit over people, but also making people the profit itself.

As the population of kidnapped and enslaved Africans grew from the mid-1600s, so, too, grew the power of science in everyday life (Valencius et al., 2016). Science and slavery combined with the help of a new phenomenon: *racism*. As noted by Painter (2010), the entire concept of race—created around the same time as the European conquests of the Americas—was used to scientifically justify the brutal treatment of African slaves. The variables of skin color, hair type, and other superficial factors that today are known to have no scientific correlation with any mean- ingful physical abilities or psychological traits (Helms, Jernigan, & Mascher, 2005), were used to justify a vicious system of domination. The deceitful pseudoscience of scientific racism was embraced by the U.S.

founding fathers, the intellectual and economic elite, and common people as well. No one better than Thomas Jefferson symbolizes this utter failure in moral and scientific reasoning, "The preamble to the Declaration of Independence, the single greatest action statement of Enlightenment philosophy, was written by a man who owned other human beings as property, knowing perfectly well it was morally indefensible" (O'Hehir, 2015). Jefferson's desire for wealth was more important than the ideals he so beautifully gushed.

If slaves of African descent weren't full human beings, but actually closer to animals, then the moral argument for abolishing slavery could be ignored. To arrive at that conclusion, a person has to embrace a madness in the irony of objectivity: the disavowing of all preconceived values must be held as the highest value. An ethic of no ethics. This amorality is at the core of the traditional scientific epistemology, and was present in scientific racism. It wasn't just flimsy biblical religious rationales that were used to defend slavery. It was an "objective" science, emanating from the natural world, that led to the racism of slavery and Jim Crow that followed.

Along with the scientific racism, and the slavery it tried to justify, came a new form of government in the Thirteen Colonies—democracy. Not since the Greeks in Athens thousands of years earlier did so many wealthy citizens gain the right to vote. The binds of millennial-old authoritarian rule began to crack. Instead of blood, the power now flowed through capital. While the American Revolution fought for a radically shared freedom, only wealthy landowners, who themselves could only be White men, might express that freedom (Zinn, 2003). It took almost a century after the revolution was won for the federal government to insure voting rights to non-landowners—who, even then, still had to be White men.

Industrial Strength Disconnection

Following the civil war—a vicious enactment of the fundamental American conflict between freedom and oppression—the culmination of much work and sacrifice was realized. At the end of the 1800s, and beginning of the 1900s, the United States made huge legal strides forward in realizing its democratic principles of freedom for all. Multiple amendments to the constitution established the right to vote—and outlawed servitude—for all U.S. citizens, regardless of wealth, country of origin, race, or sex.

Beside these changes came another dramatic shift in the United States culture: America became a powerhouse of industrial production. A new found wealth for the oligarchs—the titans of industry—would bring in a new age of exploitation of both nature and humans (Zinn, 2003). As the science of physics and chemistry influenced the invention of steam power, the mass production of steel, and electrification, these technologies coalesced into the great factories that changed the U.S.'s relationship to the world. At the center of these new means of production were the men and women who worked the industrial looms, foundries, and assembly lines. The days were long—12 to 15 hour shifts, with few, if any breaks. The toll of the dehumanization—of the psychological and social alienation—on the people that worked the factories, was devastating. As slavery and indentured servitude were outlawed, the rise of an industrialized servitude took its place (Fromm, 1955).

With the rise of factories came a crucial new value. As examined by Rose (2015), Fredrick Taylor, an industrial engineer who scientifically studied workers, suggested that it was through *standardization*—repetitively doing the exact procedure, over and over—that the key to industrial efficiency could be found. Taylor also stated: "In our scheme, we do not ask for initiative for our men. We do not want any initiative. All we want of them is to obey the orders we give them ..." (as cited in Rose, 2015 p. 46). Taylor's beliefs regarding the authoritarian-enforced regulation of the worker powerfully influenced the U.S. workforce, as well as other areas such as education and healthcare. There would be no authentic indivi-duality—only alienated individuals swarming around the standardized average (Fromm, 1955).

Along with the new American ethic of standardization, came another: *consumption*. From its first commodities of yarn and cloth, to shoes, sewing machines, ready-made clothes, through bicycles, the factory—and the workers within them—the United States' relationship with itself was changed. The need to possess things, while modest at first, was bolstered by the psychology of advertising, and grew throughout the 20th century (Cushman, 1990, 1996). Buying things out of necessity gave way to buying things for pleasure, which gave way to buying things as expressions of a person's identity.

The Psychology of Objectivity

As factories spread, so did a new field of science: psychology. From its beginning, the assertion that psychology is the scientific study of some-thing—consciousness, behaviors, experience—has been paramount (Sokal, 1992). Whatever the "it" psychology chooses to observe—and that has changed frequently over the last century—it is to be observed objectively. Regardless of whether the focus was sensing and perceiving stimuli, learning nonsense syllables, expressing emotion, or defining intelligence —psychologists were *supposed* to be hypothesizing and testing, and inter-preted from a detached perspective.

In 1893, G. Stanley Hall—who created the first American psychology laboratory ten years earlier—pulled together a small group of wealthy, White, male psychologists to create the APA (Pickren & Rutherford, 2010). There were debates from the beginning about how best to define the scope of this new science (Camfield, 1994, Evans, 1992), as well as what was its relationship to philosophy—the traditional home of the study of the mind and behavior (Miller, 1992; Sokal 2018): a monistic, narrowly defined version, as argued by Hall, versus a pluralistic, open version that would include philosophy, as embodied by James (Sarason, 1975). Hall mostly won that battle, and an obsession with a logical-positivist inspired psychology began.

Science promises the control of the surrounding world, and so much of the time it delivers. Why wouldn't these early psychologists be drawn to the scientific method's shiny display of power? And what is that power? While there are many different explicit aspects to it—the use of a testable hypothesis, followed by a measured, transparent collection of data, in an orderly, replicable manner to be shared, criticized, and replicated by others (see MacDonald, 2013 for a succinct review)—there are important psychological and relational characteristics of psychology's scientific method as well. These inner qualities—curiosity, skepticism, and imagination—and relational qualities—observation, manipulation, and detachment—are essential, but usually passed over by the positivist psychological scientist. The only value that is explicitly acknowledged by psychology is the impartial nature of objectivity.

Sociopathic Objectivity

It is ironic that throughout much of the history of psychology neither a systematic theoretical, nor scientific, exploration of objectivity has taken place. Even as the subjective nature of science, with its powerful biases, have been clearly demonstrated (Rosenthal, 1966), scientific psychologists have mostly ignored the core implications of a "value-free" science. Not until humanistic (Bugental, 1971; Rogers, 1955; Smith, 1992), feminist (Gavey, 1989; Gergen, 1988), and culturally sensitive critical psychologists (Gergen, 1985; Prilleltensky, 1989; Teo, 2015) began to gain a voice in psychology—however weak—did the ideal of a morally detached perspective begin to be questioned (Gergen, 1985; Prilleltensky, 1989; Teo, 2015). These perspectives were, of course, summarily dismissed by mainstream scientific psychology for not being scientific. As with the external criticisms of detached objectivity in other academic disciplines, such as philosophy (Derrida, 1982; Feyerabend, 1993; Foucault, 1976, 1979, 1980; Kuhn, 1996), sociology (Burr, 1995), archaeology (Hodder, 1990), anthropology (Geertz, 1973), literary studies (Eagleton, 1983), and critical race theory (Crenshaw, 1995), only those perspectives outside of the hard science of psychology have been willing or able to criticize objectivity. These criticisms have centered on the strategic rhetorical advantages of objectivity, and the ethnocentric, racialized, genderized, and/or politicized position of power it grants the privileged scientist (McGown, 1991). The critics of objectivity are dismissed as objects worthy of delegitimatizing—of dehumanizing. The critic's subjective experiences are denied. In a double-bind display of privilege, they are voided out in the subjectively launched objective gaze of the positivistic scientist.

From within the context of the well-established postmodern criticism of objectivity, I suggest an additional criticism. I suggest that a key power of science is its insistence that the human scientist disassociate from their ethical reasoning in the hypothesizing, data collecting, and theoretical interpretation of the world around them. It is the scientist's willingness to disconnect from an integrated ethics that is a source of scientific power. Science becomes a value-driven method of detachment, while at the same time demanding it is value-free. In what appears to be a sociopathic void of morality, the insistence that the scientist become psychologically divorced from values such as compassion and fairness is the toxic antisocial ingredient of traditional science.

Rejecting the Dark Sciences

The APA didn't have ethical guidelines until the 1950s. For the first half-century of its existence, morality was not a primary focus of discussion or study (Pickren & Rutherford, 2010). Perhaps this was an attempt to distance itself from the philosophy it was actively demanding it was not (Miller, 1992). There is likely no greater example of how psychology, devoid of active ethical guidance, could go so terribly wrong than psychology's involvement with eugenics in the early 1900s, and a century later, its involvement with torture (Yakushko, 2018).

The pioneering psychologists of scientific measurement, excited to show off their new science, first attempted to publicly measure "mental functioning" at Chicago's World Fair in 1893 (Mülberger, 2014). The epistemological and theoretical bases of this "functioning" were laden with implicit ethical and political values of *eugenics* (Rose, 2015). This pseudos-cientific theory is really just an extension of the scientific racism used to defend American slavery (Jackson & Weidman, 2004). The belief that nature has created a hierarchical structure for humans, based on *inherited* intellectual and moral reasoning abilities, and that those abilities could be measured by the psychologist, are both scientifically and ethically untenable, at best. Yet some of the most celebrated scientific founders of American psychology—Pearson, Spearman, Cattell, Yerkes, Goddard—were open supporters of this outrageous perspective (Buss, 1976; Pickren & Rutherford, 2010; Rose, 2015). These same individuals would pioneer the future studies of intelligence. Based on methical and statistic assumptions of eugenicists, there has rightfully been much criticism regarding the definitions, methods, and outcomes of intelligence testing (Gould, 1981). An open and honest reconciliation of American psychology's racist and classist past, and how it is implicitly perpetuated in the present, has not yet occurred (Yakushko, 2018).

Unfortunately, the scientific racism of eugenics were not the only casualties of a science unmoored from an integrated ethical model. Here are just a small sample of the failures: the Tuskegee study, which for decades studied untreated syphilis on poor African American men—even when there were treatments available (Brandt, 2006); Friedman's use of ice pick lobotomies on psychiatric patients for over a decade (Caruso & Sheehan, 2017; Gostin, 1982); forced sterilization of psychiatric patients (Dolan, 2007; Moss, Stam, & Kattevilder, 2013); military research on soldiers exploring the effects of chemical and psychological agents (Khatchadourian, 2012); Milgram's and Zimbardo's studies of obedience and social roles (Kitchener & Kitchener, 2012); Murray's studies of the inducement of sustained psychological trauma in interrogations using college students (Chase, 2000). This is saying nothing about the sheer horror of the mistreatment of nonhuman research subjects, like primates, dogs, pigeons, rats, and mice (Masson, 1995).

Many may hope the effects of an ethically untethered practice of science and treatment is a thing of the past—at least with humans. However, that would simply not be true. While there has been significant movement away from a completely amoral stance of science, through the implementation of the Belmont report's ethical guides to research (United States, 1978), and the APA's creation and development of ethical standards for psychological practice in the 1950s, not enough has been done. One need only look to the APA executive board's disastrous support of torture in the early 2000s, and the demonstration of a complete lack of moral integrity or courage in its decade long cover up (Arrigo, Eidelson, & Bennett, 2012; Hoffman et al., 2015; Pope, 2018; Welch, 2010). Given the APA history of ignoring social justice and human rights for the first half of its existence (Leong, Pickren, & Vasquez, 2017) and its peripheral use of ethics in the second half, what has transpired should not be a surprise.

Ethics-Based Science of Psychology

Miller (2000) has been advocating for the explicit, central position for ethics in professional psychology for decades. His seminal work (Miller, 1992) on the importance of philosophy within the theoretical, epistemological, and ethical aspects of psychology is very much relevant today. His exploration of the role of ethics in psychology—almost always concealed —demonstrates a need to openly embrace them. Prilleltensky (2001), Simon (2003), Cushman (1996), and Kitchener and Kitchener (2012) also advocate for an essential position of ethics in psychology.

A postpositivist science (Ryan, 2006) that recognizes the "theory-laden" aspects of scientific observation, as well as a need for diverse epistemologies and methods, has a strong, if relatively short, history (Eagly & Riger, 2014). A reflexive approach (Etherington, 2004) that acknowledges the unavoidable subjective, cultural, and ethical perspectives of the researcher should be required of all research, regardless of design. No longer can the fantasy of a value-free scientist continue. A postpositivistic science—which can still use the basics of hypothesis formulation, data collection, and interpretation—needs to integrate an explicit ethical system. As suggested by Teo (2011), psychologists must avoid *epistemological violence* in the scientific endeavor (see also Yakushko, Hoffman, Consoli, & Lee, 2016).

Science is vital in a functioning democracy, as it provides a space to explore and debate what is real, truthful, pragmatic, and useful (Simon, 2003). Scientific evidence is crucial for the functioning of a society. Through science, many of the answers to the questions of these current economic, social, and environmental problems can be informed, if not directly solved. Politics—the enactment of a code of ethics in the governing of groups of people—benefits from a robust, transparent, and open science. With that said, ethics must come before even evidence. As just reviewed, an evidence-based science, as opposed to an ethics-based one, will eventually lead to dark and terrible things.

Humanistic and Humanitarian Values as Core

Ethics are principles that guide how a person should act in the world, and at the same time, create the world a person acts in. They are not just values that guide behavior, but designs used in the construction of practices, relationships, and institutions that affect the world. By espousing a value of detachment, scientists helped construct a detached world. By embracing a science of care, a world of care can be created. There is no a priori reason to believe that the effects of a science of compassion will be worse than the dispassionate science it is replacing. In fact, it's reasonable to believe that it will be better.

The APA's ethical principles of Beneficence/Nonmalfeasance, Fidelity/Responsibility, Integrity, Respect for Rights and Dignity, and Justice are worthy principles (APA, 2002). They overlap with the individual-oriented humanistic values (e.g. empathy, positive regard, authenticity, responsibility) and socially oriented humanitarian values (e.g. democracy, justice, solidarity, diversity/inclusion) that should be at the very center of psychology, regardless of one's theoretical or epistemological perspective (Rubin, St. John, Vallejos, & Sebree, 2015. The APA, as the flagship organization of psychology in the United States, should filter all of its activities through these ethics. From the influencing of public policy, the accrediting of schools and training programs, the organization of its conventions, the publication of its professional literature, and the governing of both its council and executive boards, humanistic and humanitarian values should be primary throughout the APA.

Embracing a Justice-Based Practice of Psychology

The concept of justice has been studied in psychology for decades (see Colquitt et al., 2013; Colquitt et al., 2001). Exploring the social variety of justice, Louis, Mavor, La Macchia, and Amiot (2013) found it to be an integral, yet undefined notion in psychology: "all psychologists—and all psychologies—are innately concerned with justice, and yet there is ... no consensual understanding of social justice" (p. 14). This lack of common definition is echoed by Thrift & Sugarman (2018).

For the purposes of this discussion, justice is loosely defined in the spirit of Rawls (1999), understood to be the maximation of liberty and equality for all individuals interrelatedly, with any social and economic inequalities favoring the disadvantaged. As with all virtue-based ethical models, an individual virtue should be contextualized by the virtues that accompany it. As many are advocating for humanistic and humanitarian virtues, justice is further defined in relation to these same values. Therefore, justice is to be tempered with other tenets such as compassion, generosity, and responsibility.

Within the general understanding of psychology as an ethical endeavor, the practices of psychology, such as psychotherapy and testing, are embedded within justice, as are the situations and experiences those practices attempt to alleviate (e.g. emotional distress, relational difficulties, cognitive problems). Therefore, psychologists are not seen as needing to hide their ethical-political beliefs and activities from the public, less their "neutrality" be compromised (Haeny, 2014). Instead, they are encouraged to actively attempt to minimize the social causes of psychological suffering (Albee, 1982; Allen & Dodd, 2018; Kenny & Hage, 2009; King, 1968; Nadal, 2017; Prilleltensky, 2012). In fact, there are thoughtful calls to integrate ethics and advocacy into APA's traditional scientific-practitioner model of doctoral training (Bamonti et al., 2014; Fassinger & Brien, 2000; Mallinckrodt, Miles, & Levy, 2014).

As a way to help focus the etiological assumptions, as well as the intervention strategies, for the individuals seeking psychological services, the following three interacting levels of justice are suggested (St. John, Vallejos, & Rubin, 2017).

Psychological Justice

Unfortunately, many times, the advocacy for even a basic acknowledgment of a person's inner, subjective world is necessary. Regardless of the institutionalized dehumanizing forces that suggest otherwise, all people are assumed to have an array of emotional experiences, and a range of consciousness states; these deeply meaningful aspects of self should be respected (Bollas, 1995; Kavanaugh, 2012; Miller, 2005). Educational, medical, occupational, and other social institutions should, at very least, not pointlessly restrict the inner experiences of people, and when possible, support their expression and growth (Bugental, 1971; Maslow, 1958; Rogers, 1955; Schneider, 2013). People are not to be reduced to biological machines, but seen as complex human beings.

Social Justice

Regardless of race/ethnicity, gender/sexual identity, economic status, ability/disability, religious affiliation or age, all people, and their communities, should be treated fairly and with dignity (APA, 2003; Hoffman, 2016; Smith, 2005; Sue et al., 2007; Zinn, 1994). A person's autonomy, as long as it does not interfere with the autonomy of others, is supported. The protection of socially vulnerable individuals and communities from physical, economic, and psychosocial assault is key. The advocacy for equal access to the law, its protection, and the political rights bestowed on all people by the Constitution of the United States is essential. The demand that individuals adjust, through psychological or psychiatric treatment, to the status quo of a politically exploitative and abusive culture is not considered legitimate, and is outright rejected (King, 1968; Prilleltensky, 1989, 2012; Smith, Chambers, & Bratini, 2009).

Ecological Justice

The advocacy for the recognition of the interconnection of all life, and the crucial role that diversity plays for the survival of all living beings, is emphasized (Capra, 1996). The protection of natural and wild environments, and the species that live there—independent of their importance for human survival or comfort—is primary (Martusewicz, Edmundson, & Lupinaccic, 2011; Rifkin, 2009; Roszak, 1992). The recognition that socially and economically marginalized individuals and communities are usually the first to experience ecological problems, is also a key area of activism.

Let America Be America Again

Donald Trump represents the usually submerged aspect of America's criminal attachment to egoism. He inadvertently, but daily, exposes the cult of selfishness, and the void of compassion, that carries with it the power of exploitation for profit. He is a symbol of what ethnocentric tyranny brings to the world: unnecessary ecological, social, and psychological suffering. The sunken historical aspects of America, symbolized by Trump's presidency, will pull everyone down if not politically reversed. No amount of value-free observation will keep it afloat. It's time for the United States to truthfully reconcile with its disassociated past. A past dangerously alive in the present.

As an overly-educated White man, with and from a middle-class family in the United States, I certainly have a particular perspective. As a human being, with my cultural and personal experiences, I *bring forth* a certain view of the world (Maturana & Varela, 1980). As hard as I work to expand my conscious understanding of the world, and the people and places I perceive in it, I still bring my interpretation. I also recognize that other people have their own unique viewpoints too, and try to respect them. How well that goes is, in large part, due to the ethical models brought to the table. Connecting can often be difficult.

And disconnection is often enticing. But as tempting as it is to get lost forever in a digital haze of Instagram posts, Amazon deals, and Starbucks—or however else one prefers to disconnect—the time for chronic detachment from the world is long over. It really is killing us to ignore it. That's true with nature, as well as the daily grind of economic and educational injustice, racism, and sexism all around. It is the time to choose a different path, one that will address our ecological crisis, while also helping bring a compassionate world of liberty and fairness to all people.

Martin Luther King, Jr. was fond of quoting Theodore Parker (NPR, 2010): "Let us realize the arc of the moral universe is long, but it bends toward justice." It is a beautifully hopeful sentiment, and I believe it. But he knew better than most that justice won't be realized without a fight. The bend of the arc that Dr. King promises can only be obtained if enough people apply the force required to move it—including those within the profession of psychology (King, 1968).

So here's to bringing the force of compassion, liberty, and justice to the America that never was, but to the America that someday might be (Hughes, 1936/2004).

References

Albee, G. W. (1982). Preventing psychopathology and promoting human potential. *The American Psychologist, 37*(9), 1043–1050.

Allen, L. R., & Dodd, C. G. (2018). Psychologists' responsibility to society: Public policy and the ethics of political action. *Journal of Theoretical and Philosophical Psychology, 38*(1), 42–53.

American Psychological Association. (2002). Ethical principles of psychologists and code of conduct. *American Psychologist, 57*, 1060–1073.

American Psychological Association. (2003). Guidelines on multicultural education, training, research, practice, and organizational change for Psychologists. *American Psychologist, 58*(5), 377–402.

American Psychological Association. (2019). *Mission statement.* Retrieved from www.apa.org/about/apa/strategic-plan

Arrigo, J. M., Eidelson, R. J., & Bennett, R. (2012). Psychology under fire: Adversarial operational psychology and psychological ethics. *Peace and Conflict: Journal of Peace Psychology, 18*(4), 384–400.

Baldwin, J. (Writer) & Peck, R. (Director). (2017). *I am not your Negro* (Motion Picture). France, United States, Belguim: Mangolia Pictures; Amazon Studio.

Bamonti, P. M., Keelan, C. M., Larson, N., Mentrikoski, J. M., Randall, C. L., Sly, S. K., Travers, R. M., McNeil, D. W. (2014). Promoting ethical behavior by cultivating a culture of self-care during graduate training: A call to action. *Training & Education in Professional Psychology, 8*(4), 253–260.

Bochner, S. (1973). *Mathematics in cultural history.* In *Dictionary of the history of ideas.* New York, NY: Charles Schribers Sons.

Bollas, C. (1995). *Cracking up: The work of unconscious experience.* New York, NY: Hill & Wang.

Boorstin, D. J. (1983). *The discoverers: A history of man's search to know his world and himself.* New York, NY: Random House.

Brandt, A. M. (2006). Racism and research: The case of the Tuskegee Syphilis study. *The Hastings Center Report, 8*(6), 21.

Bugental, J. F. T. (1971). The humanistic ethic—the individual in psychotherapy as a societal change agent. *Journal of Humanistic Psychology, 11*(1), 11–25.

Burr, V. (1995). *An introduction to social constructionism.* London: Routledge.

Buss, A. R. (1976). Galton and the birth of differential psychology and eugenics: Social, political, and economic forces. *Journal of the History of the Behavioral Sciences, 12*(1), 47–58.

Cahill, T. (1996). *How the Irish saved civilization.* New York, NY: Anchor.

Camfield, T. M. (2018). The American Psychological Association and World War I: 1914 to 1919. In W. E. Pickren, & A. Rutherford (Eds.), *125 years of the American Psychological Association* (pp. 87–114, Chapter x). Washington, DC: APA. Retrieved from https://tcsedsystem.idm.oclc.org/login?url=https://search-proquest-com.tcsedsystem.idm.oclc.org/docview/1929453090?accountid=34120

Capra, F. (1996). *The web of life: A new scientific understanding of living systems.* New York, NY: Anchor Book.

Carbon Countdown Clock. (April 7th, 2019). Retrieved from https://350madison.org/carboncountdown-clock/

Caruso, J. P., & Sheehan, J. P. (2017). Psychosurgery, ethics, and media: A history of Walter Freeman and the lobotomy. *Neurosurgical Focus, 43*(September), E6.

Chase, A. (2000). Harvard and the making of the unabomber. *The Atlantic, 285*(6), 41–65.

Colquitt, J. A., Scott, B. A., Rodell, J. B., Long, D. M., Zapata, C. P., Conlon, D. E., & Wesson, M. J. (2013). Justice at the millennium, a decade later: A meta-analytic test of social exchange and affect-based perspectives. *Journal of Applied Psychology, 98*(2), 199–236.

Colquitt, J. A., Wesson, M. J., Porter, C. O. L. H., Conlon, D. E., & Ng, K. Y. (2001). Justice at the millennium: A meta-analytic review of 25 years of organizational justice research. *Journal of Applied Psychology, 86*(3), 425–445.

Crenshaw, K. (1995). Mapping the margins: Intersectionality, identity politics, and violence against women of color. In K. Crenshaw, N. Gotanda, G. Peller, & K. Thomas (Eds.), *Critical race theory: The key writings that formed the movement* (pp. 357–383). New York, NY: The New Press.

Cushman, P. (1990). Why the self is empty: Toward a historically situated psychology. *American Psychologist, 45*(5), 599–611.

Cushman, P. (1996). *Constructing the self, constructing America: A cultural history of psychotherapy.* Reading, MA: Addison-Wesley/Addison Wesley Longman.

Derrida, J. (1982). *Margins of philosophy* (A Bass, Trans.). Chicago, IL: University of Chicago Press.

Devega, C. (November 9th, 2016). White rage against the machine: President-elect Donald Trump is a historical shock—unless you study American history. *Salon*. Retrieved from www.salon.com/2016/11/09/white-rage-against-the-machine-president-donald-trump-is-historical-shock-born-in-american-history/

Diamond, J. (1999). *Guns, germs and steel: The fates of human society*. New York, NY: Norton.

Dolan, D. V. (2007). Psychiatry, psychology, and human sterilization then and now: "Therapeutic" or in the social interest? *Ethical Human Psychology and Psychiatry*, *9*(2), 99–108.

Eagleton, T. (1983). *Literary theory: An introduction*. Minneapolis, MN: University of Minneapolis.

Eagly, A. H., & Riger, S. (2014). Feminism and psychology: Critiques of methods and epistemology. *The American Psychologist*, *69*(7), 685–702.

Etherington, K. (2004). *Becoming a reflexive researcher: Using ourselves in research*. London: Jessica Kingsley.

Evans, R. B. (1992). Growing pains: The American Psychological Association from 1903 to 1920. In R. B. Evans, V. S. Sexton, & T. C. Cadwallader (Eds.), *The American Psychological Association: A historical perspective* (pp. 73–90, Chapter xvi). Washington, DC: American Psychological Association.

Fassinger, R. E., & Brien, K. M. O. (2000). Career counseling with college women: A scientist-practitioner-advocate model of intervention. In D. A. Luzzo (Ed.), *Career counseling of college students: An empirical guide to strategies that work* (pp. 253–265). Washington, DC: American Psychological Association.

Feyerabend, P. (1993). *Against method*. London: Verso.

Foucault, M. (1976). *The archaeology of knowledge* (A. M. Sheridan Smith, Trans.). New York, NY: Harper & Row.

Foucault, M. (1979). *Discipline and punish* (A. M. Sheridan, Trans.). New York, NY: Vintage Books.

Foucault, M. (1980). *Power/knowledge*. (C. Gordon, Ed.). New York, NY: Pantheon Books.

Fromm, E. (1955). *The sane society*. New York, NY: Rinehart & Company.

Gavey, N. (1989). Feminist poststructuralism and discourse analysis: Contributions to feminist psychology. *Psychology of Women Quarterly*, *13*(4), 459–475.

Geertz, C. (1973). Thick description: Toward an interpretive theory of culture. In C. Geerz (Ed.), *The interpretation of cultures: Selected essays* (pp. 3–30). New York, NY: Basic Books.

Gergen, K. (1985). The social constructionist movement in modern psychology. *American Psychologist*, *40*, 255–265.

Gergen, M. M. (1988). Building a feminist methodology. *Contemporary Social Psychology*, *13*(2), 47–53.

Gostin L. O. (1982). Psychosurgery: A hazardous and unestablished treatment? A case for the importation of American legal safe-guards to Great Britain. *Journal of Social Welfare Law*, *4*, 83–95.

Gould, S. J. (1981). *The mismeasure of man*. New York, NY: W. W. Norton.

Haeny, A. M. (2014). Ethical considerations for psychologists taking a public stance on controversial issues: The balance between personal and professional life. *Ethics and Behavior*, *24*(4), 265–278.

Hammerstein, N. (1996). The enlightenment. In H. de Ridder-Symoens (Ed.), *Universities in early modern Europe, 1500–1800* (pp. 621–663). Cambridge, UK: Cambridge University Press.

Helliwell, J., Layard, R., & Sachs, J. (2019). *World happiness report 2019*. New York, NY: Sustainable Development Solutions Network.

Helms, J. E., Jernigan, M., & Mascher, J. (2005). The meaning of race in psychology and how to change it: A methodological perspective. *The American Psychologist, 60*(1), 27–36.

Hodder, I. (1990). *The domestication of Europe*. London: Basil Blackwell.

Hoffman, D. H., Carter, D. J., Lopez, C. R. V., Benzmiller, H. L., Guo, A. X., Latifi, S. Y., & Craig, D. C. (2015). *Report to the special committee of the board of directors of the American Psychological Association: Independent review relating to APA ethics guidelines, national security interrogations, and torture* (revised). Chicago, IL: Sidley Austin LLP. Retrieved from www.apa.org/independent-review/revised-report.pdf.

Hoffman, L. (2016). Multiculturalism and humanistic psychology: From neglect to epistemological and ontological diversity. *The Humanistic Psychologist, 44*(1), 56–71.

Hughes, L. (1936/2004). *Let America be America again*. New York, NY: George Braziller.

Jackson, J., & Weidman, N. (2004). *Race, racism and science: Social impact and interaction*. New York, NY: Rutgers University Press.

Kavanaugh, P. (2012). *Stories from the bog: On madness, philosophy and psychoanalysis*. New York, NY: Rodopi.

Kenny, M. E., & Hage, S. M. (2009). The next frontier: Prevention as an instrument of social justice. *Journal of Primary Prevention, 30*(1), 1–10.

Khatchadourian, R. (2012). Operation Delirium—The New Yorker. *The New Yorker*. 1–33. Retrieved from www.newyorker.com/magazine/2012/12/17/operation-delirium

King, M. L., Jr. (1968). The role of the behavioral scientist in the civil rights movement. *American Psychologist, 23*(3), 180–186.

Kitchener, R. F., & Kitchener, K. S. (2012). Ethical foundations of psychology. In S. J. Knapp, M. C. Gottlieb, M. M. Handelsman, & L. D. VandeCreek (Eds.), *APA handbooks in psychology. APA handbook of ethics in psychology, Vol. 1. Moral foundations and common themes* (pp. 3–42). Washington, DC: American Psychological Association.

Klein, N. (February 13th, 2019). The battle lines have been drawn on the Green New Deal. *The Interceptor*. Retrieved from https://theintercept.com/2019/02/13/green-new-deal-proposal/

Komesaroff, P. (1993). *Objectivity, science and society*. London: Routledge.

Kuhn, T. (1996). *The structure of scientific revolutions*. Chicago, IL: The University of Chicago Press.

Lavine, T. S. (1984). *From Socrates to Sartre: The philosophical quest*. New York, NY: Bantam.

Leach, J. (1974). Explanation and value-neutrality. In A. C. Michalos (Ed.), *Philosophical problems of science and technology* (pp. 341–364). Guelph: University of Guelph.

Leong, F. T. L., Pickren, W. E., & Vasquez, M. J. T. (2017). APA efforts in promoting human rights and social justice. *American Psychologist, 72*(8), 778–790.

Lerner, G. (1986). *The creation of patriarchy*. New York, NY: Oxford University Press.

Louis, W. R., Mavor, K. I., La Macchia, S. T., & Amiot, C. E. (2013). Social Justice and Psychology: What Is, and What Should Be. *Journal of Theoretical and Philosophical Psychology*, *34*(1), 14–27.

MacDonald, D. A. (2013). Philosophical underpinnings of transpersonal psychology as a science. In H. Friedman, & G. Hartelius (Eds.), *The Wiley-Blackwell handbook of transpersonal psychology* (pp. 312–329). Hoboken, NJ: John Wiley & Sons.

Mallinckrodt, B., Miles, J. R., & Levy, J. J. (2014). Training and education in professional psychology the scientist-practitioner-advocate model: Addressing contemporary training needs for social justice advocacy. *Training and Education in Professional Psychology*, *8*(4), 303–311.

Martusewicz, R.A. & Edmundson, J. & Lupinaccic, J. (2011). *EcoJustice education: Toward diverse, democratic, and sustainable communities*. 1–336. London: Routledge.

Maslow, A. (1958). Towards a humanistic psychology. *ETC: A Review of General Semantics*, *14*(1), 10–22.

Masson, J. M. (1995). *When elephants weep: The emotional lives of animals*. New York, NY: Delacorte.

Maturana, H., & Varela, F. (1980). *Autopoiesis and cognition*. Dordrecht: D. Rejdel.

McGown. J. (1991). *Post-modernism and its critics*. Ithaca, NY: Cornell University Press.

McNeill, W. H. (1991). *The rise of the west*. Chicago, IL: University of Chicago Press.

Miller, R. (1992). Introduction to the philosophy of clinical psychology. In R. Miller (Ed.), *The restoration of dialogue: Readings in the philosophy of clinical psychology* (pp. 1–27). Washington, DC: American Psychological Association.

Miller, R. (2000). Scientific vs. clinical-based knowledge in psychology: A concealed moral conflict. *American Journal of Psychotherapy*, *55*(3), 344–356.

Miller, R. (2005). Suffering in psychology: The demoralization of psychotherapeutic practice. *Journal of Psychotherapy Integration*, *15*(3), 299–336.

Milton, G. (2000). *Big Chief Elizabeth: The adventures and fate of the first English colonists in America*. New York, NY: Farrar, Straus & Giroux.

Moss, E. L., Stam, H. J., & Kattevilder, D. (2013). From suffrage to sterilization: Eugenics and the women's movement in 20th century Alberta. *Canadian Psychology/Psychologie Canadienne*, *54*(2), 105–114.

Mülberger, A. (2014). Introduction: The need for contextual approaches to the history of mental testing. *History of Psychology*, *17*(3), 177–186.

Nadal, K. L. (2017). "Let's get in formation": On becoming a psychologist-activist in the 21st century. *American Psychologist*, *72*(9), 935–946.

NPR. (2010). Thedore Parker and the "moral universe". *NPR: All Things Considered*. Retrieved from www.npr.org/templates/story/story.php?storyId=129609461

O'Hehir, A. (July 4th, 2015). Two cheers for the Declaration of Independence: The weird, contradictory and radical vision of human equality that America couldn't handle. *Salon*. Retrieved from www.salon.com/2015/07/04/

Painter, N. I. (2010). *The history of White people*. New York, NY: W. W. Norton.

Pickren, W. E., & Rutherford, A. (2010). *A history of modern psychology in context*. Hoboken, NJ: John Wiley & Sons.

Pope, K. S. (2018). A human rights and ethics crisis facing the world's largest organization of psychologists. *European Psychologist*, 1–15.

Porter, R. (1996). The scientific revolution and the universities. In H. de Ridder-Symones (Ed.), *Universities in early modern Europe, 1500–1800* (pp. 531–556). Cambridge, MA: Cambridge University Press.

Prilleltensky, I. (1989). Psychology and the status quo University of Manitoba. *American Psychologist*, *44*(5), 795–802.

Prilleltensky, I. (2001). Value-based praxis in community psychology: Moving toward social justice and social action. *American Journal of Community Psychology*, *29*(5), 747–778.

Prilleltensky, I. (2012). Wellness as fairness. *American Journal of Community Psychology*, *49*(1–2), 1–21.

Rawls, J. (1999). *A theory of justice*. Cambridge, MA: Belknap Press.

Rifkin, J. (2009). *The empathic civilization: The race to global consciousness in a world in crisis*. New York, NY: Tarcher/Penguin Group.

Rogers, C. (1955). Person or science? A philosophical question. *American Psychologist*, *10*, 267–278.

Rose, T. (2015). *The end of average: How we succeed in a world that values sameness*. San Francisco, CA: HarperOne/HarperCollins.

Rosenthal, R. (1966). *Experimenter effects in behavioral research*. East Norwalk, CT: Appleton-Century-Crofts.

Roszak, T. (1992). *The voice of the earth*. New York, NY: Simon & Schuster.

Rubin, S., St. John, D., Vallejos, L., & Sebree, D., Jr. (2015). *Humanitarian psychology for the global 21st century*. Paper presented at the 8th Annual Society for Humanistic Psychology Conference, Chicago, IL.

Ryan, A. (2006). Post-positivist approaches to research. In *Researching and Writing your thesis: A guide for postgraduate students* (pp. 12–26). MACE: Maynooth Adult and Community Education. Retrieved from http://mural.maynoothuniversity.ie/874/

Sarason, S. (1975). Psychology to the Finland Station in the heavenly city of the eighteenth century philosophers. *American Psychologist*, *58*, 1072–1080.

Sarason, S. B. (1981). An asocial psychology and a misdirected clinical psychology. *American Psychologist*, *36*(8), 827–836.

Schneider, K. J. (2013). *The polarized mind: Why it's killing us and what we can do about it*. Colorado Springs, CO: University Professors Press.

Shepard, P. (1992). *Nature and madness*. San Francisco, CA: Sierra Club Books.

Simon, L. (2003). *Psychology, psychotherapy, psychoanalysis, and the politics of human relationships*. Santa Barbara, CA: Praeger.

Smith, L. (2005). Psychotherapy, classism, and the poor: Conspicuous by their absence. *The American Psychologist*, *60*(7), 687–696.

Smith, L., Chambers, D. A., & Bratini, L. (2009). When oppression is the pathogen: The participatory development of socially just mental health practice. *American Journal of Orthopsychiatry*, *79*(2), 159–168.

Smith, M. B. (1992). The American Psychological Association and social responsibility. In R. B. Evans, V. S. Sexton, & T. C. Cadwallader (Eds.), *The American Psychological Association: A historical perspective* (pp. 327–345). Washington, DC: American Psychological Association.

Sokal, M. (1992). Origins and early years of the American Psychological Association: 1890 to 1906. In R. B. Evans, V. S. Sexton, & T. C. Cadwallader (Eds.), *The*

American Psychological Association: A historical perspective (pp. 43–71). Washington, DC: American Psychological Association.

Sokal, M. M. (2018). Origins and early years of the American Psychological Association: 1890 to 1906. In W. E. Pickren, & A. Rutherford (Eds.), *125 years of the American Psychological Association* (pp.41–68, Chapter x). Washington, DC: American Psychological Association.

St. John, D., Vallejos, L., & Rubin, S. (2017). *The American shadow grows long: Authoritarianism, bigotry, and the humanitarian resistance.* Paper presented at the 10th Annual Society for Humanistic Psychology Conference. Pittsburgh, PA.

Sue, D. W., Capodilupo, C. M., Torino, G. C., Bucceri, J. M., Holder, A. M. B., Nadal, K. L., & Esquilin, M. (2007). Racial microaggressions in everyday life: Implications for clinical practice. *The American Psychologist, 62*(4), 271–286.

Teo, T. (2011). Empirical race psychology and the hermeneutics of epistemological violence. *Human Studies, 34*(3), 237–255.

Teo, T. (2015). Critical psychology: A geography of intellectual engagement and resistance. *American Psychologist, 70*(3), 243–254.

Thrift, E., & Sugarman, J. (2018). What is social justice? Implications for psychology. *Journal of Theoretical and Philosophical Psychology, 39*(1), 1–17.

United States. (1978). *The Belmont report: Ethical principles and guidelines for the protection of human subjects of research.* Bethesda, MD: The Commission.

Valencius, B. C., Spanagel, D. I., Pawley, E., Gronim, S. S., & Lucier, P. (2016). Science in early America: Print culture and the sciences of territoriality. *Journal of the Early Republic, 36*(1), 73–123.

Welch, B. L. (2010). Moral drift and the American Psychological Association: The road to torture. *Social Justice, 37*, 175–182. Retrieved from http://search.ebsco host.com/login.aspx?direct=true&db=i3h&AN=65442004&site=ehost-live

Winks, R, Brighton, C., Christopher, J., & Wolff, R. L. (1992). *A history of civilization: Pre- history to 1715.* Englewood Cliffs, NJ: Simon & Schuster.

Yakushko, O. (2018). *Eugenics and its evolution in history of Western psychology: A critical archival review.* In review.

Yakushko, O., Hoffman, L., Consoli, M. L. M., & Lee, G. (2016). On methods, methodologies, and continued colonization of knowledge in the study of "ethnic minorities": Comment on Hall et al. (2016). *American Psychologist, 71*(9), 890–891.

Zinn, H. (1994). *You can't be neutral on a moving train: A personal history of our times.* Boston, MA: Beacon Press.

Zinn, H. (2003). *A people's history of the United States.* New York, NY: HarperPerennial.

Part III

Applications in Multicultural Contexts

12 Indigenous Psychology

Louise Sundararajan

Indigenous psychology (IP) is an emerging academic project as well as an intellectual movement across the globe. In its initial phase, the IP movement called attention to the different psychologies around the world (Allwood & Berry, 2006; Kim, Yang, & Hwang, 2006), and to the problems generated by rampant exportation of North American and Northern European psychologies to other countries (Enriquez, 1992; Heelas & Lock, 1981; Holland & Quinn, 1987; Martín-Baró, 1994; Moghaddam, 1987; Sinha, 1986). The IP movement also highlighted the dangers in using concepts and methods that showed limited sensitivity to the realities of the developing nations and that denied the possibilities of inclusive conceptualization (Marsella, 1998; Misra & Gergen, 1993). In sum, what drives the IP movement is the increasing realization that there are "other" non-Western ways of being, understanding the world, relating with others, and doing psychology (Sundararajan, 2005, 2008, 2013, 2015; Sundararajan, Misra, & Marsella, 2013; Ting & Sundararajan, 2018; Wertz, 2011).

It is possible to distinguish between *indigenous psychology* as the psychology developed within a particular, local culture; *indigenized psychology*, referring to the assimilation and accommodation of a "foreign" psychology to a local psychology; and *psychologies of indigenous peoples* as the study of indigenous populations (First Nations) (e.g., Palmater, 2011). I have used the term IP for all three forms. This formulation of IP has far reaching implications: It destroys any illusion of IP as a homogenous phenomenon; it also suggests that IP as defined here embodies both the tension and synergy of cultural pluralism, which lies at the core of any genuine global psychology. Consequently, anyone who adheres to a master script of IP does injustice to it. A prime example is Jahoda's (2016) treatment of this subject. Approaching IP as a noun—a static, finished product—Jahoda (2016) failed to appreciate it as an evolving, dynamic movement. He followed one particularly problematic definition of IP (Kim & Berry, 1993), as he himself pointed out, and when that version of IP led him to a dead-end street, he declared IP to be infeasible. Likewise, mistakenly looking for IP along geographical and national divides, Jahoda (2016) found only one full-fledged IP of a particular country—Filipino psychology (Enriquez, 1993). This reinforced his suspicion as to whether IP really existed. Most importantly, following a narrow definition of science in terms of experimental and quantitative approaches, Jahoda (2016) disqualified IP as science, due to the latter's "more flexible re-definition of 'science'" (p. 177). But from the IP point of view, a broader definition of science that embraces many disciplines beyond psychology is necessary, since culture is a complex phenomenon, the understanding of which requires the insights from multiple disciplines.

The Task Force

The idea of a task force was born in my email exchanges with Anthony Marsella, a prominent leader in IP, before we met in person. Encouraged by Tony, I took the initiative to start and chair the Task Force on Indigenous Psychology when I became president of Division 32 (Society for Humanistic Psychology) in 2010. My first email on the Task Force was dated November 22, 2010, addressing to the following charter members— I had hoped to recruit five, but ended up with seven: Wade Pickren, Miraj Desai, Louis Hoffman, Kwang-Kuo Hwang, John Christopher, Frederick J. Wertz, and Anthony Marsella. I circulated the following suggestions from Tony Marsella:

* Hold a symposium at APA [This has happened every year since then];
* Sponsor a conference and publish papers [This never happened];
* Write a book for the cultural and international psychology series [*Palgrave Series on Indigenous Psychology* was launched in 2017];
* Write a white paper on the topic [multiple papers have been published since];
* Form a small organization of like-minded thinkers [the Task Force was born];
* Identify the issues and solutions [ongoing discussions on the IP-list];
* Get prepared for a lot of work and little reward [still true today].

With sixteen charter members who came together within a month or so, the Task Force on Indigenous Psychology was up and running without a hitch. Within one year, the Task Force had 62 members from over 20 countries around the globe. In two years, the Task force has evolved into a burgeoning international community of researchers in cross-cultural, cultural, and indigenous psychology, as well as related fields, such as anthropology, sociology, and linguistics. What brings this group of people together is their concern and interest in moving the field of IP forward.

Vision and Mission

With currently more than two hundred members around the globe, the Task Force has a website (www.indigenouspsych.org) and a dedicated publication outlet: *Palgrave Studies in Indigenous Psychology.*[1] These developments help to advance the objectives in our mission statement below:

- Making a mission statement or manifesto for indigenous psychology that is congenial to the indigenous psychologies across the globe.
- Dissemination of knowledge concerning indigenous psychology through conferences, journals, and edited volumes.
- Promoting online debates and exchanges across the globe on issues concerning indigenous psychology.
- Serving as resources, via our website, for the global community of indigenous psychologists.

A Future Forecast

To make a systematic assessment of this emerging field of IP and its future trends, the Task Force conducted a survey by means of the Delphi Poll. The Delphi Poll technique is one form of expert forecasting that consists of multiple—in our case two—rounds of survey. In the first round, identified experts answered questions regarding their assessment of a particular subject, in this case IP. This is followed by the second round where the responses from the first round are aggregated into a more objective form with the average responses shown in order to obtain a second assessment and work towards convergence. The idea is that the best ideas are obtained and then revisited so that the result is the most likely prediction (Rowe & Wright, 1999). Our survey consisted of two types of questions—quantitative and qualitative: One is on a Likert scale that can be checked off quickly; the other raises open-ended questions for reflection. In combination, these questions provide a clearer sense of where the IP field is going, and where it needs to go.

Fred Leong was instrumental in the development of the survey. Having participated in Heath, Neimeyer, and Pedersen's study (1988) on multicultural counseling utilizing the Delphi Poll, he first made the suggestion, and subsequently offered his SurveyMonkey account for the survey.

Timeline

In 2012, the Delphi Poll Committee was formed to generate a questionnaire. The committee, chaired by Louise Sundararajan, consisted of five members: Fred Leong, James Liu, Dharm Bhawuk, Peter P. Li, and Kwang-Kuo Hwang.

The survey was conducted twice:

- 1st round, 2/1/13 to 10/20/13: 72 out of a total of 115 members of the IP Task Force participated.
- 2nd round, 2/15/15 to 6/15/15: 49 out of a total of 163 members of the IP Task Force participated.

Results of the Delphi Poll

Quantitative analysis. The quantitative analysis was done by Kuang-Hui Yeh, Research Fellow and Professor, Institute of Ethnology, Academia Sinica, Taiwan. No significant difference was found between the two rounds of the poll. See Table 12.1 for results of the first round.

Qualitative analysis. The qualitative analysis was done by Radhika Lu Sundararajan, Assistant Professor, Director of Global Health, Medical School, University of California, San Diego (now at Cornel Medical School). The results are presented in full below to give you an up-close acquaintance with the Task Force in terms of their feelings and thoughts concerning IP. This personal approach, I believe, would be the best introduction to the subject matter of IP.

Overview. Analysis was undertaken employing an inductive approach towards category construction using a content analysis framework. Using this approach, codes were not developed a priori. Nvivo 10 software (QRS International Pty Ltd, Victoria Australia) was used to organize study data, but not for the development or generation of codes. Open-ended survey responses were repeatedly reviewed for content pertaining to defining, advancing, and developing the field of indigenous psychology. Based on survey responses, descriptive categories were constructed to characterize respondents' thoughts about problems faced by the field of indigenous psychology. These categories were revised, elaborated, and refined through successive returns to the dataset. Four categories were developed and are presented here under two larger themes: the *hegemony of Western psychology* and the *issue of diversity* in indigenous psychology. The first theme showed no change across the two rounds. The second theme showed slightly different emphasis—the first round focused on diversity; the second round on the tension between the particular and the universal.

In the first round, two major themes were noted as pertaining to the field of indigenous psychology: the hegemony of Western psychology and the issue of diversity. Within the theme of Western hegemony, two categories were identified: (1) demonstrating relevance of indigenous psychology; and (2) increasing the visibility of indigenous psychology. Two categories were also identified under the theme of diversity: (1) the problems with diversity in indigenous psychology; and (2) the benefits of diversity in indigenous psychology.

Item	Number of Valid Respondents	Mean	Standard Deviation
What is INDIGENOUS PSYCHOLOGY: Within the next 10 years how much do you think the importance given to this question will INCREASE or DECREASE?	70	2.71	1.874
Identity of INDIGENOUS PSYCHOLOGY: Within the next 10 years how much do you think the perceived difference between INDIGENOUS PSYCHOLOGY and Cross-cultural psychology will INCREASE or DECREASE?	69	1.67	2.027
Identity of INDIGENOUS PSYCHOLOGY: Within the next 10 years how much do you think the need for INDIGENOUS PSYCHOLOGY to differentiate itself from other related disciplines will INCREASE or DECREASE?	66	2.12	2.057
Theory development: Within the next 10 years how much do you think theory building in INDIGENOUS PSYCHOLOGY will INCREASE or DECREASE?	68	2.34	1.759
Theory development: Within the next 10 years how much do you think the importance given to theory building in INDIGENOUS PSYCHOLOGY will INCREASE or DECREASE?	66	2.83	1.494
Method: Within the next 10 years how much do you think quantitative methods in the study of INDIGENOUS PSYCHOLOGY will INCREASE or DECREASE?	67	0.78	2.262
Method: Within the next 10 years how much do you think qualitative methods in the study of INDIGENOUS PSYCHOLOGY will INCREASE or DECREASE?	67	2.67	1.796
Method: Within the next 10 years how much do you think combined use of quantitative and qualitative methods will INCREASE or DECREASE?	64	2.31	1.901
Application and Intervention: Within the next 10 years how much do you think indigenous psychology-based application and interventions will INCREASE or DECREASE?	68	2.09	1.843

(*Continued*)

Table 12.1 (Cont.)

Item	Number of Valid Respondents	Mean	Standard Deviation
Within the next 10 years how much do you think the importance given to curriculum on INDIGENOUS PSYCHOLOGY will INCREASE or DECREASE?	65	1.72	1.596
Within the next 10 years how much do you think textbooks on INDIGENOUS PSYCHOLOGY will INCREASE or DECREASE?	65	1.92	1.534
Within the next 10 years how much do you think workshops on INDIGENOUS PSYCHOLOGY will INCREASE or DECREASE?	65	2.29	1.578
Within the next 10 years how much do you think research publications on INDIGENOUS PSYCHOLOGY will INCREASE or DECREASE	65	2.58	1.379
Within the next 10 years how much do you think INDIGENOUS PSYCHOLOGY researchers in academic positions will INCREASE or DECREASE?	65	1.48	1.415
Within the next 10 years how much do you think INDIGENOUS PSYCHOLOGY researchers serving on the editorial board of journals will INCREASE or DECREASE?	65	1.66	1.253
Within the next 10 years how much do you think INDIGENOUS PSYCHOLOGY researchers serving on the editorial board of journals will INCREASE or DECREASE?	64	1.87	1.409
Within the next 10 years how much do you think journal citations of INDIGENOUS PSYCHOLOGY-related publications will INCREASE or DECREASE?	65	2.45	1.705
Within the next 10 years how much do you think the perceived need for indigenizing psychology will INCREASE or DECREASE internationally?	64	2.06	1.632
Number of valid respondents (without any missing value)	57		

Hegemony of Western Psychology. Participants describe the mainstream psychological tradition as emerging from Western, Enlightenment-based, empirical ideals. This hegemonic discourse impacts indigenous psychology in two distinct ways, as discussed in the subthemes, in efforts to demonstrate indigenous psychology's relevance and in those aimed to increase the field's visibility.

The first subtheme under the hegemony of Western psychology was *demonstrating relevance of indigenous psychology*. In considering the advancement and development of indigenous psychology, participants emphasize the importance of demonstrating the field's relevance and potential to expand or improve upon current, mainstream psychology models. The following quote suggests how researchers can make an impact on mainstream audiences:

> [We need] articles, books, etc. that show how "accepted" or "mainstream" models, theories, explanations, definitions can be expanded, improved, changed with indigenous concepts … [thereby] getting mainstream readers, editors, etc. to realize that they are missing something.
>
> (Q1 and 9, #45)

The relevance of indigenous psychology is tied to the process of distinguishing the field from other types of psychological inquiry. Many respondents were wary that indigenous psychology lacked identity except as a reaction to, or rejection of, Western hegemony. The following responses illustrate concern that the discipline could be construed as "reactionary":

> It is not really a coherent movement because it does not share a core sets of goals or ideas about what it IS so much as it shares ideas about what it is NOT (Western mainstream).
>
> (Q13, #32)

> We need to be careful not to get caught up in differentiating between western and indigenous psychologies to the extent that indigenous psychology becomes more of a reactive psychology … That as indigenous peoples we pursue the legitimization of our psychologies and support each other globally to identify the distinctive features of psychology not as a reaction to western, "mainstream" psychology but as an indigenous right to have our epistemologies, ontologies and methodologies validated.
>
> (Q13 and 6, #41)

The second subtheme was *increasing the visibility of indigenous psychology*. Participants suggested that the field of indigenous psychology could be advanced by promoting the subject and scholarship through high profile publications and grant funding. In this sense, the field must "compete" within the mainstream hegemonic framework where such ventures confer disciplinary legitimacy. These researchers describe the barriers faced by indigenous psychologists in attempts to appeal to a broader audience:

> While most of the publications and researchers are from the West, the indigenous psychology voice is insignificant.
>
> (Q9, #8)

> Obtaining funding and wide scale acceptance, again, [is] countering the perception that indigenous psychology is not relevant to psychological science in the mainstream.
>
> (Q15, #31)

Respondents also state that increasing visibility could also be achieved through interdisciplinary collaboration, with anthropology and cross-cultural psychology, for example, to forge a more "robust" impact.

The issue of diversity. Diversity refers to a concept that includes notions of pluralism, variation, and difference; this theme is central to the participants' beliefs about the field of indigenous psychology. However, the topic of diversity is considered in two contrasting ways, as either a problem with, or benefit to, the field of indigenous psychology.

The first subtheme identified under the issue of diversity was *the problems with diversity in indigenous psychology*. Diversity is considered a problem with regard to defining and implementing the field of indigenous psychology. Participants express concern that indigenous psychology struggles with its identity because the field lacks coherence. The diverse backgrounds, approaches, methods, and interests of those involved in indigenous psychology research preclude the derivation of a uniform identity or working definition. Even the use of the term *indigenous* is contentious, and derogatory to some—garnering reactions similar to those evoked by self-imposed identities such as *psychological science*—however, self-mocking and self-criticisms are signs of growth-orientedness of a group. Lack of agreement on basic tenets of what the field does and does not include raised concern that its theoretical impact will be limited. These participants describe the operational problems created by the diversity within the field:

> The variety of cultures [in indigenous psychology] may make a cohesive theoretical view difficult.
>
> (Q10, #28)

> There have been numerous historical and even competing definitions at any given time, so then when one adds to these ambiguities and

contentions of all the cultural approaches to the discipline, matters even get more complicated.

(Q10, #38)

The second subtheme under issues of diversity is *the benefits of diversity in indigenous psychology*. Diversity is considered beneficial in the scope and potential intellectual contribution of indigenous psychology. As indigenous psychology poises itself in contrast to "universalizing" Western psychology, it emphasizes its ability to analyze and appreciate the range of human experiences. Participants state that focus on diversity is the strength and appeal of indigenous psychology as an alternative to Western, ethnocentric traditions. The following quotes illustrate the perceived benefit of diversity in the field:

> The world is changing; and the western bio-medical model, though valuable, has a more limited role to play. Diversity is the reality of today, so we should honor that with our approaches to psychology.
>
> (Q2, #43)

> This particular approach to diversity fosters the vision of a global psychology that embodies unity in diversity—a unity that transcends blood and soil; a diversity that celebrates epistemological differences among cultures and even within the same culture.
>
> (Q3, #27)

The second round. The response rate of the second round was half that of the first round, possibly because we asked the participants to write down their names whereas the first round was anonymous.

Hegemony of Western psychology. Participants note the "dominant," oppressive influence of Western psychological frameworks. This hegemonic discourse impacts efforts to define and practice IP through processes of marginalization and devaluation.

Marginalization from mainstream psychology. Participants report difficulty in demonstrating the relevance of IP to psychology more broadly. They note that IP is unlikely to gain mainstream acceptance because of its emphasis on theory development rather than empirical research or pragmatic application. The following quotes demonstrate perceived relationships between *mainstream psychology* and the field of IP:

> The Western scientific model does not question itself, recognize that it possesses a unique worldview and values that accompany that worldview. Thus, this limits the perspective toward recognizing the importance of this area [IP].
>
> (Q13 #12)

I think it is a hard sell to mainstream psychology to incorporate indigenous psychology. I think it will grow, but more on the fringes. (Q11, #24)

Participants explain this marginalized status as the result of the dominant Western positivistic paradigms where qualitative or ethnographic data are devalued in favor of quantitative methodology. The following response suggests that strong natural science biases in the discipline of psychology may necessarily relegate a field like IP to the fringes:

IP and cultural studies necessarily require deeper exploration at the conceptual level through qualitative methods before they can be tested at the broader level through quantitative methods. However, as long as the natural science bias/dominance continues in psychology, I am afraid all things related to "culture" will always be marginalized as "folk" psychology.

(Q7 #4)

Tension between specificity and generality. Participant responses reflect an ongoing tension between opposing concepts of specificity and generality. Specificity refers to diverse, unique, and distinctive characteristics, such as culturally, spatially, and temporally specific details of indigenous psychologies. Specificity also relates to the debate regarding definitions for terminology within the discipline. Generality represents broad, inclusive, and widely applicable theories or principles, and lack of strict definitions. Tension between these concepts is noted in defining the identity and purpose of IP as a discipline and its broader relevance to psychology and knowledge production. There is also tension between practitioners who disagree about specificity or generality as the ideal principle guiding the development of this field.

Specificity or generality in defining the field of IP. In considering how to define IP, participants face a rift between the values of cultural specificity and generality. That is, whether IP should seek to emphasize the particularities of an indigenous psychology or develop generalizable theories that are more widely applicable. One participant described this as the debate between "contextualism" and "universalism" (Q3 #15). The following quotes further illustrate this tension:

I think we need to work toward an approach that is inclusive, but not so inclusive to become meaningless. To accomplish this, we need to allow for change within indigenous approaches and what could be considered new indigenous approaches. We also need to avoid having any litmus test items that must be adhered to in order to be considered a true indigenous psychology.

(Q4 # 25)

We may be our own worst enemy. Because IP has necessarily focused on advancing the local knowledge, it remains in the margins as it cannot be generalized or applied broadly.

(Q9 #3)

Perhaps diversity is both our strengths and liability. With multiple perspectives, it is difficult to develop a unified, essentialized theory or will be quickly deconstructed/criticized.

(Q5 #4)

Advocating for specificity in moving the field forward. Many participants advocate for specificity as a way to advance development of IP as a field. These respondents indicate that misunderstandings about the term *indigenous* prevent greater acceptance or understanding of what the field represents, and state that the field lacks a "common language." They note the importance of defining terminology for developing a "coherent" field with a "unified voice":

Cultural identity versus national identity versus ethnic identity are all being lumped into indigenous psychology. If we embrace multiple identities of IP, then we are also embracing a not so "concise" definition of IP.

(Q2 #19)

The murky definition of indigenous psychology is a key one. I suspect that there are lots of rifts and fissures among those who fall under that rubric. I'm pretty sure that there are latent disagreements that will turn out to be pivotal.

(Q15 #40)

Advocating for generality in moving the field forward. Many other participants advocate for generality as a guiding principle in the development of IP, and do not demonstrate concern about strictly defining goals or terms. These respondents are proponents for a flexible or *mosaic* approach to IP, arguing that the field is predicated on acceptance and appreciation of local, variable, and culturally specific psychologies. As such, agreement between practitioners on how to define terminologies is not crucial to the development of the field, and may in fact be antithetical to the concept of IP:

The need to define ONE indigenous psychology rather than accepting many local definitions is a problem.

(Q1 #24)

I suggest a mosaic approach, in which there are a collection of values, themes, or principles that are identified as being associated with indigenous psychology. This would allow for a flexible definition without going as far as to say that indigenous psychology can refer to anything claimed to be indigenous.

(Q2 #25)

Relevance for Clinical Practice

One important and significant contribution of IP scholarship to clinical practice lies in demonstrating the intimate connection between culture and humanistic practice. Sundararajan, Misra, and Marsella (2013) proposed indigenous models of health and treatment as alternative to the dominant Western models of mental health. Inspired by the works of the El Salvador psychologist Martín-Baró (1994), Blanco, Blanco, and Díaz (2016) published an article in the *American Psychologist* to challenge the *Diagnostic and Statistical Manual of Mental Disorder*'s model of psychological trauma. Christopher, Wendt, Marecek, and Goodman (2014) showed how without proper understanding of a local culture, good intentioned attempts of international relief work can do more harm than good.

Most important, IP scholarship factors in social justice as an essential ingredient of health and well-being. This theme finds an eloquent expression in Marsella and Yamada (2007):

> There can be no mental health where there is powerlessness, because powerlessness breeds despair; there can be no mental health where there is poverty, because poverty breeds hopelessness; there can be no mental health where there is inequality, because inequality breeds anger and resentment; there can be no mental health where there is racism, because racism breeds low self-esteem and self-denigration.
>
> (p. 812)

Along this line, the term *happiness donut*, coined by Sundararajan (2005, p. 35), gains predictive power by exposing the moral vacuum in American positive psychology. This moral vacuum was subsequently found by anthropologists (e.g., Yang, 2015) in the nation-wide promotion of Western positive psychology in China, where psychologizing was used by the state as a means to put the responsibility for happiness on the individuals whose livelihood was on the line under state-wide economic restructuring. The intimate connection between social justice and physical and mental health is also addressed by Ting and Sundararajan (2018) in their study of ethnic minority groups in China.

Conclusion

After this brief historical tour, and having listened in on the thoughts and feelings of the Task Force members, the reader will agree, I hope, that the Task Force is steered by visions that have deep roots in humanistic psychology:

- Epistemological diversity: Based on one of the central values of the Society for Humanistic Psychology (Division 32 of the American Psychological Association), the Task Force signifies a shift of emphasis from gene-based to meme-based definition of diversity. This particular approach to diversity fosters the vision of a global psychology that embodies unity in diversity—a unity that transcends blood and soil; a diversity that celebrates epistemological differences among cultures and even within the same culture.

- Dialogue: Psychology, like any other language game, is a living conversation, for which translation is the key to the perpetuation and permutation of the discourse. As Western psychology is translated into other cultures, the more we make sure that the influence is going both ways, and the more we allow conflicting voices to inhabit the terms we use in psychology, the more likely it is that alternative ways of doing psychological science will emerge.

Note

1 See http://indigenouspsych.org/News/HR_A41373_Indigenous_Psych_image2.pdf

References

Allwood, C. M., & Berry, J. W. (2006). Origins and development of indigenous psychologies: An international analysis. *International Journal of Psychology, 41,* 243–268.

Blanco, A., Blanco, R., & Díaz, D. (2016). Social (dis)order and psychological trauma: Look earlier, look outside, and look beyond the persons. *American Psychologist, 71,* 187–198.

Christopher, J. C., Wendt, D. C., Marecek, J. & Goodman, D. M. (2014). Critical cultural awareness: Contributions to a globalizing psychology. *American Psychologist, 69,* 645–655.

Enriquez, V. G. (1992). *From colonial to liberation psychology: The Philippine experience.* Quezon City: University of the Philippines Press.

Enriquez, V. G. (1993). Developing a Filipino psychology. In U. Kim & J. W. Berry (Eds.), *Indigenous Psychologies Research and experience in cultural context* (pp. 152–169). Newbury Park, CA: Sage Publications.

Heath, A. E., Neimeyer, G. J., & Pedersen, P. B. (1988). The future of cross-cultural counseling: A Delphi poll. *Journal of Counseling and Development, 67,* 27–30.

Heelas, P., & Lock, A. (Eds.). (1981). *Indigenous psychologies: The anthropology of the self.* London, UK: Academic Press.

Holland, D., & Quinn, N. (Eds.). (1987). *Cultural models in language and thought.* Cambridge, UK: Cambridge University Press.

Jahoda, G. (2016). On the rise and decline of "indigenous psychology". *Culture & Psychology, 22,* 169–181.

Kim, U., & Berry, J. W. (Eds.). (1993). *Indigenous psychologies: Research and experience in cultural context.* Newbury Park, CA: Sage.

Kim, U., Yang, K-S., & Hwang, K-K. (Eds.). (2006). *Indigenous and cultural psychology: Understanding people in context.* New York, NY: Springer.

Marsella, A. J. (1998). Toward a "global-community psychology"/meeting the needs of a changing world. *American Psychologist, 53,* 1282–1291.

Marsella, A. J., &Yamada, A. M. (2007). Culture and psychopathology: Foundations, issues, and directions. In S. Kitayama & D. Cohen (Eds.), *Handbook of cultural psychology* (pp. 787–818). New York, NY: Guilford Press.

Martín-Baró, I. (1994). *Writings for a liberation psychology.* Cambridge, MA: Harvard University Press.

Misra, G., & Gergen, K. J. (1993). On the place of culture in psychological science. *International Journal of Psychology, 28,* 225–243.

Moghaddam, F. M. (1987). Psychology in the Three Worlds. *American Psychologist, 47,* 912–920.

Palmater, P. (2011). *Beyond blood: Rethinking indigenous identity.* Saskatoon, SK: Purich.

Rowe, G., & Wright, G. (1999). The Delphi technique as a forecasting tool: Issues and analysis. *International Journal of Forecasting, 15,* 353–375.

Sinha, D. (1986). *Psychology in a third world country: The Indian experience.* New Delhi, India: Sage.

Sundararajan, L. (2005). Happiness donut: A Confucian critique of positive psychology. *Journal of Theoretical and Philosophical Psychology, 25,* 35–60.

Sundararajan, L. (2008). The plot thickens–or not: Protonarratives of emotions and the Chinese principle of savoring. *Journal of Humanistic Psychology, 48,* 243–263.

Sundararajan, L. (2013). The Chinese notions of harmony, with special focus on implications for cross-cultural and global psychology. *The Humanistic Psychologist, 41,* 25–34.

Sundararajan, L. (2015). *Understanding emotion in Chinese culture: Thinking through psychology.* New York, NY: Springer SBM.

Sundararajan, L., Misra, G., & Marsella, A. J. (2013). Indigenous approaches to assessment, diagnosis, and treatment of mental disorders. In F. A. Paniagua & A. M. Yamada (Eds.), *Handbook of multicultural mental health* (2nd ed., pp. 69–87). San Diego, CA: Elsevier.

Ting, R. S-K., & Sundararajan, L. (2018). *Culture, cognition, and emotion in China's religious ethnic minorities: Voices of suffering among the Yi.* (Palgrave Studies in Indigenous Psychology Series). New York, NY: Springer Nature.

Wertz, F. J. (2011). The qualitative revolution and psychology: Science, politics and ethics. *The Humanistic Psychologist, 39,* 77–104.

Yang, J. (2015). *Unknotting the heart/unemployment and therapeutic governance in China.* Ithaca, NY: Cornell University Press.

13 Humanistic Perspectives on Sexuality

Sara K. Bridges and Christina M. New

With the sexual revolution of the 1960s and 1970s came an assertion that both women and men have the right to be, and perhaps should be, comfortable with their own sexuality. Different ways of being sexually open became options and the more puritanical ideologies of the 1950s became a thing of the past. No longer was sex supposed to be an activity confined to Saturday night bedroom behavior. Instead, sexuality was something to be enjoyed, shared, and experienced freely without guilt or fear of negative judgment. In this way, sexuality began to be recognized as an innate right and a biologically natural occurrence both between people and with the self alone. The work of Masters and Johnson (1966, 1970) furthered this biological stance. From their perspective, sex was as natural as any other bodily function (e.g., respiration or digestion), and as such should be discussed and studied just as freely. As being sexual became a natural part of living and a right rather than a privilege, opportunities for personal growth in a sexual way for both women and men became increasingly possible. However, along with the opportunity for sexual freedom has come somewhat of a mandate for men and women to have (and embody) sexual comfort, knowledge, and skill. Additionally, there has been a push to have an optimal level of sexual desire, particularly for women (Bridges & Horne, 2007).

Conversations about too much or too little sexual desire have become commonplace, as though sexuality were a prescriptive recipe. Unfortunately, the mandate for positive sexuality existed then, and continues to exist today, without an accompanying psychological or relational support structure available to help women and men understand their personal meanings about sexuality and to assist them in finding sexual comfort, knowledge, skill, or desire. Thus, the unintended consequence of making sexuality more acceptable and natural by approaching it from a biological-only standpoint has been the categorization of sexuality from a "medical" mind frame that has neglected the underlying personal and interpersonal meanings associated with sexuality in general and sexual difficulties in specific. Further, while the right to sexuality is asserted from a medical, as well as a mainstream media standpoint, it comes with caveats. The underlying message is that the pursuit of sexual satisfaction and connection is only acceptable if one fits within the confines of what is considered normal, meaning that one must be the right age, race, ethnicity, ability, orientation, gender identity, and socioeconomic status to enjoy the "right" of sexuality. All else outside this is subjected to judgment of being inappropriate. This chapter will examine the effects of medical approaches to sexuality and explore a humanistic model that can help to identify personal meanings and subjective experiences of sexuality.

Traditional Approaches

Both Kinsey (1947) and Masters and Johnson (1976) brought sexuality into the forefront through medical channels. Understanding the difficulties most people had talking about sexuality or feeling okay studying it, they emphasized the physiological and anatomical aspects of sexuality by comparing it to other bodily functions such as respiration and digestion (Kinsey, 1947). This move allowed for the advancement in scientific study of sexuality beyond reproduction; however, another perhaps less desirable outcome was the medicalization of sexuality in general. "Appropriate" discussions of sexuality became objective and treatment for sexual problems, even those relationally based, stayed in the medical/remediation of problems arena rather than remaining subjective or interpersonally based. The inclusion of sexuality-based problems in the *Diagnostic and Statistical Manual of Mental Illness* (DSM) helped to keep a reductionistic, behaviorally based, medical understanding central to medical providers and clinicians. Thus, although the move to talk more openly and less puritanically about sexuality was achieved, the ability to talk about sexuality more holistically and personally remained problematic for both clinicians and their clients.

Because the medical model became the predominate and approved way of working with sexual issues, most of the therapy around that time followed a medical, problem-focused approach (Kleinplatz, 2001). Treatments and techniques aimed to remediate difficulties that came from disordered or dysfunctional parts. Through this process, "patients" were created and diagnoses were given. For some, having a diagnosis was a relief; by labeling the experience it seemed as though a prescriptive solution should be available, not unlike the common cold or a broken bone. Yet for others, these diagnoses became prophetic rather than a means to receiving help (i.e., the diagnosis of Female Sexual Interest/ Arousal Disorder could lead to a feeling of helplessness and avoidance of connection with partners). Further, diagnosis contained the potential to reduce people to a problem narrative and risked dehumanizing the person as a whole (Kleinplatz, 2001; Yalom, 2001).

Diagnosis did lead to some effective treatments for some sexual problems (i. e., dilators for vaginismus) and some pharmacologic treatments are quite effective for treating certain physiological difficulties (i.e., PDE5 inhibitors such as sildenafil (Viagra)). However, the unintended consequences of having effective treatments such as these is that there becomes a clear demarcation between what makes sexuality functional versus dysfunctional, and it imposes a definition of what "normal" sexuality looks like (Barker, 2011). In this type of narrow messaging about sexuality there runs a greater risk of dehumanizing and limiting clients (Barker, 2011). For example, people can be sexually active and satisfied without penetration and yet both of the above-mentioned treatments are for diagnosable disorders; thus, the message is that if penetration is not possible and not treated there necessarily is something wrong. So, what then are some alternatives to traditional diagnosis and treatment of difficulties with sexuality?

Humanistic Approaches

Peggy Kleinplatz (1996, 2001, 2013) has taken the lead in humanistic approaches to understanding sexuality. Her work has focused on critiquing the medical models for defining sexuality as a goal-oriented endeavor (with mutual orgasm as the pinnacle of sexual success) rather than as a way of increasing mutual and individual pleasure. As a sex therapist herself, Kleinplatz does recognize that some medical treatments for sexual difficulties can work; however, she also recognizes that limiting the definition of successful treatment to successful penetration does a great disservice to the true diversity possible when it comes to being sexually fulfilled. As the understanding of sexuality moves away from simple function versus dysfunction, and the influences of larger systems of family, society, culture, and religion is better understood, the medical model has become insufficient for a holistic understanding of sexuality. A more complex understanding of sexuality has led to an increase in systemic approaches (Weeks & Gambescia, 2015) that seem to understand the holistic nature of sexuality. The approaches value how characteristics of an individual, their background, culture, and religion can influence sexuality.

Other writers have also been influential in helping humanistic approaches rise to a more prominent place in the study and understanding of sexuality. In particular, Leonore Tiefer (2006) and Meg Barker (2011) have written about humanistic and existential approaches to sexuality and have posited that humanistic psychology can help by challenging the medical model and offering creative research practices, a respect for sexual diversity, and an understanding that although the physiological aspects of sexuality are similar from person to person, there is significant variability in the meanings that are made from sexual experiences and understandings. Tiefer's *The New View of Women's Sexual Problems* educational campaign (2006) directly challenged the medicalization and commercialization of sexual problems and worked to bring attention back to the holistic aspects of sexuality and away from the marketing efforts of the pharmaceutical industry.

Barker (2011) takes an existential view of sexuality and critiques the "normalization" of sexuality as being solely focused on heterosexual, able-bodied sexuality, while relegating other ways of being sexual as "less than," dysfunctional, or completely non-existent. Instead, she forwards the existential idea that sexuality can be explored phenomenologically in order to gain a full understanding of the client's actual lived experience and worldview (Barker, 2011). To do this, therapists must be able to bracket their own understandings of sexuality and also deconstruct societal expectations and pressure to perform and view sexuality through a very particular lens.

Explicitly, Western societal expectations about sexuality seem to have shifted some in the last few decades; however, little has actually changed about who, what, and how sexuality is expressed (Kleinplatz, 2013). The same distinct societal barriers to healthy sexuality exist currently and their influence has permeated the lived experience of the individual. Specifically, there is pressure to be sexually knowledgeable, but not too much so, for fear of being seen as promiscuous. This is especially true for women. Additionally, there is encouragement to be open about sexuality, yet secretive, especially in the face of sexual trauma. Lastly, it is socially communicated and reinforced to look the "part" of socially approved sexuality (i.e., the right size, shape, gender, ability, ethnicity, etc.). These all stand as barriers to the expression of one's own understanding and unique experience of sexuality. Thus, simply working with individuals or couples from a traditionally medicalized sex therapy approach, not only is reductionistic and dehumanizing, it also comes with the risk of missing the very real impact of societal and cultural factors.

It is worth noting explicitly that humanistic and existential approaches complement sex therapy work with lesbian, gay, bisexual, and transgender (LGBT) individuals and couples, as well as those who embody other ways of being sexual and experiencing gender. Particularly from a humanistic perspective, it should also be noted that experiences are not the same across lesbian, gay, bisexual, transgender, and nonbinary individuals. Often, the use of LGBT+ is used indiscriminately in a manner that hides aspects of differences between the people who identify with different labels. In this text, LGBT (lesbian, gay, bisexual, transgender), LGB (lesbian, gay, transgender), and LGBT+ (lesbian, gay, bisexual, transgender, and all other non-heterosexual non-cisgender identities) are used intentionally to reflect the intended population of reference.

While same sex attraction and relationships are becoming more "acceptable" in the past decade in general, (Gallup, 2015; Pew Research Center, 2016), and gender identity is becoming of greater consideration in our social climate (Allen, 2008; James et al., 2016), those who identify as gay, lesbian, bisexual, transgender, or nonbinary often face discrimination and prejudice. The societal and cultural influences that are essential to consider for all clients may show up in unique ways for LGBT+ individuals who are living and have been socialized in a hetero/cis-normative culture. While sexuality among LGB individuals merely reflects the sexual variance within the species and is likely supported by many traditional/heteronormative therapeutic approaches, the impact of identity related discrimination and limited role models cannot be ignored as possible influential factors on both identity and sexuality development (Berry & Lezos, 2017; Bond & Miller 2017; Kollmann & Hardré, 2012). In addition, LGBT+ individuals are often subjected to questioning about the legitimacy of their "non-normative" attractions and/or identity regardless of the connection to sexuality. These additional variables may impact how sexuality is understood or embodied by clients.

Further, for many LGB individuals, their sexual and emotional attractions are not widely accepted or modeled, thus seeking clinical support for sexual difficulties may be additionally complicated by feelings of internalized homophobia or fear of being discriminated against by their provider (Lee & Kanji, 2017). Humanistic approaches honor the influence that discrimination and shame associated with one's sexual/emotional attraction may have on an individual's presenting needs during sexuality therapy.

Similarly, the spectrum of transgender individuals further misaligns with a purely medicalized perspective. Special considerations within this population include, but are not limited to, how sexuality is defined by individuals who have transcended or do not fit the gender binary as well as how sexuality is enacted amidst physiological changes due to cross-sex hormone use, or how gender-affirming surgeries or lack thereof influence the enactment and experience of sexuality (Berry & Lezos, 2017; Williams, Weinberg, & Rosenberger, 2016). These non-hetero/cis-normative experiences, in addition to the discrimination, invalidation, and internalized shame that transgender individuals may experience, influence their feelings and experience of their sexuality.

As clinical education on sexuality and therapy work with LGBT+ individuals continues to grow, clinical spaces for all clients will become inherently more inclusive. Specifically, the more that research can include LGBT+ identities, the more our thinking about sexuality and identities will expand. Through this, therapists and mental health professionals will continue to redefine the clinical understanding of the multitude of places in which one's identities and sexualities are constructed. As this occurs, the ground will be fertile for a more inherently humanistic approach to therapy in sexuality and beyond.

The following case example will demonstrate the differences between a traditional sex therapy approach and a humanistic therapy approach. This aims to illustrate how a humanistic approach to sexuality can help address both apparent and underlying issues.

Case Example

Lena and Stephanie presented for couples' therapy because they both were feeling unsatisfied in their relationship. They are both 36-year-old cisgender women who have two children who were adopted at birth. Their children are Toya and Tevan, ages ten and eight respectively. Lena and Stephanie have been living together since they graduated from college 13 years ago; they married three years ago, just as soon as they were legally able. Lena identifies as African American and Stephanie identifies as Caucasian, stating that she was raised "super white" when asked about her upbringing. Lena said she comes from a middle class fairly traditional southern African American family who, while not accepting, does not totally reject her relationship with Stephanie. Stephanie reports that her family disowned her in college when she started the relationship with Lena.

Lena made the initial appointment for therapy stating that she and Stephanie were no longer as physically intimate as either one of them would like, and this was causing a rift between them. In the first appointment, Lena also stated that Stephanie was always "fine" with whatever Lena wanted to do sexually but would not initiate or ever really talk about what she wanted. Stephanie said she did not have any preferences and actually would be mostly okay if they did not have a physical/sexual part of their relationship as long as this was okay with Lena (which it was not). Both women agreed that raising children was difficult and that work pressures and fears about the current conservative political climate were impacting their ability to relax and sink into being together. However, Lena believed that it was a breakdown in communication and that the real problem was Stephanie's unwillingness to express her true wants and needs.

Therapeutic Directions

Traditional sex therapy would approach the sexual difficulties between Lena and Stephanie from a behavioral and potentially relational approach. While not ignoring the family backgrounds and pressure from societal expectations, the main focus would be on the ways in which their sexual relationship was not meeting their needs and the origin of low sexual desire. Techniques such as Sensate Focus would be used to help the couple learn how they both want to be touched. Additionally, this approach would focus on helping the couple to feel satisfaction and pleasure through their partners. Sensate Focus is a technique originally designed by Masters and Johnson to help couples move away from the mechanical demand characteristics in a sexual relationship and move instead to the pleasure that can come from touching one's partner and allowing themselves to be touched. It is a slow, progressive behavioral technique that can be quite effective when there are few underlying concerns within the relationship.

Additionally, traditional sex therapists and couples therapists trained in issues related to sexuality might work with this couple on their communication skills and the expression of wants and needs in the relationship. Using approaches such as implementing "I statements" or the DESC model (Describe, Express, Specify, and Consequences), the goal would be to help Lena and Stephanie not only express their sexual wants and needs, but also to ameliorate the problematic communication patterns that are keeping them away from the intimacy and connection that is believed to be necessary for satisfactory sexual experiences. Frequently, these types of interventions can be useful for making incremental changes within the relationship. Sex can happen more frequently, communication becomes a bit more open, and couples report feeling somewhat better about the nature of the relationships. Yet, as has been mentioned previously, this approach follows the assumptions in sex therapy that sex needs to happen within a particular range of frequency to be healthy (not too much or too little), that sexual difficulties are always psychological or biological in nature, and that the therapist is an expert on the client's sexuality, perhaps even more than the clients themselves (Kleinplatz, 2001).

However, it could also be argued that more long-lasting transformational change is possible when both partners in the relationship are seen from a holistic humanistic–existential perspective. In particular, understanding the personal meanings and constructions of sexuality could be beneficial. In the case of Lena and Stephanie, exploration of the pervasive impact of familial and societal influences could lead to a deeper understanding of sexuality and its role in their relationship. Constructivist psychotherapy, which has been identified as having many commonalities with existential therapy (Lincoln & Hoffman, 2018), could be quite useful in this case. In this approach, there is great focus on personal meaning made by the individual or couple. Additionally, the therapist takes a nonexpert stance during therapy, accompanying clients on the journey towards understanding their own sexuality. Understanding both one's own core meanings around sexuality and the origin and function of sexual meanings in their partners can be an important step in moving beyond an objectivist reductionistic view of sexuality. Extending beyond the traditional approaches can help improve connection and communication by building both empathy and perspective taking (Kelly, 1991; Leitner, Begley, & Findley, 1996).

Yet, sometimes understanding meaning-making is difficult without a clear understanding of deeply held beliefs or positions that were learned early on. Coherence therapy can be useful when wanting to explore the depths of an underlying difficulty that may be fueling the current relational difficulties (Bridges, 2016). This methodology looks for how the current difficulty is actually a solution that was created to address a deeper suffering earlier in life (Ecker, Ticic, & Hulley, 2012). This model is an extension of constructivist theory in that it contends that the constructs or ways of viewing the world are created as solutions to the overarching need for safety, well-being, or justice at a young age. These solutions, or constructs as they are known, are then applied to situations in the future. For example, through Coherence Therapy, Lena and Stephanie began to understand that there was a vitally important reason for Stephanie to never express her wants and needs, nor to even recognize these needs herself. Growing up, Stephanie learned that the solution to getting in trouble by her parents was to never express her own wants and needs. Her family struggled with finances, and rather than letting their children be okay with wanting things and not being able to have them, they shamed their children for having any wants or needs at all. Stephanie quickly learned that having wants and expressing them to her parents resulted in shocking outpourings of anger by her parents followed by profound rejection, which felt awful. She learned that the solution to the rage was to hide all her wants and needs or even further, to deny (even to herself) that she had any wants or needs at all. This solution worked well at reducing the amount of anger or rejection she received from her parents; however, as she matured and became involved with Lena, not being able to express wants or needs led to dissatisfaction, disappointment, and a rift in her relationship. Before the actual agency behind not voicing her wants was discovered, Stephanie believed there was something wrong with her and Lena believed that Stephanie was holding back in their relationship. Moreover, Stephanie attributed her stoicism to being "super white" and felt shame for not being able to be as natural and connected to her body as Lena was to hers. Because Coherence Therapy is designed to find the original learning or construct that makes the current situation necessary, the actual risk of expressing Stephanie's wants and needs was discovered. Once the true agency and wisdom of the symptom (not communicating her needs or wants) was recognized (understanding that not revealing her own wants and needs to another person is a way to avoid anger and rejection), the blame between Lena and Stephanie dissipated. What emerged was the possibility for understanding of the pain that Stephanie expected, as well as the availability of adult resources to demonstrate two things: that expressing wants and needs does not always end up with anger and rejection, and that if one does receive anger and rejection there are adult resources available to cope with those feelings that were not available when the initial learning happened. This allows for more freedom of expression and openness to possibility in the relationship.

Clearly, however, there were other aspects of their relationship that needed to be addressed, yet learning that there were underlying constructs that necessitated the symptoms humanized their difficulties and allowed room for future understanding about meanings. Societal and family issues also seemed to be a factor and those could be addressed in subsequent sessions.

[margin note: WANTS & NEEDS]

Future Directions

Sexuality and sexual images are pervasive in Western culture; however, just because it is everywhere does not mean there is true understanding, knowledge, or comfort of what it means to be a sexual being. Additionally, typical Western social structures do not provide support for gaining understanding, knowledge, or comfort about sexuality and often penalize and shame people for not knowing what they "should" know. Thus, it's difficult to see how people could come to understand their own meanings around sexuality and feel satisfied in their sexual lives, however they are defined. As more and more people are using the internet to find out about sexuality in general (Kleinplatz, 2013), informational sites and blogs that encourage holistic sexual meaning-making and discovery would be a positive step. Research that addresses the multiple ways in which people understand sexuality could also be useful.

Further, most therapists are not trained specifically in sexuality and courses in sexuality are not required in most states for licensure (Russell, 2012). Therapists must seek out their own training in sexuality to ensure they understand the potential physiological explanations for sexual trouble, as well as the more holistic intra and interpersonal difficulties that can arise (Bridges & Neimeyer, 2003). Training in diversity and the many ways culture, ethnicity, ability, and religion can play a key role in the meaning of sexuality is also necessary. Finally, because therapists live in the same sexually saturated society, doing one's own work around sexuality could only benefit therapists and their clients as they move towards a deeper understanding of sexuality and its varied meanings.

Key Points

- Traditional sex therapy can be effective, but risks reducing sexuality to physiology and the medicalization of sex.
- Humanistic approaches allow clinicians to work with the whole person and their sexual meanings.
- Understanding and addressing sexual meaning-making is central to helping clients navigate problematic issues regarding sexuality.
- Personal training and exploration are needed for therapists to be prepared to work with the sexual issues of their clients.

References

Allen, M. (2008). Transgender history: Trans in ancient times. In The bilerico project. Retrieved from http://bilerico.lgbtqnation.com/2008/02/transgender_history_trans_expression_in.php

Barker, M. (2011). Existential sex therapy. Sexual and Relationship Therapy, 26(1), 33–47.

Berry, M. D., & Lezos, A. N. (2017). Inclusive sex therapy practices: A qualitative study of the techniques sex therapists use when working with diverse sexual populations. *Sexual & Relationship Therapy, 32*(1), 2–21.

Bond, B. J., & Miller, B. (2017). From screen to self: The relationship between television exposure and self-complexity among lesbian, gay, and bisexual youth. *International Journal of Communication, 11*, 94–112.

Bridges, S. K. (2016). Coherence therapy: The roots of problems and the transformation of old solutions. In H. E. Tinsley, S. H. Lease, & N. S. Giffin Wiersma (Eds.), *Contemporary theory and practice of counseling and psychotherapy* (pp. 353–380). Thousand Oaks, CA: SAGE Publications.

Bridges, S. K., & Horne, S. G. (2007). Sexual satisfaction and desire discrepancy in same sex women's relationships. *Journal of Sex & Marital Therapy, 33*(1), 41–53.

Bridges, S. K., & Neimeyer, R. A. (2003). Exploring and negotiating sexual meanings. In J. S. Whitman & C. J. Boyd (Eds.), *The therapist's notebook for lesbian, gay, and bisexual clients* (pp. 145–149). New York, NY: Hawthorn Press.

Ecker, B., Ticic, R., & Hulley, L. (2012). *Unlocking the emotional brain.* New York, NY: Routledge.

Gallup. (2015). Gay and lesbian rights. Retrieved from www.gallup.com/poll/1651/gaylesbian-rights.aspx

James, S. E., Herman, J. L., Rankin, S., Keisling, M., Mottet, L., & Anafi, M. (2016). *The report of the 2015 U.S. transgender survey.* Washington, DC: National Center for Transgender Equality. Retrieved from https://transequality.org/sites/default/files/docs/usts/USTS-Full-Report-Dec17.pdf

Kelly, G. A. (1991). *The psychology of personal constructs* (Vol. 1, First published in 1955). New York, NY: Routledge.

Kinsey, A. C. (1947). Sex behavior in the human animal. *Annals of the New York Academy of Sciences, 47*, 635–637.

Kleinplatz, P. J. (1996). Transforming sex therapy: Integrating erotic potential. *The Humanistic Psychologist, 24*(2), 190–202.

Kleinplatz, P. J. (2001). Introduction: A critical evaluation of sex therapy: Room for improvement. In P. J. Kleinplatz (Ed.), *New directions in sex therapy: Innovations and alternatives* (xi–xxxiii). Philadelphia, PA: Brunner-Routledge.

Kleinplatz, P. J. (2013). Three decades of sex: Reflections on sexuality and sexology. *Canadian Journal of Human Sexuality, 22*(1), 1–4.

Kollmann, S., & Hardré, P. (2012). LGB in the land of the free: Exploring the social and educational implications of identity development. *International Journal of Diversity in Organizations, Communities & Nations, 11*(6), 79–94.

Lee, A., & Kanji, Z. (2017). Queering the health care system: Experiences of the lesbian, gay, bisexual, transgender community. *Canadian Journal of Dental Hygiene, 51*(2), 80–89.

Leitner, L. M., Begley, E. A., & Findley, A. J. (1996). Cultural construing and marginalized persons: Role relationships and ROLE relationships. In D. Kalekin-Fishman & B. M. Walker (Eds.), *The construction of group realities: Culture, society, and personal construct theory* (pp. 323–340). Melbourne, FL: Robert E. Krieger Publishing.

Lincoln, J., & Hoffman, L. (2018). Toward an integration of constructivism and existential psychotherapy. *Journal of Constructivist Psychology.* doi:10.1080/10720537.2018.1461719.

Masters, W. H., & Johnson, V. E. (1966). *Human sexual response.* Boston, MA: Little, Brown.

Masters, W. H., & Johnson, V. E. (1970). *Human sexual inadequacy.* Boston, MA: Little, Brown.

Masters, W. H., & Johnson, V. E. (1976). Principles of the new sex therapy. *The American Journal of Psychiatry, 133*(5), 548–554.

Pew Research Center. (2016). Support steady for same-sex marriage and acceptance of homosexuality. Retrieved from www.pewresearch.org/fact-tank/2016/05/12/support-steady-forsame-sex-marriage-and-acceptance-of-homosexuality/

Russell, E. B. (2012). Sexual health attitudes, knowledge, and clinical behaviors: Implications for counseling. *The Family Journal, 20*(1), 94–101.

Tiefer, L. (2006). Sex therapy as a humanistic enterprise. *Sexual and Relationship Therapy, 21*(3), 359–375.

Weeks, G. R., & Gambescia, N. (2015). Toward a new paradigm in sex therapy. In K. M. Hertlein, G. R. Weeks, & N. Gambescia (Eds.), *Systemic sex therapy* (2nd ed., pp. 32–52). New York, NY: Routledge/Taylor & Francis Group.

Williams, C. J., Weinberg, M. S., & Rosenberger, J. G. (2016). Trans women doing sex in San Francisco. *Archives of Sexual Behavior, 45*, 1665–1678.

Yalom, I. D. (2001). *The gift of therapy.* London, UK: Piatkus.

14 Exploring Disability from the Lens of Humanistic Psychology

Juliet Rohde-Brown

The survival rate of injured and congenitally disabled persons is growing as well as other populations who would identify within the construct of disability. There is concern in the field of psychology as questions around resources and quality of life are explored as well as attitudinal and physical confinements and opportunities for healthy personal and community life. Hoffman, Cleare-Hoffman, and Jackson (2015a) are among those who voice the necessity for an expansion of humanistic psychology's wings to include much more dialogue and collective agency around issues of diversity and to highlight inquiries around what the term "multicultural" actually means in psychological terms. To address this question in the particular realm of humanistic psychology, these authors have stressed the inclusion of sociopolitical contexts on every level of discussion. One of the areas long ignored in multicultural contexts, but currently entering into the spotlight, is that of disability.

Constructs on Disability

Olkin (1999), although not explicitly identified with humanistic psychology, has been a voice for considering what she refers to as a "new paradigm" in the area of disability research and practice, often referred to as the "social model," as it heightens the focus on power and privilege imbalances (pp. 26–27). In a copious review of the history of how disability has been recognized and met with in the United States, Olkin shares that this paradigm experienced its seed in the early 1900s. In the 1970s, more importance was placed on disability with the Rehabilitation Act. Yet, there has been scant literature on the topic in the psychological journals. This is curious, since for some time disabled individuals have been the largest represented group in the mosaic of categorizations of diversity. This beckons the question of why this population may have been historically pushed aside, even in the realm of humanistic psychology.

Integrating perspectives into inquiries of what embodiment means on the continuum of "disability" may serve to broaden awareness to include considerations of the idiosyncratic, archetypal, nuanced, and even subtle nature of being. The perpetuation of "otherness" creates a great deal of suffering at interpersonal and intrapersonal levels. As a general rule, being in relationship with one's own notions of "disablement" or with disowned parts of oneself often results in anxious denial and projection, and is reflected in the ways in which "others" are related to individually and collectively as well.

Stolorow (2015) has proposed a "phenomenological contextualism" (p. 395). This philosophical idea beckons one to consider reflections on Olkin's (1999) lamentation regarding the tendency in the field of psychology to fail to recognize disability as occurring along a continuum, resulting in the notion that "you either have one or you don't" (p. 296). Attention to the contexts from which definitions and views of disability emerge may highlight that this construct is nuanced and often subjectively biased. Meaning derives from organizing patterns of phenomena across time and within intersubjective, social, historical, and cultural contexts (Lyddon, 1995). When an individual shares an interpretation of a phenomenon, personal experience moves into a co-created experience and a social construction occurs. Family environments are the first place that interpretations of life and personal responsibility are developed. Olkin and Pledger (2003) lament that "the relationship between the model of disability that families hold and the psychosocial functioning of those families is virtually unexplored" (p. 302).

The term "disability" tends to depend on who is creating the definition or making the decision that a particular disability exists. These decisions often emerge in families and other group contexts. Constructs of disability may include, but should not be limited to, physical or learning disabilities, substance abuse, medically related confinements due to illness, autistic spectrum considerations, those who are severely psychotic, developmentally delayed or brain-injured, and those who may have a difficult time expressing their needs. More and more families are facing the real possibility of caring for another family member's basic daily physical, emotional, and even communication needs when disability is extreme.

Family members often find themselves in the position of having to be the dominant voice for their loved one when it comes to medical and/or care decisions. How they use language has implications on many levels. It is easy to fall into framing the loved one as a "wounded one" and psychologists may fall into the same predicament when working with such families. A humanistic psychologist who may be working therapeutically with an "intercultural family (disabled and nondisabled)" may invite dialogue and reflection on how their assumptions have affected their way of being with each other and expectations about the world at large (Olkin & Pledger, 2003; Rohde-Brown & Frain, 2014).

Aside from the meaning-making that intercultural families may be assisted with in humanistic-oriented therapy, there are real systemic concerns for these families and individuals in the realm of additional health vulnerabilities, financial decline, stigma, and disparities in access to competent and compassionate care in the larger community. In the United States there are disparities in regard to who may even be eligible for access to health care resources and when these disparities are considered not only from the standpoint of disability, but with the added component of racism, the divides in care are even more striking (Perrin, 2013). As Disability Rights Education and Defense Fund (DREDF) Staff Attorney, Yee (2011), validates "race and disability together may have a previously unaccounted cumulative impact on creating health disparities" (p. 2). Adding gender, socioeconomic status, and LGBTQ contexts on top of race and ethnicity amplifies imbalances in who may receive quality care. A quote from Yee states:

> It is vitally important to distinguish between disability as a natural part of the human condition, and disability-related health disparities that can lead to compromised care, ill health, institutionalization, and premature death. These are not consequences that inevitably follow the simple fact of impairment.
>
> (p. 1)

Health care disparities exacerbate the insults of those already marginalized. Cities and towns are full of those uncared for in wheelchairs under freeway passes, as homeless veterans with missing limbs and others attempt to find comfort and care to the best of their abilities, sometimes trapped in the cycle of addiction, thereby extrapolating an already traumatized psyche and body. Some experience financial hardship due to high costs of medical and psychological care, throwing individuals and families out of the safety of a home, a car, and a way to earn an adequate income.

Disparities extend beyond the U.S. to other countries, as can be expected. Yee and colleagues at DREDF have been conversing with international organizations and gathering data from many different countries. The purpose of this endeavor is to compare and contrast health care disparities and work toward reducing this phenomenon by bringing attention to such and inviting voices from those impacted (see DREFT website for statistics regarding disparities in the U.S. and other countries). This type of research and advocacy resonates with humanistic values and visions. Perrin (2013) asserts that knowing about and having empathy for these disparities is not enough, for "humanistic psychology must leave academia, engage the community, and reengineer systems that stifle justice" (p. 54). He wisely adds the component of race-based traumatic stress to the mosaic of multiple minority identities, which may or may not include disability, and strongly suggests that "advocacy" be added to the lexicon of how psychologists describe themselves, positioning humanistic psychology at the helm because of its "holistic philosophy" and directing attention to "mesa, micro, and macro" contexts (p. 60). An example given for where humanistic psychologists may actively participate with facilitating workshops and other endeavors on a macro level is an organization entitled Dismantling Racism Works (DRW). While Western psychologists and psychiatrists move more toward attempting to impose Western modalities in global contexts, as opposed to inquiring into what is indigenous to a particular geographical area and culture, humanistic psychologists are counteracting this movement by turning to global actions (Bedi, 2018).

At a community level, such approaches as *in vivo immersive cultural plunge* may be utilized to assist in the sensitization of psychologists and psychologists in training, by immersing them in intensive events with multimedia presentation, breakout groups, the sharing of stories of oppression, and interactive discussion. Psychodrama may be included as well (Payne, 2017).

At the individual or small group level, part of clinical work, then, starting with a *mesa* framework would be to explore systemic aspects of suffering and oppression intrapsychically and interpersonally in the here and now. Further, within clinical work, this would involve investigating how White people and people of color may internalize arrows of injustice, which then may have an impact on their sense of self and identity (Perrin, 2013). Therapists would begin with themselves, exploring where they may have inflicted oppressive stances and violence or been the recipient of such. How these insults may have included responses or internalizations around a multiplicity of minority frameworks would be an important part of this personal reflection. Coming back to how one's philosophical stance on life impacts therapeutic work with others would be suggested for humanistic psychologists who wish to walk the talk of the core principles of humanistic philosophical foundations (Hoffman, Stewart, Warren, & Meek, 2015b). The question of selfhood would ultimately emerge in this kind of deep contemplation.

Social Contexts of Selfhood and Disability Identity

The late philosopher Allan Watts (1968) wrote, "basically, then, 'self' is not only the body but the whole energy system which embodies itself in all bodies" (p. 76). The self, for instance, may ultimately be seen as an interpretation, as something illusory that human beings construct, and this construction occurs through our meaning-making and our ways of describing that process within a social context. People often flail in that they can come to believe that they are fixed in one's selfhood, rather than constantly changing. Hoffman et al. (2015b) state,

> Cultural competency and sensitivity in therapy and psychological theory mandate that therapists develop the flexibility to work with clients with a variety of conceptions of the self. The practice of therapy often assumes a particular view of self. As therapists often unfamiliar

with the diverse conceptions of the self, they may assume a certain understanding of the self and impose it on clients without recognizing that they are doing so.

(p. 125)

When it comes to disability and self-hood, assumptions may thwart authentic inquiry as well. With all good intention and with attempts to be empathic and sensitive to diversity, the injury of one's words or the placing of one's gaze is often not recognized or understood as an injustice. It takes active and honest communication to bring awareness to micro aggressions that occur in interpersonal interactions. Inquiring into lived experience is directly in accordance with humanistic psychology's collaborative way of working, which serves to reduce false separations and engage pluralistic ways of knowing. Constructs around "dis"ability benefit from inclusive contemplative inquiry, long a practice in humanistic psychology. "Cultural complexes" will bleed into therapeutic interactions (Samuels, 2004, p. 210). Thus, as suggested above, with reflection on one's own personal narrative around the sociopolitical aspects of one's lived experience, a compassionate attunement to the diverse lived experience of others may be less elusive.

Merleau-Ponty (1958) wrote, "There is a consciousness of myself which makes use of language and is humming with words" (p. 466). Assumptions distinctly have an impact on one's use of language and the ways in which one describes experience. Dunn and Andrews (2015) propose that the person-first language of psychology does not gel with the identity-first language of disability culture. The main observation with those bringing voice to this concern is that, unlike rehabilitation studies, mainstream psychological theory, education, and practice has hardly given an articulated thought to how individuals wish to be considered *on their own terms*. Humanistic psychology asserts the perspective that in order to understand a phenomenon, it is best to ask the individuals in question about their own experience.

Curious to engage in further inquiry with disability culture and language preferences around self and identity from a human-centered stance, I consulted with a couple of individuals. The first person consulted was George Zambos, a case manager with a regional center in California. Born with arthrogryposis, George states that, in contrast to Dunn and Andrews' stance, he disagrees with the disability-first framework. Specifically, Dunn and Andrews advocate for changing the language from the APA recommendation of "people with disabilities" to "disabled people." They do so based on having compiled a great deal of research from within disability culture. George, however, does not resonate with referring to himself as a disabled person. He realizes that his view is "not the majority view on this." Hearing George's stance on his identity amplifies the importance of qualitative and hermeneutic research that emphasizes lived experience and people using their own voice in defining themselves and expressing meaning. It also opens up more questions about how to be able to speak about disability within radical humanistic psychological circles and to do so with respect and sensitivity.

Having grown up in a family who treated him "exactly the same way that they treated anybody else," he was rather surprised and insulted when, while walking through the library door during his attendance at university, someone said to him "If you pray hard enough, God will fix your hands!" George was struck by this person's comment and found himself reflecting that "the person who has the inability to see that I am just fine the way that I am" is "impaired in judgment," a form of "disability" of perception. George went on to say, "I never saw myself the way that this person saw me. I do not let it define me as a person. The problem is that we get labeled as disabled," as if people believe "that we can't do something" and placed in a binary category rather than being regarded in one's fullness. Indeed, Olkin and Pledger (2003) assert, "psychology must shed its emphasis on disability as abnormal, deviant, or special" (p. 303).

Coming back to the importance of family dynamics, George's overall message is "It is the mindset of the families that determine how one views oneself." In regard to his work with regional center clients and their families, he asserts, "I expect more than the client does and sometimes more than the family does. Perhaps this gives me a certain advantage in my work, especially with people with Cerebral Palsy" (G. Zambos, Personal Communication, April 29, 2015).

As an advocate for feminist approaches to disability and other aspects of diversity, Allele Coble-Temple speaks of the impact of family as well. She is an example of someone in the educational community who has fought for equality in social and professional contexts with the support of her family, such that she is one of the small, but growing number of psychologists who identify as disabled and who are in leadership positions. These psychologists speak from human experience about the sociopolitical construction of realities around disability.

Another strong voice in this field is Megan Carlos (2017), who posits that an environmental/architectural space, such as a building, serves as a powerful metaphor for how a culture makes personal and societal space for difference and alter-ability. She advocates for considerations that are more humanitarian in the actual planning and construction of buildings, whether they be homes or professional spaces. These insights may have been inspired by Temple Grandin's unique contributions to more humane treatment of cattle based on reflections about her own sensitivity to environmental space growing up on the autistic spectrum (see her book entitled *Animals Make Us Human*, 2010).

Humanistic family psychology and psychotherapy offers much, particularly when the shared care of a family member is a topic of exploration and the contextual framework of culture and international similarities and differences expands the conversation. Coming from an intercultural family in the context of disability, while at the Second International Conference on Existential Psychology in Shanghai, China, I sought to engage in discussion with a group of Chinese conference attendees who disclosed that they were from similar families. It was quite moving to witness the level of compassion and open emotional disclosure offered by the Chinese attendees in regard to their value of shared responsibility as a family and how this informed their co-constructed identity and sense of self as an interrelated being (Rohde-Brown & Frain, 2014). Indeed, from a phenomenological perspective "care can be experienced as transcendent" (Josselson, 2000, p. 99).

The Net of Being

Humanistic psychology has, since its inception, deeply espoused "interpersonal embeddedness" and a relational way of conducting psychotherapy as well as research (DeRobertis, 2015, p. 239). Approached from a humanistic perspective and description, the term "disability" begins to open up considerations of relativity and paradox. An ontological exploration into Heidegger's (1953/1996) concept of "Da-Sein," or being-ness itself, has been a significant part of an international dialogue, instigated by Louis Hoffman, Mark Yang, and Xuefu Wang. Wang's (2011) *Zhi Mian* psychology bridges east and west and offers a uniquely meaningful approach to exploring both the individual and collectivist aspects of disability through existential–humanistic dialogue. Furthering ways in which a humanistic stance may expand perceptual frameworks into transpersonal domains, Cambray (2009) and others write about complex adaptive systems, emergence, and the self-organizing processes of all living systems. Cambray expresses there is an "underlying synchronistic chord to empathic experience that can be described as a resonant field. Perhaps an additional step toward the resonance among different cultural appreciations of mind can be taken now" (p. 87).

How may a radical humanism around disability be facilitated? Rather than top-down ways of engaging with this construct, engaging in authentic dialogue and active listening may open to greater insight and care. Kalsched (2015), a depth psychologist, metaphorically amplifies Dante's description of Hell and refers to the character of "Dis" in the framework of trauma and dissociation. With much insight, he postulates that "all of the suffering instigated by Dis is to avoid another kind of suffering, a more productive kind of suffering, which might lead out of the ingrown, closed circle of Hell" (pp. 87–88). Coming back to Wang's (2011) Zhi Mian concept, one could say that a great deal of suffering comes from a sense of separateness and an inability to "face directly" and question our collective constructs in contemplative inquiry.

Within humanistic psychology, the arts provide a window into the implicit and transrational, and provide a way to expand upon the meaning of lived experience in the context of disability. The arts, creative mediums, and active imagination with dreams provide avenues toward *feeling* through engaging metaphor and the symbolic (Jung, 1916/1960; May, 1981) and *awe* (Schneider, 2011). Art and creativity relate to the visionary aspect of the human being, so honored in indigenous and mystical strains of spiritual traditions. Streams to deeper meanings within disability culture open with the arts as well. Indeed, exploring archetypal representations of disability in the art of literature and myth serves an important function for gaining greater insight into cultural stories around disability. Some propose that tracking myths around disability historically brings to light how moving from an agrarian way of life toward the dominance of industry resulted in less inclusion of disability in terms of valuing contributions to society (Ebenstein, 2006).

In many indigenous contexts, various forms of physical or mental differences have historically been perceived as a sort of giftedness or part of a shamanic calling. Ebenstein (2006) calls for an archetypal psychological approach to understanding assumptions around disability, emphasizing the Hephaestus myth for the compensatory nature and trickster element. The Hephaestus myth offers an image of "a powerful magician with access to occult power precisely because of his deformity" (p. 10). The value of including archetypal psychology in the mix of any considerations around disability is that this approach acknowledges that a "multiplicity of images is needed to explore the breadth and depth of human experience. Seeing disability through any singular perspective limits and distorts its full meaning" (Ebenstein, 2006, p. 12). Further, considering myths, metaphor, and symbolic or archetypal contemplations opens to further insights that may emerge through "imaginal history rather than actual history" and "meaningful patterns that can inform our personal and communal experience of disability" (p. 13). Bringing these types of depth/archetypal aspects from the literary world into psychotherapy and community endeavors is part of the humanistic psychology vision, which values the transpersonal and poetic and includes art as a worthy interactive endeavor for greater authenticity of feeling and as a meaning-making vehicle.

As a child, Tommy Hollenstein enjoyed taking his bicycle apart and putting it back together again. He was particularly fascinated with the wheels and how, when riding his bike, they could transport him places by spinning around and around in circles. As he entered his teens, he became an accomplished athlete, involved in competitive bicycle racing and other sports. Inspired by an art teacher in High School, he began to experiment with painting. Just as he was entering early adulthood, a bicycle accident resulted in his breaking his neck. While he was in a rehabilitation facility adapting to the changes from paralysis, he expressed that the staff "tried to teach me to paint with a mouse stick, but that wasn't broad enough because I had been in so many sports" and he had grown used to more expansive movement. As he was in the process of discharge from the rehabilitation hospital, he acquired a service dog and named him Weaver. This animal–human relationship was one of the most meaningful connections he had ever experienced. One day, while gazing at Weaver, Tommy became aware of a deep sense of gratitude for this companionate being. He relates that Weaver "gave me independence and changed my life. I never would have left my parents' house, or gotten a job, or done art if it weren't for him" (T. Hollenstein, personal communication, April 30, 2015). He had the thought that he would like to honor their life together in some symbolic way. A spontaneous idea came to him. He wished to create a collaborative painting with Weaver. He had a large canvas placed on the floor, immersed Weaver's paws in paint, and created an art piece that combined the swirling of the wheels of his wheelchair intertwined with the kinetic movement of paws as Weaver ran around on the canvas enjoying their playful endeavor.

This collaborative human–animal art piece was the catalyst for a series of "wheelchair" paintings, resulting in Tommy's first gallery showing in 2005 with a succession of art exhibits after that. An expansiveness of movement has opened in a novel way for Tommy. A valence of emotion displays itself in lively and complex spirals of color in his work. People are drawn to the fractal element of his paintings as well. Fluidity comes about through creative expression that has the potential to bring about deeper meaning and integration. As Romanyshyn says (2015), "soul moves slowly and never in straight lines. It drifts and meanders, drawn to edges and margins, pausing at thresholds and loitering at the lip of an abyss trying to hear who whispers from below" (p. 110). It was relatedness and mutual care between two beings that spurred a transcendent creative flowering in Tommy. It had nothing to do with identification around social constructions of disability and it had everything to do with the phenomenon of love. He stated that he would not place disability foremost in his identity; he would like to be known as "Tommy the artist, not Tommy the disabled artist."

Tommy's experience with Weaver and art informs conceptions of therapy in a number of ways, namely that a humanistic psychology reaches beyond the merely personal to the transpersonal and to our relationship to the non-human. Deepening inquiry into phenomenological nuances around selfhood via animal-assisted therapy is one way of inviting here-and-now contact and relational emergence from a "non-interpretive stance to allow clients to make their own meaning from their interactions with the animals" (Lac & Walton, 2011, p. 2). Not everyone is able to express meaning in words, but there is a felt sense in the field of awareness that a shift in developmental complexity has occurred and that the therapist–animal –client interaction has somehow facilitated that expansion.

Human–animal relationships have long been valued in indigenous/ shamanic healing traditions. The documentary entitled *The Horse Boy* offers a moving example of psychologist Kristin Neff's autistic son's experience with Mongolian shamans and horses after exhausting Western modes of therapy to work with his inability to regulate chaotic outbursts. Equine therapy is now embraced by Western psychology and enabling veterans with PTSD a greater sense of well-being. Many others have benefited within and outside of disability contexts. For instance, Lac (2014) has developed an existential–humanistic approach to equine therapy, particularly for working with children, stressing the element of play and exploration. She emphasizes blending Gestalt Equine Therapy with Humanistic Play Therapy as an "embodied relational process" that supports coherence and development. Ecopsychological frameworks further this consideration, as the natural world is included in therapeutic interaction and being out among trees and bodies of water, for instance, opens to an expansion of relational constructs (Chalquist, 2007; Pilisuk & Joy, 2015). Thus, in regard to working therapeutically along the continuum of disability, Lac's and others' descriptions and case examples that include the non-human offer much in regard to how humanistic psychology may approach the intersubjective field and expand upon Buber's "I–Thou" considerations.

Humanistic psychology honors and fosters inquiry that is most interested in incorporating the "difficult" questions of consciousness (Chalmers, 1996). Grounded in an authentic endeavor to "face directly" the existential givens of life and to honestly explore one's assumptions and prejudices and to do so relationally is at the forefront of this purposeful approach (Wang, 2011). Radical humanism includes recognition of the transpersonal, emphasizes contextual emergence, and is consistent with Eastern and indigenous frameworks regarding a great web of being (Cambray, 2009; Hoffman, 2008). For a review of what it means to embrace a transpersonal view within the context of humanistic psychology, see Friedman and MacDonald's (2003) special volume of *The Humanistic Psychologist* devoted to the topic as well as a recent chapter by Walsh (2015) in the second edition *The Handbook of Humanistic Psychology*. What is referred to as the human body in its development and its processes is formed "by communication networks extending within, through, and beyond the visible organism" (Levin, 1985, p. 5). A stance such as this, as with any approach to psychology, has sociopolitical implications and implications for health care.

Humanistic-centered visionaries such as the late Oliver Sacks have enlightened psychologists to music considerations in stroke rehabilitation and other neurological injuries. Psychotherapists have explored prosody of voice and rhythmic flow in therapeutic attunement (Mancia, 2006) and not simply in the listening of music, but in the creation of music. Many composers throughout history have created astoundingly beautiful and complex compositions in the context of disability (Straus, 2011). Indeed, music has been one of the most profound avenues of connection between my own brain-injured brother and myself. There is a palpable sense of something sacred in these moments of attunement with music opening us to a divine mystery. His inability to express himself with sophisticated language and syntax opens other forms of relating with each other, such as the melody and tonal quality of voice, facial expressions, and eye contact, a shared loved of music, the touching of hands, or a hug. Wallace (1999) from a Buddhist framework says aptly "experience that transcends language and conceptual frameworks can't be adequately described in the language it transcends" (p. 175).

A humanistic stance acknowledges the construction of realities, the illusory nature of such, and enables a respect and even "awe" for the pluralistic influences on a life. Thus, in case conceptualizations, one does not jump to rapid conclusions based on textbook explanations or conventional definitions of disability, rather on an integration of validated concepts blended with the idiosyncratic realities of individuals as well as nuances among and between groups. Open for exploration is the narrative, the story, the here and now, the image, the symbolic or metaphor, and meaning as an organizing context for human action. Humanistic psychology has always embraced the perspective of slowing down for active listening regarding lived experience. It developed in the context of the human potential movement, which argued against the incompleteness and objectification of operant and classical conditioning and other reductionist models of psychology and beckoned toward teleological, ontological, phenomenological, and transpersonal ways of understanding (Krippner, 2002; May, 1969; Schneider, 2011). Humanistic psychology, with the added component of advocacy that Perrin (2013) and others suggest, can withstand the paradigm shifts and ever increasing folderol of "techniques" while focusing on exploring the patterns that are meaningful in the stream of moment to moment experience.

Future Directions for Humanistic Psychology and Application

When social constructions around disability are explored from a humanistic perspective, this exploration opens up considerations of relativity and paradox. Expanding humanistic psychology into broader discussions that include disability in sociopolitical frameworks and community-based endeavors serves to empower those who work in the field of psychology and those to whom they offer care. Because existential–humanistic psychology is most concerned with the human condition, it crosses cultural boundaries and does not impose reductionist stances on human lived experience. Rather, it explores the variety of experience with an appreciation for diversity and with an openness to "awe" (Schneider, 2011, p. 437). As O'Hara (1997) aptly phrased it, humanistic psychology is "emancipatory."

Those who are passionate about humanistic psychology have been actively engaging in lively discussion about where the field of psychology is going. They stress that it is necessary to critically question the status quo and include diverse ways of knowing, including, but not limited to, non-linear paradigms and sociopolitical frameworks. Bringing to light systemic concerns in the field at large are endeavors deemed valuable and purposeful. Actively and collectively responding to injustices are paramount in importance at this time. It is conceivable that it is possible to join hands across and between theoretical and cultural differences with an intention for integration. A powerful disequilibrium in the broader field of psychology is calling for a growth spurt in awareness and spiritual maturity. Future directions for humanistic psychology and disability could be in the realm of therapeutic applications with families and with animal-assisted paradigms, ecotherapeutic approaches, music and the arts, and involvement in consultation and social policy (Hoffman, Cleare-Hoffman, & Jackson, 2015a; Perrin, 2013; Watkins, 2009). A quote from Merleau-Ponty (1945/2008) regarding freedom seems an apt way to close this chapter: "For this significant life, this certain significance of nature and history which I am, does not limit my access to the world, but on the contrary is my means of entering into communication with it" (p. 529).

Essential Lessons

1. Humanistic psychology values definitions of disability that derive from subjective experience.
2. Race, ethnicity, sexual orientation, gender, socioeconomic status interact with and amplify health care disparities in the context of disability.
3. In humanistic psychology, ontological, relational, sociopolitical, and transpersonal inquiry are the guiding foundations of exploring and working with disability.
4. Humanistic applications to therapy value the process of making meaning through integrating art, metaphor, and animal-assisted approaches.
5. Future directions for humanistic psychology include considerations for advocacy, community-based endeavors, consultation, and social policy.

References

Bedi, R. P. (2018). Racial, ethnic, cultural, and national disparities in counseling and psychotherapy outcome are inevitable but eliminating global mental health disparities with indigenous healing is not. *Archives of Scientific Psychology*, 6(1), 96–104.

Cambray, J. (2009). *Synchronicity: Nature and psyche in an interconnected universe.* College Station, TX: Texas A & M University Press.

Carlos, M. (2017, January). Accommodations for trainees with disabilities in psychological testing and assessment. *National Council of Schools and Programs of Professional Psychology, Reclaiming Our Identity: Rediscovering our Social Relevance as NCSPP and Psychologists*, Long Beach, CA.

Chalmers, D. J. (1996). *The conscious mind: In search of a fundamental theory*. New York, NY: Oxford University Press.

Chalquist, C. (2007). *Terrapsychology: Reengaging the soul of place*. New Orleans, LA: Spring Journal.

DeRobertis, E. M. (2015). Toward a humanistic–multicultural model of development. In K. J. Schneider, J. F. Pierson, & J. F. T. Bugental (Eds.), *The handbook of humanistic psychology: Theory, research, and practice* (2nd ed., pp. 227–242). Thousand Oaks, CA: Sage Publications.

Dunn, D. S. & Andrews, E. E. (2015). Person-first and identity-first language. *American Psychologist, 70*, 255–264.

Ebenstein, W. (2006). Toward an archetypal psychology of disability based on the Hephaestus myth. *Disability Studies Quarterly, 26*(4).

Friedman, H. & MacDonald, D. A. (2003). Introduction to special issue on transpersonal psychology. *The Humanistic Psychologist, 31*(2–3), 3–5.

Grandin, T. (2010). *Animals make us human: Creating the best life for animals*. New York, NY: Mariner Books.

Heidegger, M. (1996). *Being and time* (J. Stambaugh, Trans.). Albany, NY: State University of New York Press.

Hoffman, L. (2008). An existential framework for Buddhism, world religions, and psychotherapy: Culture and diversity considerations. In F. Kaklauskas, S. Nimmanheminda, L. Hoffman, & M. Jack (Eds.), *Brilliant sanity: Buddhist approaches to psychotherapy* (pp. 19–38). Colorado Spring, CO: University of Rockies Press.

Hoffman, L., Cleare-Hoffman, H., & Jackson, T. (2015a). Humanistic psychology and multiculturalism: History, current status, and advancements. In K. J. Schneider, J. F. Pierson, & J. F. T. Bugental (Eds.), *The handbook of humanistic psychology: Theory, research, and practice* (2nd ed., pp. 41–56). Thousand Oaks, CA: Sage Publications.

Hoffman, L., Stewart, S, Warren, D. M., & Meek, L. (2015b). Toward a sustainable myth of self: An existential response to the postmodern condition. In K. J. Schneider, J. F. Pierson, & J. F. T. Bugental (Eds.), *The handbook of humanistic psychology: Theory, research, and practice* (2nd ed., pp. 105–134). Thousand Oaks, CA: Sage Publications.

Josselson, R. A. (2000). Relationship as a path to integrity, wisdom, and meaning. In P. Young-Eisendrath & M. E. Miller (Eds.), *The psychology of mature spirituality: Integrity, wisdom, transcendence* (pp. 87–102). London, UK: Routledge.

Jung, C. G. (1916/1960). The structure and dynamics of the psyche. In R. F. Hull (Ed. & Trans.) Vol. 8. *The collected works of C. G. Jung* (pp. 281–297). Princeton, NJ: Princeton University Press.

Kalsched, D. (2015). *Trauma and the soul: A psycho-spiritual approach to human development and its interruption*. New York, NY: Routledge.

Krippner, S. (2002). Dancing with the trickster: Notes for a transpersonal autobiography. *International Journal of Transpersonal Studies, 21*, 1–18.

Lac, V. (2014). Horsing around: Gestalt equine psychotherapy as humanistic play therapy. *Journal of Humanistic Psychology, 56*(2), 194–209.

Lac, V. & Walton, R. (2011). Companion animals as assistant therapists: Embodying our animal selves. *British Gestalt Journal*, *21*(1), 32–39.

Levin, D. M. (1985). *The body's recollection of being*. New York, NY: Routledge.

Lyddon, W. J. (1995). Forms and facets of constructivist psychology. In R. A. Niemeyer & M. J. Mahoney (Eds.), *Constructivism in psychotherapy* (pp. 69–92). Washington, DC: American Psychological Association.

Mancia, M. (2006). Implicit memory and early unrepressed unconscious: Their role in the therapeutic process (How the neurosciences can contribute to psychoanalysis). *The International Journal of Psychoanalysis*, *87*(1), 83–103.

May, R. (1969). *Existential psychology* (2nd ed.). New York, NY: McGraw Hill.

May, R. (1991). *The cry for myth*. New York, NY: Dell.

Merleau-Ponty, M. (1958). *Phenomenology of perception*. Translated by Colin Smith. New York, NY: Routledge & Kegan Paul.

Merleau-Ponty, M. (2008). *Phenomenology of perception*. (C. Smith, Trans.) New York: NY: Routledge(Original work published 1945).

O'Hara, M. (1997). Emancipatory therapeutic practice in a turbulent transmodern era: A work of retrieval. *Journal of Humanistic Psychology*, *37*, 7–33.

Olkin, R. (1999). *What psychologists should know about disability*. New York, NY: The Guilford Press.

Olkin, R. & Pledger, C. (2003). Can disability studies and psychology join hands? *American Psychologist*, *58*, 296–304.

Payne, C. V. (2017). *Immersive cultural plunge: How mental health trainees can exercise cultural competence with African American descendants of chattel slaves-a qualitative study*. Antioch University, Ohiolink.

Perrin, P. B. (2013). Humanistic psychology's social justice philosophy: Systemically treating the psychosocial and health effects of racism. *Journal of Humanistic Psychology*, *53*(1), 52–69.

Pilisuk, M. & Joy, M. (2015). Humanistic psychology and ecology. In K. J. Schneider, J. F. Pierson, & J. F. T. Bugental (Eds.), *The handbook of humanistic psychology: Theory, research, and practice* (2nd ed., pp. 395–399). Thousand Oaks, CA: Sage Publications.

Rohde-Brown, J. & Frain, B. (2014). Facing invisible dragons: An East–West discussion on finding meaning with a sibling with developmental disability. *Journal of Humanistic Psychology*, *54*, 182–202.

Romanyshyn, R. D. (2015). Conversations in the gap between mind and soul: Grammatical reflections "in (the) place(s) of thinking". *The Humanistic Psychologist*, *43*, 109–118.

Samuels, A. (2004). What does it mean to be in "The West?": Psychotherapy as a cultural complex—"foreign" insights into "domestic" healing. In T. Singer & S. L. Kimbles (Eds.), *The cultural complex: Contemporary Jungian perspectives on psyche and society* (pp. 126–143). New York, NY: Routledge.

Schneider, K. J. (2011). Awakening to an awe-based psychology. *The Humanistic Psychologist*, *39*, 247–252.

Stolorow, R. D. (2015). The renewal of humanism in psychoanalytic theory. In K. J. Schneider, J. F. Pierson, & J. F. T. Bugental (Eds.), *The handbook of humanistic psychology: Theory, research, and practice* (2nd ed., pp. 395–399). Thousand Oaks, CA: Sage Publications.

Straus, J. N. (2011). *Extraordinary measures: Disability in music*. Oxford, UK: Oxford University Press.

Wallace, B. A. (1999). *Boundless heart: The cultivation of the four immeasurables*. New York, NY: Snow Lion Publications.

Walsh, R. (2015). Authenticity, conventionality, and angst: Existential and transpersonal perspectives. In K. J. Schneider, J. F. Pierson, & J. F. T. Bugental (Eds.), *The handbook of humanistic psychology: Theory, research, and practice* (2nd ed., pp. 105–134). Thousand Oaks, CA: Sage Publications.

Wang, X. (2011). Zhi mian and existential psychology. *The Humanistic Psychologist*, *39*, 240–246.

Watkins, M. (2009). Creating restorative ecotherapeutic practices. In L. Buzzell & C. Chalquist (Eds.), *Ecotherapy: Healing with nature in mind* (pp. 219–236). Berkeley, CA: Counterpoint Press.

Watts, A. (1968). *Does it matter? Essays on man's relation to materiality*. New York, NY: Vintage Books.

Yee, S. (2011). *Health and health care disparities among people with disabilities*. Berkeley, CA: Disability Rights Education & Defense Fund.

15 If You Live Long Enough

An Existential–Humanistic Perspective on Aging

Myrtle Heery

Reading a book is a short part of one's life's journey where the take-aways from the book might be a surprise. In this very moment, you are growing a little older and hopefully more awake while reading this book. This chapter is a lived experience of aging from an existential–humanistic perspective where the experience of aging is the teacher.

Through experience I will elaborate the following points on aging and dying:

- The fact that everyone will die contributes to making meaning in life in every culture.
- If you live long enough, you will experience impermanence and accept freedom from permanence.
- Choosing death is creating controversy that includes choice and responsibility.

Brief Overview of Emerging Aging Perspective

In 2003, the Harvard School of Public Health-MetLife Foundation Initiative on Retirement and Civic Engagement sponsored a conference on "Baby Boomers and Retirement: Impact on Civil Engagement." This conference is one of many emerging perspectives on aging that is trying to deal with the critical impact of the largest population to age: the baby boomers. The conference proceedings reported the old way of viewing aging, including the language used is obsolete:

> Words like "work," "retirement," "volunteer," and all of the lan-
> guage related to aging (e.g., "seniors") oversimplify a complex reality,
> and may serve as barriers to change. To combat the negative image of
> the frail, dependent elder that underpins a grim view of the future,
> society may have too willingly embraced the contrasting image of the
> "active senior" .... New language, imagery, and stories are needed to
> help boomers and the general public re-envision the role and value of

elders and the meaning and purpose of one's later years ... alternative images of aging and portraying individuals of all ages participating in community life ... alternatives to the narrow set of existing images that reflect current social attitudes toward aging.

(*Reinventing aging: Baby boomers and civic engagement*, 2004, p. 8)

Meanwhile, in California in 2004, panels of mental health professionals were formed by the International Institute for Humanistic Studies (www. human-studies.com) to discuss the challenges of aging with professionals and laypeople of different ages and cultures. These panels formed two editions of *Awakening to Aging* (Heery & Richardson, 2009, 2015). Neither the Harvard School of Public Health nor the International Institute of Humanistic Studies knew of the other's emerging humanistic responses to the aging challenges, but their responses included humanistic language relevant to aging that focused on cross-cultural individuals living the gifts of aging. The humanistic perspective is rich with personal stories of aging with the clinician listening with therapeutic presence (Suri, 2010, p. 175). This presence allows both the individual who is aging and their significant others assistance in their search for meaning from aging and the many levels of spirituality. To illustrate clinical opportunities when working with aging, I now shift to some personal aging stories with clients and their significant others applying the gifts of aging if you live long enough (Heery, 2011b; Heery & Richardson, 2009, 2015).

Aging Stories with Humanistic Perspective[1]

In the 1990s, my dear friend Edith celebrated her ninetieth birthday. Friends and family gathered in her home by the bay in northern California to celebrate, to remember, and to receive. Edith was a granny to many, graciously sharing her wisdom with everyone.

"Edith, how does it feel to be 90?"

"Well, when I look in the mirror I am always surprised and I ask, 'Is that you, Edith?' The person inside feels familiar but the person in the mirror keeps surprising me. You will have this experience too if you live long enough." Edith gently tipped her head back and gave a generous laugh. Yes, generous of heart for those who still recognize ourselves in the mirror and know that we are also seeing ourselves in Edith in this moment.

"*If you live long enough.*" These words awaken me again and again. What about not recognizing myself in the mirror? Or perhaps not even being able to see myself in the mirror? If I live long enough, I will attend many memorials and funerals. I have lived long enough to look over the bay and remember Edith at her memorial. Edith died at age 99.

"And what advice do you have for us for living a long and healthy life?" I asked.

"Take a nap in the afternoon, not long, just fifteen or twenty minutes. And walk every day, every day. Start this discipline now while you are young."

"Anything else?"

"Oh, I am sure there is more, but these two disciplines are what has worked for me."

I remember Edith, with her veins peeking through the thin skin on her hands. I remember the veins on my grandmother's hands, and I see the veins on my own hands steadily showing more. My hands are like a faithful old clock, reminding me daily that I am aging. A little Botox or face-lift might temporarily stop my face from aging, but I remember pictures on the cover of a tabloid (called "adult comic books" by some) at the checkout counter of a local grocery. The photos showed the hands of famous actors against their face-lifted visages. The hands spoke the truth, with all the veins proudly proclaiming their age. The faces spoke of wanting what had been and hoping for physical youth that was long gone. If you live long enough a face-lift will drop from your list of concerns. Life has a way of throwing challenges in aging that seem monumental and very unfair at times. These are the experiences that aging clients face, and that therapists must be prepared to face with them.

If you live long enough, you will laugh harder and cry deeper. Experiences arrive that scare most people and, paradoxically, enliven them. It is startling to be told that you or the person closest to you is going to die, but that message awakens the recipient. Death is no longer the shadow following at a distance but is standing close. "THE CHOICES DON'T stop. Life is choices, and they are relentless. No sooner have you made one choice than another is upon you" (Gawande, 2014, p. 215).

The greatest challenge in being told you have a life-threatening illness is keeping a distance to the fears that will arise in one's mind. Being mindful of these fears helps one to experience the rise and fall of recurrent fears. It may cause one to begin experiencing the impermanence of emotional states and steady oneself in the reality that thoughts, emotions, and life is impermanent. As a clinician it is an opportunity to teach mindfulness meditation during a session and to also bring into the client's awareness the experience of how the therapy hour is not the same as it was at the beginning of the hour (Heery & Gyatso, 2015).

In Garth Stein's (2008) novel *The Art of Racing in the Rain*, his character Eve is on her deathbed at the end of a long bout with cancer; she speaks to her dog Enzo:

> "Do you see?" she asked. "I'm not afraid of it anymore. I wanted you with me before because I wanted you to protect me, but I'm not afraid of it anymore. Because it's not the end."
>
> She died that night. Her last breath took her soul, I saw it in my dream. I saw her soul leave her body as she exhaled, and then she had no

more needs, no more reason; she was released from her body, and, being released, she continued her journey elsewhere, high in the firmament where soul material gathers and plays out all the dream and joys of which we temporal beings can barely conceive, all the things that are beyond our comprehension, but even so, are not beyond our attainment if we choose to attain them, and believe that we truly can.

(pp. 161–162)

If you live long enough, you will move through fear and on into the deep quiet of what is. Walking away from Western medicine is a walk many people take when faced with the possibility of dying. Some might label this as crazy, others might applaud the decision, and still others might remain silent, not knowing what to say and wanting to reclaim their denial of death. As a clinician, it is critical to accept how the client is settling into the fact of their own death. This acceptance first requires the clinician to accept their own death (Heery, 2014b; Reilly, 2015).

No one beats death but rather they may learn to live side by side with death—ready to go and truly ready to live more fully. Being told you will die is an opportunity for rebirth to live more fully in the moment. This fact is a highly valued cornerstone of existential–humanistic psychotherapy.

Each person experiences lessons of impermanence. At some point in life, everyone will be given the opportunity of surrendering to impermanence and to the mystery of life. How can one prepare for this experience of surrender to impermanence to a person whose whole life is based in denial of impermanence? One preparation is to try a form of meditation and or prayer as a means of listening from inside. The inner listening experience strengthens the reality of impermanence. Over and over in silence they may experience how emotions and thoughts change and there can be a point of steady awareness watching this change. There are many words for this steady point, such as "soul," but beyond the word is the repeated experience of this steady point observing the impermanence. This experience brings great solace to those who have death denial and live with waves of anxiety and depression (Heery & Gyatso, 2015). One is no longer attached to their emotions and thoughts but live from a steady point deep inside that brings great relief without any medication or diagnosis. Bev Miller (2015) voiced the spiritual dimension of aging and dying.

> I have led and organized grief groups since I started working with hospice. Being with people in grief has been my training. My faith has brought me to these groups and sustained me. I offer people hope and sacred space where they have the freedom to do their own internal work. I believe in people's ability to work through and heal. That is what I offer—holding their hope until they have the strength and recognition to hold it themselves.
>
> (pp. 132–133)

If you live long enough you will experience liberation from permanence. One might experience impermanence in various forms. Perhaps a marriage of many years ends either by divorce or death of a spouse. One's life seems to end, yet being alive is movement. One may grieve the loss of permanence by leaning on family, friends, faith, and written and/or spoken words of wisdom. The choice of reactions is wide and varied. One could resist by being angry, "why me?" Or one could allow the process of choice and responsibility and surrender and acceptance to emerge. The experiencing self, how one experiences the loss at the time and the remembering self, and how you remember and make meaning of the loss over time will make peace with each other (Kahneman, 2011).

One may begin looking for the rainbow(s) that are right in front of oneself. They may meet new people who could be some of the greatest teachers of their life and give more opportunities to say, "Thank you." I am so deeply grateful to knowing well two women, ages 95 and 98, and one man, age 94. These individuals continue to guide me in aging with dignity and grace. All are active in enhancing the lives of others. They are not in the least interested in self-promotion but are interested in how I am doing and what can they do to help me. Each one of them consistently offers me a look and words of wisdom. Their support has been a great impetus for my writing about aging.

If you live long enough you will have more opportunities to say thank you. For some, as they age, they might need to wear adult diapers, which someone half their age may have to put on you. They might be fed by someone else. If they cannot speak, they may learn to say thank you with their eyes or those aged hands whose knotted veins can no longer be denied. They might experience gratitude for someone else's hands' sensitivity in helping through their aging. Particularly for clients who have valued their independence, they may need assistance accepting that they no longer can do for themselves what they are accustomed to doing and rely upon others.

If you live long enough, you will become humble. Even if one has "no intention of dying" and lives with great care, they will die. No matter what country or city they live in, one day they will die. How each person is influenced by this fact is unique to their nature, their bodies, and the limited and unlimited choices that they make or do not make. I remember a dear friend responding humorously to death denial with, "You and Mr. Jesus are the only two I know that are not going to do it." Often, many people in the lives of those who are facing death try to protect them from the reality of death or do not want to discuss it with them. Therapists need to be able to be with clients honestly and authentically as they face these difficult realizations.

I have held hands with my own death through a near-fatal car accident in 1980 and almost drowning in an ocean riptide at age eight. My death has not come yet but it will one day; that is certain. I am humbled and deeply grateful that I am still here to tell my story, still here on this earth, working, loving and sharing with others all the paradoxical gifts of aging.

If you live long enough you will tell your story of living, aging, and dying. As one ages they enter the great mystery school where they often take the keenest pleasure in holding another's hand for an hour, in laughing as they start a stream of urine, in finding it breathtaking to watch a leaf fall from a tree, or in applauding the great blue heron's return to nest in the same gnarled tree for the third, fourth, or fifth time. As a clinician using the existential–humanistic perspective, the client's repetitive telling of their story is essential to the healing process (Suri, 2010). The literature on story telling with the aging is growing in existential–humanistic psychology, giving substance to this emerging new positive perspective on aging with emphasis on the clinicians use of the present moment (Heery, 2011a, 2014b; Pinnell, 2015; Suri, 2010).

If you live long enough, you will live in the moment. One may not remember people, places, events, books, yesterday, or the words they just said. They may be lost in a state of consciousness that seems miserable to some and enlightened to others. But they will at times experience deep peace at what is in the moment. My dear mentor, Jim Bugental, in his later years would spend long portions of his day waiting for the blue heron to return to the tree in their backyard then marvel at its beauty. The bird became a great solace to Elizabeth, his wife, after Jim died. The bird would come at moments when she would be missing Jim and the bird's presence brought her into the moment of beauty of the now and remembering how much Jim treasured this beautiful bird (Heery, 2011a).

If you live long enough, you will experience isolation and community. Individuals who are aging often become more curious about what is happening to friends and family emotionally, physically, and spiritually in the aging process. It might satisfy their curiosity through reading and education in a variety of forums: classes on aging, discussions with friends, meditation, prayer, and consulting various professionals to confront your issues of aging. They will begin to understand how much alike people are in aging, including cross-cultural perspectives, as shared by therapist Anne Contreras (2015) about her parents from the Philippines.

> I remember the first moment I noticed that my father was no longer "present." My parents came to visit the Philippines. It had been ten years for them both since their last visit. I was living/working as a yoga and meditation instructor in Manila at the time. I had met them at the airport when their international flight arrived at 3:30am … about an hour outside of Manila, my mother had mentioned that she had not had the opportunity to sleep at all on the flight and was going to rest in the room. …
>
> Twenty minutes later, my father asked where my mother was and decided to join her in their room. Five minutes later, my mother,

sleepy-eyed and jostled, came out with my father who was angry. She told me he did not want to sleep or stay at the resort. She kept asking him to go to sleep with her but my father kept saying no and that he did not want to stay at the resort. Instead, he wanted to stay at his mom's house. My grandmother (his mother) known as *Lola* in the Filipino culture, died in 1989. It was as if I had been punched in the stomach and could no longer breathe. It was in that moment that I felt both fear and sadness. I realized that my father was no longer really present anymore.

I looked at my father and said to him, "Dad, you do not live here anymore. You live in San Francisco." He stared at me and paused. I continued, "You arrived this morning from San Francisco by plane and we are here in a resort. Mom is resting. We are all resting right now." … It was this moment that I realized my father was no longer there. His physical presence was however, his state of mind showed and presented otherwise. It was then that I became aware of my father's mortality, the person I use to put on a pedestal and consider my rock. In the transpersonal sense, this is also when I realized that I was meeting my own mortality. It was uncomfortable and challenging to swallow. I thought to myself that moment, "so, this is how it will be now." I took a deep breath as tears continued to well in my eyes and continued to say "okay, this is what it is." I made peace with it by accepting exactly what was happening and decided to work with whatever that moment was presenting.

(pp. 89–90)

When one's turn comes to die they embark on one of the greatest journeys of their life, helping those who dearly love them to remember and live the gifts they have given to these loved ones. One will make difficult decisions about their body or relinquish those decisions to others. Instead of being offered "false hopes, leading families to empty bank accounts, sell their seed crops, and take money from their children's education" (Gawande, 2014, p. 192), hopefully they will be offered the newest paradigm in western medicine by their health practitioner, "ask, tell, ask" (Gawande, 2014, p. 207), which includes oneself and their significant others in making conscious choices about the quality of living and dying.

Yalom (2008), in his afterword to *Staring at the Sun*, a book focused on facing death, ended with this thought:

It is my hope that by grasping, really grasping, our human condition—our finiteness, our brief time in the light—we will come not only to savor the preciousness of each moment and the pleasure of sheer being but to increase our compassion for ourselves and for all other human beings.

(p. 277)

If you live long enough you and your significant others might step into a large, emerging debate about death with dignity. The right to die laws are in effect in California, Oregon, Washington, Vermont, Montana, and New Mexico. Internationally, Switzerland for decades has had a highly successful hospital assisting patients and their families in dying with dignity (see www. dignitas.ch). Assisted suicide in the United States is seen by some as abuse, by others with terminal painful illnesses as emotional and physical relief. This subject is opening to the largest population now to age: the boomers. What the boomers are and will be doing with their right to die is still emerging. There are some resources, such as notdeadyet.org and compassionandchoices.org, that provide information on the different sides of the debate. Internationally, there is the world federation of right to die societies (www.worldrtd.net). This is an invitation for readers to awaken to this topic that deserves an entire book filled with diverse stories to help make this critical decision. My story is that I know people who have chosen both sides of this debate. The diversity of this topic is moving and needs to be approached with one answer does not fit all circumstances. Clinicians working with clients who are facing death must be able to engage clients and, at times, their families with difficult conversations about these topics.

If you live long enough you will experience gratitude to the authors of this book. Reading a book is a short part of one's life's journey and here we are at the end of this short journey together. Endings create space for beginnings. So now is the time to live what matters to you.

Clinical Applications

The most important part of the clinical application of this model of existential–humanistic therapy to the aging population is to search closely your own comfortable and uncomfortable feelings, attitudes, and values that you carry about your aging and dying. This searching process will eventually bring you face to face with many known and unknown dimensions of how you hold your own death anxiety (Heery, 2011b). This deep therapeutic work by the clinician on one's own aging and dying brings an awakened therapeutic presence to the work with clients (Heery, 2014b). Awake to the fact life does end in death and this fact enriches the presence of living.

Experiencing one's own aging and death anxiety is the most valuable application of this work a clinician can have. During the clinical hour with a client who is working on their aging and dying, the most common sharings are rich with gratitude from my clients with my ease and comfort with aging and dying. I have heard many, many moving stories in my forty years of clinical practice, including sudden deaths, suicides, long-term cancers, loss of body parts while aging, and, the most moving, the loss of a child to accident, disease, and or murder. All of these stories have given me the life I have now. I am eternally grateful to my clients and the many years of mentorship with my mentor, James F. T. Bugental, PhD, who was thirty years my senior and died while I was actively learning from him. The slow process of his dying gave me great humility to not know. To stand alone with not knowing and to paradoxically know I am held in this truth by all those who have gone before me. Wisdom slowly arrives with aging and I am deeply grateful to the fact I am aging and dying slowly with some wisdom to apply clinically.

Conclusion

If you live long enough, you will awaken to aging and live consciously. Death and dying can become the greatest gift of aging. It can wake one up to face fears being denied. My hope is that these shared experiences in this chapter have empowered the courage to view the clinical hour with an opportunity to:

- Bring aging, death and dying into the clinical hour
- Teach the tool of mindfulness or meditation for freedom from permanence
- Explore openly as needed the choice of death controversy.

Note

1 Portions of this section were adapted from Heery (2015).

References

Contreras, A. (2015). All your training leads to now. In M. Heery & G. Richardson (Eds.), *Awakening to aging: Glimpsing the gifts of aging* (2nd ed., pp. 82–90). Petaluma, CA: Tonglen Press.

Gawande, A. (2014). *Being mortal.* New York, NY: Metropolitan Books, Henry Holt.

Harvard School of Public Health-MetLife Foundation. (2004). *Reinventing aging: Baby boomers and civic engagement.* Retrieved from www.hsph.harvard.edu/chc/reinventingaging/Report.pdf

Heery, M. (2011a). Pointing with my elbow: Remembering James F.T. Bugental, 1916–2008. *Journal of Transpersonal Psychology, 43*(2), 124–127.

Heery, M. (2011b). Baby boomers on conscious aging. *Journal of Transpersonal Psychology, 43*(2), 256–259.

Heery, M. (Ed.). (2014a). *Unearthing the moment: Mindful applications of existential–humanistic and transpersonal psychotherapy.* Petaluma, CA: Tonglen Press.

Heery, M. (2014b). A humanistic perspective on bereavement. In K. J. Schneider, J. F. T. Bugental, & J. Fraser Pierson (Eds.), *The handbook of humanistic psychology* (2nd ed., pp. 535–549). Thousand Oaks, CA: Sage.

Heery, M. (2015). If you live long enough. In M. Heery & G. Richardson (Eds.), *Awakening to aging: Glimpsing the gifts of aging* (2nd ed., pp. 172–195). Petaluma, CA: Tonglen Press.

Heery, M., & Gyatso, P. (2015). A practice for aging—Impermanence: An interview with Palden Gyatso. In M. Heery & G. Richardson (Eds.), *Awakening to aging: Glimpsing the gifts of aging* (pp. 161–171). Petaluma, CA: Tonglen Press.

Heery, M., & Richardson, G. (Eds.). (2009). *Awakening to aging: Glimpsing the gifts of aging.* Colorado Springs, CO: University of the Rockies Press.

Heery, M., & Richardson, G. (Eds.). (2015). *Awakening to aging: Glimpsing the gifts of aging* (2nd ed.). Petaluma, CA: Tonglen Press.

Kahneman, D. (2011). *Thinking, fast and slow.* New York, NY: Farrar, Straus, Giroux.

Miller, B. (2015). The gift of faith: Waiting on god. In M. Heery & G. Richardson (Eds.), *Awakening to aging: Glimpsing the gifts of aging* (pp. 124–134). Petaluma, CA: Tonglen Press.

Pinnell, C. (2015). Mutato nominee De Te Fabula Narratur: With the name changed the story applies to you. In M. Heery & G. Richardson (Eds.), *Awakening to aging: Glimpsing the gifts of aging* (pp. 151–160). Petaluma, CA: Tonglen Press.

Reilly, R. (2015). What's aging all about anyway? In M. Heery & G. Richardson (Eds.), *Awakening to aging: Glimpsing the gifts of aging* (pp. 42–55). Petaluma, CA: Tonglen Press.

Stein, G. (2008). *The art of racing in the rain.* New York, NY: HarperCollins.

Suri, R. (2010). Working with the elderly: An existential–humanistic approach. *Journal of Humanistic Psychology, 50*(2), 175–186.

Yalom, I. D. (2008). *Staring at the sun: Overcoming the terror of death.* San Francisco, CA: Jossey-Bass.

16 Religious and Spiritual Diversity and Humanistic Psychology

Drake Spaeth

Hoffman, Cleare-Hoffman, and Jackson (2015) noted that until recently humanistic psychology has had a long, uncomfortable history of not attracting diverse individuals from varied cultural contexts, although appreciation for diversity has been a part of the paradigm from its inception. They emphasized that if humanistic psychology is to fully demonstrate its commitment to inclusion of diversity it must (a) attract individuals representing various forms of diversity, (b) encompass a range of ideas and epistemologies (ways of knowing), and (c) incorporate approaches that authentically challenge and transform humanistic psychology, so that it does not remain static. It would follow then that with regard to psychotherapy, people who would be clients would also be diverse with diverse ways of knowing and being and would challenge therapists to stretch and eschew mainstream clinical concepts, practices, and approaches that do not serve them well. With regard to religion and spirituality, humanistic psychology has been demonstrating progress toward fulfillment of the criteria of Hoffman and colleagues (2015).

Comas-Diaz (2015) stated that multicultural and humanistic therapy share in common an emphasis on the importance of social context in individual experience, a holistic view of the person that strives to integrate fragmented internal and external experience, and liberation from what restricts full expression of personhood. She argued for a more intentional and conscientious partnership between the two as essential for a required paradigm shift in achieving a more inclusive psychotherapy (Comas-Diaz, 2015). All three factors—context, holism, and liberation—are important for beneficial experience with religion and spirituality. After all, the context of ceremony, ritual, and other religious or spiritual practice can be conducive to holistic, unhindered, and unfragmented connection with the sacred or mysterious—to produce a sense of liberation from the mundane and an experience of beauty (see also Chapter 10). Religion and spirituality would therefore seem to hold a central place in Comas-Diaz's vision. The next section will briefly describe some recent work on religion and spirituality prior to considering contemporary developments to humanistic approaches to religious and spiritual diversity.

Some Current Approaches to Religion and Spirituality in Psychotherapy

Barnett (2016), referring to numerous surveys that indicate that therapist sensitivity and competence with religious and spiritual issues and aspects is very important to those who seek therapy, stated unequivocally that religion and spirituality are relevant and important in clinical work. His assertion certainly makes sense. With regard to religion in its organized aspects—dogma, tradition, structure and community—therapists can support clients in cognitive, emotional, behavioral, and social struggles with concepts, values, and aspects of religion. They can also facilitate psychological strategies for clients to feel or become more involved with or connected to religious communities and institutions. They can help weigh the costs and benefits or navigate the challenges of converting from one religion to a different one. With regard to spirituality in its less organized and defined hunger for meaningful connection to God or something powerful within themselves or the universe, therapists can support clients in their desire for individual freedom in seeking pathways into the sacred dimensions of their lives. However, Barnett (2016) also emphasized the need for therapists to be ethically discerning about their boundaries of competence and what they are willing and able to integrate into sessions of clients' religious and spiritual practices. Therapists cannot act as clergy or spiritual leaders, but they can consult and collaborate with clergy as needed.

While spirituality could be regarded as an individual longing for the sacred and the consequences of that longing both within and outside of religious frameworks, Frederick (2014) regarded spirituality as a disavowal of the organized and dogmatic aspects of religion in favor of a more flexible and idiosyncratic incorporation of the transcendent dimensions of the sacred in life experience. He endorsed the work of Sperry and others in recognizing how processes of spiritual transformation mirror psychological goal setting and models of change in supporting clients on their journeys of self-discovery and self-awareness. However, he exclusively focused on spirituality within a Christian context.

Sperry (2013) provided a useful taxonomy that endeavors to classify different approaches to the relationship between psychology and spirituality. How a therapist includes/incorporates religion and spirituality into psychotherapy depends on their perspective in terms of where they identify in the taxonomy. According to Sperry, perspectives on this relationship fall into five categories:

1. Those which consider psychology and spirituality to be essentially the same with psychology having primacy over spirituality are psychologically reductionistic and espouse no need for special considerations for spirituality. An example, according to Sperry, would be Freudian psychoanalysis.

2. The second category would consider the two to be essentially the same, but with spirituality having primacy. An example would be Jungian depth psychology, what Sperry would consider to be a spiritually reductionistic approach.

3. The third category considers them to be different, with psychology having primacy. These would be non-reductionistic approaches, into which Sperry places existential–humanistic positions such as that of David Elkins, discussed in the next section of this chapter.

4. The fourth category considers them to be different, with spirituality having primacy. Also non-reductionistic, Sperry places many trans-personal psychology perspectives in this category.

5. The fifth category considers them to be different, with neither having primacy and neither being reducible to the other. He regards these as holistic and includes his own perspective. When clients present in therapy with psychological challenges, psychotherapeutic strategies are called for; when they present with concerns around ultimate questions, spiritually oriented strategies are warranted (Sperry, 2013).

Sperry (2013) also advocated for a spiritually sensitive approach that is sensitive to developmental stages of spirituality in clients. He, like Frederick, offered a Christian framework. Sperry (2014) offered additional clarifications that spiritually oriented psychotherapy is warranted when clients are coping with significant losses or problems, having a crisis of faith or life meaning, or seeking self-development or spiritual growth. Sperry further specified that spiritual interventions should be sensitive to life stages—whether externally oriented to community in adolescence or internally focused in middle age and later adulthood (Sperry, 2014).

While these approaches would likely work well with a range of clients, they are limited by overt and exclusive application to a Christian context and lack of inclusiveness of other religious contexts. The next section focuses on contemporary humanistic approaches which more conscientiously incorporate diversity.

Humanistic Approaches to Religious and Spiritual Diversity

Whether or not Sperry's (2013) taxonomy ultimately proves to be useful in the long term, as humanistic psychology is broadly considered in terms of overlapping concepts on existential, depth, transpersonal, and indigenous psychology, it may become more challenging to place it in Sperry's model. Of course, confusion about the relationship among religion, spirituality, and psychotherapy is not new, particularly in the context of existential–humanistic therapy. Hoffman (2010) pointed out that existential aspects of this paradigm have been misunderstood to be religious or spiritual in nature, when they are not. In fact, Hoffman pointed out that existentialism is quite capable of critiquing problematic aspects of religion as well as appreciating positive aspects. Both Hoffman and Temple and Gall (2018) advocate for the utilization of the phenomenological method of being open to how clients describe their lived experiences of religion and spirituality while bracketing the therapists' personal assumptions and biases in order to deepen and enrich therapeutic alliance. Temple and Gall showed how authentic phenomenological therapeutic engagement with clients' lived experiences of their struggles with the existential givens of isolation, death, freedom, and meaning of life can provide a container of support in which clients may actualize personal spiritual fulfillment and constructive engagement with their religious traditions while liberating themselves from more oppressive aspects of religious dogma and tradition. Most importantly, this phenomenological approach provides a judgment and value-free container in which clients can move toward greater authenticity and insights about spiritual challenges while remaining rooted in their unique cultural context, whatever it is. Therapists are able to support religious and spiritual challenges even if they do not share the same religious or spiritual beliefs and values of the client. The cultural/ spiritual competence of therapists depends heavily on their ability to engage in a phenomenological approach.

Engagement in such work has led to deeper understanding of this dimension of client's lived experiences within respective diverse religious and spiritual contexts. Schneider (2009, 2015) showed how this way of working with clients consistently reveals the prevalence and universality of the experience of awe in terms of religion and spirituality. Awe is a combination of humility and wonder experienced in engagement with the givens of existence (isolation, death, freedom, meaning of life) and seems to promote positive outcomes in encounters with these givens and increase appreciation of and connection to beauty (Schneider, 2015). Personal stories of spiritual transformation frequently encompass this dimension. Schneider (2017) further proposed that awe is a needed remedy for the dehumanizing impact of engagement with technology and the robotic revolution. Exploring with clients their lived experiences of awe can be a powerful way of helping them address their spiritual challenges in a diverse array of religious contexts.

David Elkins has been doing extensive work with religion and spirituality in the context of humanistic psychology and has been dedicated to opening the field to religious and spiritual diversity for the past three decades. Some of his earlier work was dedicated to moving toward a humanistic spirituality based on ideas of Maslow, Dewey, James, Jung, and others (Elkins, Hedstrom, Hughes, Leaf, & Saunders, 1988). Elkins and colleagues also developed a measure designed to assess the spirituality of those not affiliated with traditional religion, derived from prior review of humanistic theoretical, empirical, and phenomenological work. They sought informal validation that the dimensions of spirituality identified in the measure were meaningful by obtaining agreement from members of

Buddhist, Catholic, Protestant, and Jewish religious traditions. Their work yielded a definition of spirituality that emphasized "a transcendent dimension that is characterized by certain identifiable values in regard to self, others, nature, and whatever one considers to be the ultimate" (p. 10). These early efforts by Elkins and colleagues worked toward a quantitative way of engaging commonalities and differences in humanistic spirituality that was consistent with and built upon phenomenological endeavors, but perhaps overlooked a wider diversity of religious and spiritual traditions. For instance, indigenous cultures typically regard the sacred dimension of life as more immanent than transcendent. In other words, it is at the center of and embodied in physical existence rather than separate from or above it.

Elkins (1998, as cited in Elkins, 2015) showed an evolution and expansion in consideration of religious and spiritual diversity in concepts and descriptions of spirituality in what he considered to be six key aspects of spirituality, and even shows some commonly with Schneider's work on awe:

First: Spirituality is universal. By this, I mean that spirituality is available to every human being. It is not limited to one religion, one culture, or one group of people. In every part of the world, one finds those who have cultivated their souls and developed their spiritual lives.

Second: Spirituality is a human phenomenon. This does not mean that it has no divine component, but it does mean that spirituality is an inborn, natural part of the human being. It also means that authentic spirituality is grounded in our humanity; it is not imposed from above or from without.

Third: The common core of spirituality is found at the inner phenomenological level. Spirituality manifests in countless outer forms—from the rain dances of Native Americans to the prayer services of Southern Baptists, from the whirling dervishes of Islam to the meditating monks of Zen Buddhism, from the ecstatic worship services of charismatic churches to the solemn silent meetings of the Quakers. But underneath these outward forms, there is common longing for the sacred, a universal desire to touch and celebrate the mystery of life. It is in the depths of the soul that one discovers the essential and universal dimensions of spirituality.

Fourth: Spirituality has to do with our capacity to respond to the numinous. The essential character of spirituality is mystical, a fact easily overlooked in a scientific and material age. Spirituality is rooted in the soul and cultivated by experiences of the sacred: it feeds on poignancy, wonder and awe. Its very nature is an expression of the mystery of life and the unfathomable depths of our own being.

Fifth: There is a certain mysterious energy associated with spirituality. Every culture has recognized a life force that moves through all creation. Mystics, poets, artists, shamans, and others are familiar with this force and have described it through the centuries. The soul comes alive when it is nurtured by this sacred energy, and one's existence becomes infused with passion, power, and depth.

Sixth: The aim of spirituality is compassion. The word *compassion* literally means "to suffer with." Spiritual life springs from the tenderness of the heart, and authentic spirituality expresses itself through loving action toward others. Compassion has always been the hallmark of authentic spirituality and the highest teaching of religion. Loveless spirituality is an oxymoron and an ontological impossibility. (Elkins, 2015, pp. 687–688, citing Elkins, 1998, pp. 32–33)

Elkins (1998) further built a case for movement away from rigid adherence to traditional dogmatic religion in favor of spirituality within and without religious traditions, which he regarded as being both universally appealing to individuals with diverse lived experiences as well as sensitive to the uniqueness and idiosyncrasies of those experiences. Drawing on past research and personal experience, he described eight pathways to lived experience of the sacred in life, namely (a) the sacred feminine, (b) the arts, (c) the body, (d) psychology, (e) mythology, (f) nature, (g) relation-ships, and (h) experiences known as *dark nights of the soul* or periods of despair, depression, and anxiety that can precede transformative spiritual insight or transformation. These pathways clearly have a cross-cultural appeal and can enrich the spiritual dimension of diverse religions, and they are useful outside of religion as well.

The last item in Elkin's list calls to mind the concept of *spiritual emergency* espoused by Grof and Grof (1989) as well as Lukoff (1985, 1998). This view advocates that some apparent manifestations of psychoses and other mental health challenges are actually evidence of deeply spiritual transformation in process, calling for (and sadly rarely receiving) supportive psycho-spiritual therapy rather than medication and pathology-based interventions. For a full discussion of this concept, which is often shared by depth psychology as well as transpersonal perspectives, see the above cited works as well as Viggiano and Krippner (2010) and Smith (2016). Smith (2016) is notable for its powerful advocacy for a combination of Jungian concepts with Whiteheadian philosophy and the utilization of the methods of cultural anthropology for cross cultural support of spiritual crises and emergencies in diverse religious and spiritual contexts.

Elkins (2015) further emphasized that therapists who wish to integrate spiritual perspectives into therapeutic work need to be willing to have an active spiritual life and practice as well in order to heal at the level of soul. Moreover, therapy can be a type of apprenticeship for clients in learning to care for their own spiritual lives—seeking to find their way through their own lived experiences. A phenomenological stance is a growth-facilitating context for their own practice. Therapists also need to be able to recognize and support clients who avoid painful realities by hiding behind a veneer of spirituality (Elkins, 2015).

Indigenous Psychology and Decolonizing Approaches to Indigenous Spirituality

One of the most exciting developments in contemporary perspectives on religious and spiritual diversity in humanistic psychology has been the entry of indigenous psychology into humanistic psychology, enriching and expanding its global purview, social justice, and other important aspects. Chapter 12 covers these aspects more thoroughly. In terms of working with religiously and spiritually diverse clients, respectful integration of indigenous wisdom regarding spirituality has increased the potential for clients from indigenous religious traditions to benefit from contemporary psychotherapy and has provided rich alternatives to traditional pathology-based approaches in psychotherapy. They also open the possibility of deeper phenomenological engagement with traditions that experientially embrace an immanent concept of the sacred as opposed to one that is more exclusively transcendent. They challenge psychology's insistence on keeping itself separate from spirituality, meshing well with humanistic psychology's emphasis on personal lived experience. They also invite therapists of European ancestry to encounter and explore their own pre-Christian, indigenous European roots, expanding their own lived experience of their personal spirituality.

Katz (2017) pointed out that indigenous spirituality does not emphasize categories and separations. It does not express a preference for so-called normal consciousness over other consciousness states, and is therefore not prone to even unintentionally pathologizing variations from what is regarded as normal. Consciousness that is expanded through ritual, ceremony, dance, drumming, chanting or other spiritual practices experientially engage individuals in new experiences that help them know their unity with the natural world. They help individuals experience the fluid, mysterious sacred within. This is, of itself, healing and therapeutic. They are so deeply personal that they cannot be dictated to by an external source or authority. Katz's view here seems to mirror that of Elkins, which is symbolic of the promise of rich dialogue between indigenous and humanistic psychology.

In the endeavor to integrate diverse indigenous spiritual traditions into psychotherapy, it is critically important not to contribute to the multi-generational trauma of indigenous peoples by using the universal aspects of spiritual experiences to justify misappropriation of cherished traditions or inappropriate use of indigenous sacred objects and ceremonies where they do not belong. Indigenous healers should be identified by their proper names and therapists should never presume to be competent or eligible to do indigenous work for which they have not been trained or initiated. For example, frequent participation in sweatlodge ceremonies does not qualify a therapist to facilitate this ceremony. Therapists should not perpetuate the historical harm of colonization by doing such things. Linklater and Mehl-Madrona (2014) provide a great example and full explanation of the importance of decolonizing therapy when integrating indigenous traditions.

Working with Religiously and Spiritually Diverse Clients: Case Examples

The following are case examples of three clients, with names and superficial aspects of identities altered, selected from actual experiences of the author in his work as a psychologist over the past 21 years. These examples are provided to illustrate pertinent applications and aspects of this chapter.

Rowan

Rowan is a 47-year-old Caucasian woman of German ancestry experiencing frequent panic attacks, a prolonged period of depression, and grieving from the loss of a significant other three years prior. Rowan and her husband are polyamorous; both are open to having secondary long-term romantic relationships with others. Her deceased friend was also an intimate partner. While these issues are also a source of distress for Rowan, of more immediate concern to Rowan herself is her inability to find employment during the past year after being unexpectedly laid off from her position as a financial manager of a medical firm. Rowan privately practices Wicca, a contemporary Pagan religion that aligns with pre-Christian indigenous European nature-based spiritual practices. Some Wiccans also espouse a personal practice of magic as means of achieving personal balance with seasonal, solar, and lunar cycles and promoting health and prosperity. Rowan occasionally joins with established Wiccan groups but primarily embraces a lively, solitary spiritual practice. Rowan's therapist understands that polyamorous lifestyles are common—although by no means obligatory—among various Pagan religions. Since polyamory itself has not been a focus of concern for Rowan or her husband, he does not treat it as such.

The therapist learns that Rowan experiences a fairly constant state of helplessness and immobility in which she becomes quickly discouraged and demoralized after job searches prove fruitless. Her self-esteem has deteriorated. She complains that her well-meaning spouse is unable to understand and support her in the intuitive, special way that her deceased lover could. Perceived expectations and pressure from her husband to "get over it and move on" engender panic and helpless feelings in social situations, arousing memories of emotional abuse by significant others when she was very young.

The therapist asks open-ended questions about personal magic routines and listens to her responses. She acknowledges feeling disconnected from magic and spirituality altogether, and wonders about re-engaging with magic as a way to attract a new job. In collaboration with the therapist and in alignment with the moon waxing over toward full, she daily counts out a number of bean seeds and every morning ritually places an exponentially increasing number of them into a small cauldron, counting the beans to attract the outcome of securing a position as a "bean-counter." Ten days into this practice, she becomes a bookkeeper for an international company after having become more excited, empowered, and invested in her job search.

Over the course of eight months, the therapist non-judgmentally supports her grief for her lost partner as a natural process that has no expiration date. She designs and carries out a ritual of personal closure and farewell. Her panic attacks and depression cease. Note how "magical thinking" is here honored rather than pathologized. Whether or not the therapist regards magic as literal or as a metaphor for cognitive empowerment is bracketed. Unconditional positive regard can then work its own inevitable magic! A non-judgmental, phenomenological stance of active curiosity and interest in the context of a genuine, caring relationship is what is of authentic help to her.

Julio

Julio is 32-year-old Mexican-American man who immigrated with his family to the U.S. when he was eight years old. His religious tradition is Santeria, a syncretic blend of Catholicism and a Caribbean version of African Yoruba that focuses on a reverence for orishas (African spirits) who are intentionally connected to Catholic saints. Many of his friends and some of his family believe that he is simply a devout Catholic.

Julio came to therapy feeling that he has been suffering excessive bad luck, bizarre somatic and health issues, and persistent feelings of anxiety. His godmother, not a relative but a mentor in his faith, has stated that spirits have told her that Julio's troubles stem from interference from his deceased grandmother, an angry ancestral spirit who feels that she has not been properly and fully honored by Julio in specific spiritual practices. His godmother's explanation caused him great anxiety because she is largely unaware that Julio was severely physically and verbally abused by his grandmother for a period of time when he was very young. Julio desires only to forget her and not honor her in his practices. On the other hand, he reveres his godmother and wishes to resolve the curse he believes he is under.

After the therapist establishes a strong rapport with Julio, he agrees to work with the therapist on *unfinished business* he has with his grandmother through empty chair work, in which he is able to address his grandmother as well the parts of himself that suffer shame and trauma from the abuse. Although this therapy work is difficult for him, Julio enjoys it as well, stating that it feels sacred to him. He is now able to honor the ancestral nature of his grandmother while by no means forgiving her for the abuse, which is a balance that he experiences as empowering. He begins having greater spiritual fulfillment and no longer feels that he is under a curse.

Note how the therapist accepts Julio's belief in the curse and does not challenge his belief in the reality of spirits and their impact on Julio's life. Instead the therapist utilizes gestalt therapy techniques, supportive of Julio's private sacred work. The integrity of the religious aspects of Julio's tradition is preserved and his connection to spirituality enriched.

Summary and Future Directions

The utilization of a phenomenological approach to working with religious and spiritually diverse clients is advisable and an inherent strength of humanistic psychology. Earlier and more mainstream approaches were limited by their tendency to adhere to Christian religious and spiritual frameworks often without recognizing some of the inherent biases when generalizing to other religious groups. Humanistic and indigenous psychology perspectives both espouse a preference for personal stories of lived experience and move away from rigid dogmatic aspects of religion in favor of a more fluid spirituality within and without religious frameworks. Indigenous psychology promises to enrich the engagement of humanistic psychology with diverse religious and spiritual traditions. The invitation of future work in humanistic psychology lies in intersectional studies among religion and spirituality with other diversity contexts such as race, ethnicity, sexual orientation, gender, age, and ability.

Essential Lessons

- There are benefits to utilizing a phenomenological approach for working with religiously and spiritually diverse clients.
- Working with personal stories of lived experiences connected to religious and spiritual diversity will continue to enrich insight and understanding of the relationship among psychology, religion, and spirituality, as well as effectively broaden the purview of humanistic psychology.
- Having a rich personal spiritual life is essential for therapists working with religious and spiritual diversity.
- Engagement in more intersectional research and conceptual work would be of benefit to beneficial therapeutic engagement with religiously and spiritually diverse clients.

References

Barnett, J. E. (2016). Are religion and spirituality of relevance in psychotherapy? *Spirituality and Clinical Practice, 3*(1), 5–9.

Comas-Diaz, L. (2015). Humanism and multiculturalism: An evolutionary alliance. In K. J. Schneider, J. F. Pierson, & J. T. Bugental (Eds.), *The handbook of humanistic psychology: Theory, research, and practice* (2nd ed., pp. 386–394). Los Angeles, CA: Sage.

Elkins, D. (1998). *Beyond religion: A personal program for building a spiritual life outside the walls of traditional religion.* Wheaton, IL: Quest Books.

Elkins, D. (2015). Beyond religion: Toward a humanistic spirituality. In K. J. Schneider, J. F. Pierson, & J. T. Bugental (Eds.), *The handbook of humanistic psychology: Theory, research, and practice* (2nd ed., pp. 681–692). Los Angeles, CA: Sage.

Elkins, D., Hedstrom, L., Hughes, L., Leaf, J., & Saunders, C. (1988). Toward a humanistic–phenomenological spirituality: Definition, description, and measurement. *Journal of Humanistic Psychology, 28,* 5–18.

Frederick, T. V. (2014). Spiritual transformation: Honoring spiritual traditions in psychotherapy. *Spirituality in Clinical Practice, 1*(2), 109–115.

Grof, S. & Grof, C. (1989). *Spiritual emergency: When personal transformation becomes a crisis.* New York, NY: TarcherPerigree.

Hoffman, L. (2010). *Existential psychology, religion, and spirituality: Method, praxis, and experience.* 118th Annual Convention of the American Psychological Association, Sand Diego, CA, August 2010. Berlin, Germany: Research Gate.

Hoffman, L., Cleare-Hoffman, H., & Jackson, T. (2015). Humanistic psychology and multiculturalism: History, current status, and advancements. In K. J. Schneider, J. F. Pierson, & J. T. Bugental (Eds.), *The handbook of humanistic psychology: Theory, research, and practice* (2nd ed., pp. 41–55). Los Angeles, CA: Sage.

Katz, R. (2017). *Indigenous healing psychology: Honoring the wisdom of the first peoples.* New York, NY: Simon & Schuster/Healing Arts.

Linklater, R. & Mehl-Madrona, L. (2014). *Decolonizing trauma work: Indigenous stories and strategies.* Nova Scotia, Canada: Fernwood Publishing.

Lukoff, D. (1985). The diagnosis of mystical experience with psychotic features. *Journal of Transpersonal Psychology, 17*(2), 155–181.

Lukoff, D. (1998). From spiritual emergency to spiritual problem: The transpersonal roots of the DSM-IV category. *Journal of Humanistic Psychology, 38*(2), 21–50.

Schneider, K. J. (2009). *Awakening to awe: Personal stories of profound transformation.* Lanham, MD: Jason Aronson.

Schneider, K. J. (2015). Rediscovering awe: A new front in humanistic psychology, psychotherapy, and society. In K. J. Schneider, J. F. Pierson, & J. T. Bugental (Eds.), *The handbook of humanistic psychology: Theory, research, and practice* (2nd ed., pp. 73–81). Los Angeles, CA: Sage.

Schneider, K. J. (2017). *The spirituality of awe: Challenges to the robotic revolution.* Lumsden, Saskatchewan: Waterfront Press.

Smith, C. M. (2016). *Psychotherapy and the sacred: The active use of spiritual resources.* Seattle, WA: Amazon Publishing.

Sperry, L. (2013). Psychotherapy sensitive to spiritual issues: A postmaterialist psychology perspective and developmental approach. *Spirituality in Clinical Practice, 1,* 4–14.

Sperry, L. (2014). Spirituality in clinical practice: Practice considerations. *Spirituality in Clinical Practice, 1*(2), 80–81.

Temple, M. & Gall, T. (2018). Working through existential anxiety toward authenticity: A spiritual journey of meaning-making. *Journal of Humanistic Psychology, 58*(2), 168–193.

Viggiano, D. B. & Krippner, S. (2010). The Grof's model of spiritual emergency: Has it stood the test of time? *International Journal of Transpersonal Studies, 29*(1), 118–127.

17 Multiculturalism and Intersectionality

Weaving New Webs of Relationship and Solidarity

Joel Federman

In late February 2017, a meme began circulating in United States social media of a photograph of two people on a New York subway, sitting next to each other and minding their own business (@boubah360, 2017). One person was a woman dressed in all black, wearing a traditional Muslim hijab covering her face. The other person was a well-known New York drag performer named Gilda Wabbit, dressed in a leather jacket, blue dress, and a bright orange wig. The photographer who first posted the image captioned it with a message to U.S. President Donald Trump: "This is how freedom looks like, Mr. President, we have no problem with diversity and we embrace the freedom of religion" (@boubah360, 2017). In response, a far-right Twitter account re-posted the image, with a new caption that quickly went viral: "(T)his is the future the liberals want" (as quoted in BBC Newsbeat, 2017). The ensuing debate on the meaning of this image, which circulated on various social media for several weeks, typifies a broad contemporary cultural divide in the United States, as well is in many other countries, between monocultural and multicultural worldviews.

In this chapter, I explore how this kind of contemporary cultural divide exemplifies a broader and deeper divide between two kinds of worldviews, which I characterize as *open and closed ways of being*. I suggest how this understanding of open versus closed ways of being can be applied to several different contemporary cultural conversations and issues. In addition, I make a case for the value of maximally multicultural, inclusive, and cosmopolitan cultural norms, along that continuum of relatively open versus closed ways of individual and cultural being.

Appreciation of difference is not a value or attitude that exists in a vacuum. Rather, it is part of a person's broader intellectual, emotional, and behavioral worldview. This worldview can be mapped along a continuum involving open and closed attitudes, emotions, and beliefs. A central political dynamic of the contemporary world is the struggle between a more open, multicultural, cosmopolitan culture and worldview versus a closed, monocultural, hyper-nationalist one. Multicultural and monocultural worldviews pose very different and opposite approaches to the meaning of community: open versus closed, or inclusive versus exclusive. Each of these cultures and worldviews comes with its own set of proposed politics and policies. The cosmopolitan worldview embraces and even celebrates cultural, ethnic, sexual, gender, religious, and other forms of diversity as both a value in itself, and also as a measure of a healthy community. A cosmopolitan approach is characterized by openness toward other human beings in whatever manifestation in which they are encountered. This interrelational openness can be directed solely toward others encountered in a local setting, all the way up to a more universal compassion toward all other human beings (Federman, 1999). In contrast, a hyper-nationalist or monoculturalist worldview embraces a static and monolithic understanding of a particular culture as an ultimate norm and primary value, and also as its measure of community health. For hyper-nationalists, diversity is seen as a threat to cultural unity. The hyper-nationalist worldview as described here has often been labeled "populism," and has transformed cultural and political landscapes in North America, Europe, the Middle East, Asia, and South America (Kyle & Gultchin, 2018).

This dynamic between inclusive and exclusive, open and closed, visions of community is as old as the hills, and as universal as humanity. It was seen in the contrast between the cultures of ancient Athens and Sparta, with Sparta as a hyper-nationalist and militarist culture, and Athens as the far more open society that brought diverse cultures together, and was the birthplace of both Western philosophy and democracy—despite upholding slavery and gender inequality. In Africa, more recently, this same contrast is exemplified on the one hand by the kind of tribal prejudice that informed the inter-tribal genocide in Rwanda of more than 800,000 members of the Tutsi minority population during a 100-day period in 1994 (U.N. Security Council, 1999). On the opposite end of the spectrum, there is the more open and embracing worldview of *Ubuntu*, the Xhosa word meaning a form of cultural harmony summed up by the phrase, "I am because we are" (Africa and the World, n.d.). As Archbishop Desmond Tutu of South Africa summarized this philosophy, "Ubuntu speaks particularly about the fact that you can't exist as a human being in isolation. It speaks about our interconnectedness. You can't be human all by yourself" (as cited in Randoph, p. 24).

The notion of the human potential for a more fully open way of being has roots in the humanistic psychology tradition, specifically Carl Roger's (1961) formulation that the meaning of a "good life" involves a set of three "characteristic qualities" (p. 187) that imply an open way of being. First, for Rogers, a good life involves an "increasing openness to experience," (p. 187), as opposed to a defensive posture toward life and other people. Second, it means an "existential" approach to life, involving an "increasing tendency to live fully in each moment, (and) an absence of rigidity, of tight organization, of the imposition of structure on experience" (p. 189). Third, it involves a trusting of self, of one's inner life and intuitive skills, to engage directly with life experience.

Through the Johari Window toward Transformative Social Change

The gay rights pioneer Harvey Milk recognized that a key strategy for the advancement of civil and cultural rights for sexual and gender minorities to occur was for those minorities to come out of the closet and be open about who they are and who they love (Jones, 2016; Shilts, 2008). By telling one's stories, one by one, in families and in communities, they are able to change hearts and minds about the stereotypes and prejudices that afflict these populations.

This is often a very difficult process, and it involves great courage. Usually, it first involves a process of self-discovery—first coming out to oneself before one can come out to others. This is a comparable spectrum of human development to one described by Luft and Ingham (1955), as "The Johari Window," in which an individual moves from self-unawareness to self-disclosure to disclosure to others (see Figure 17.1).

I suggest that thinking about this developmental schema can be extended to add a few more phases to the process, an extended Johari process, in which one moves from self-disclosure to identification with the larger community, and then to engaging in processes of transformative social change, involving broader theoretical and practical efforts to understand and address the history and contemporary impact of oppression and structural violence in all its forms, and the development of more liberatory and just social structures and relationships.

Joining one's own community may involve a separation from the larger community in order for healthy development to occur. This process was outlined by Beverly Daniel Tatum (1997), in her book, *Why Are All the Black Kids Sitting Together in the Cafeteria?* Very often the self-separation of young black people in middle schools and high schools is viewed as something undesirable. But Tatum points out that it is often part of a

1. Open Known to self and to others	2. Blind Not Known to self but known to others
3. Hidden Known to self but not to others	4. Unknown Not known to self or others

Figure 17.1 Johari Window

healthy process of identifying with others when one exists as an individual in a marginalized group in a racist society. It becomes a kind of parallel adolescent identity development process by which marginalized adolescents form peer-to-peer support groups. During this process, Black adolescents become immersed within their own identity grouping as a way of navigating an externally hostile (racist) social world. This process ideally leads toward an emergent adult identity in which individuals can engage in relations with others outside their grouping in a healthy and prosocial manner. As Tatum (1997) writes:

> One emerges from this process into the internalization stage, characterized by a sense of security about one's racial identity. Often the person at this stage is willing to establish meaningful relationships across group boundaries with others, including Whites, who are respectful of this new self-definition.
>
> (p. 76)

Tatum (1997) notes that this process of Black adolescent identity development in racist societies can be fruitfully applied to other classes of individuals and groups who have been historically and contemporaneously oppressed within a given society: "Though racial identity models ... were developed with African Americans in mind, the basic tenets of such models can be applied to all people of color who have shared similar patterns of racial, ethnic or cultural oppression" (p. 132). Just like with other adolescent development processes, it is this differentiation from one's culture of origin, or the dominant culture, that allows a person to eventually further differentiate, be oneself as an individual, and then join the larger community in a healthy way. In their review of theories and research on racial and ethnic identity, Yip, Douglass, and Sellers (2014) cite research pointing to the prosocial advantages of such racial and ethnic identity development, while also noting other, more mixed and sometimes negative psychological and social results of such identification.

Relevance of Johari Window to Clinical Settings

This usage of the Johari Window has specific applications for mental health professionals. For clinicians, the Johari window has applications for the therapist and for the client, and particularly with regard to intersectionality. Individuals in the helping professionals have a higher ethical obligation to be aware of their biases and how these may emerge when working with clients. At times, the interplay of various forms of difference may allow a therapist to justify their biases to themselves. For example, it is possible to ignore the role racism plays in social oppression by focusing on socioeconomic status (SES), and denying the role of race in the marginalization of people of color. This kind of obfuscation can protect the clinician from looking more deeply at their biases.

It is also important that therapists help clients explore how the various aspects of their identity development—personal and affiliation-based—impact their experience and understanding of themselves. In addition, it is helpful to be aware of how these may influence their experience of the therapy process, including the development of the therapeutic alliance. The intersection of cultural issues, such as gender identity development and racial identity development, add a layer of complexity to one's experience. For example, a transgender individual who also is a Christian person of color with a lower socioeconomic (SES) background may be more isolated from community resources, such as religious/spiritual support and access to healthcare resources, while having an increased likelihood of stress from discrimination and hate incidents. After experiencing prejudice and discrimination based upon varied aspects of their identity, it may be more difficult to develop a solid therapeutic alliance. Bringing an awareness of intersectional oppressions into the therapeutic process can help support diverse clients.

Building Solidarity across Societal Divides

While racism, sexism, homophobia, transphobia, xenophobia, and other forms of social exclusion—closed and monocultural ways of being—are generally the province of the political and cultural right, the political left is not immune to its own form of exclusionary politics and behaviors, to closed ways of being. Smucker (2017) notes that in their quest for ideological purity, those on the left often engage in their own form of the politics of exclusion by creating seemingly infinite ideological purity tests for measuring the correctness of their views. Smucker describes the way that some members of progressive social movements have tendencies to become so "caught in (a) pattern of emphasizing how different they are (that they) start to prize their own marginalization ... If society is bad, then marginalization within society must be good" (p. 94). With this attitude of self-imposed marginalization, movements for social change often limit their capacity to create large scale social transformation by limiting the expansiveness of their coalitions to the ideologically pure.

At the same time, there have been broad and longstanding efforts within progressive social movements to build more inclusive and open communities and societal structures. This kind of cross-community coalition building is something that Reverend Martin Luther King, Jr. and Harvey Milk, one of the first openly LGBTQ elected officials in the United States, understood and utilized to great effect, both in their rhetoric and in their day-to-day political action. In his "I Have a Dream" speech, King (1963) spoke of a time when "*all* of God's children, black men and white men, Jews and Gentiles, Protestants and Catholics, will be able to join hands." King built coalitions with Christian and Jewish leaders such as the Reverend Glenn Smiley of the Fellowship of Reconciliation, who rode with him on the first integrated bus ride in Montgomery, Alabama, and Rabbi Abraham Joshua Heschel (Heschel, n.d.), who was his long-time friend and ally. He also supported labor efforts, including the United Farm Workers and the Memphis sanitation workers' campaigns for better working conditions, and was building toward a broad-coalition Poor People's Campaign when he was assassinated on April 4, 1968.

Similarly, when Harvey Milk spoke about social change, he often referred to what he called the "us's," the collective grouping of those who have been dispossessed and marginalized within society: "Without hope," he said, "not only gays, but the blacks, the seniors, the handicapped, the us'es, the us'es will give up" (quoted in Shilts, 2008, p. 363). Milk appointed a lesbian as his campaign manager and built coalitions with labor organizations, beginning with LGBTQ support for the Coors boycott in 1977 and Latino migrant farmworkers in fighting for their shared causes.

More currently, social justice activists such as William J. Barber II, in building broad social coalitions such as the Poor People's Campaign, have affirmed the value and necessity of inclusivity and solidarity. In his sermon, "When the Stones Come Together," Barber (2018) argues that only by speaking, organizing, and preaching beyond the choir will those on the left, and particularly those in oppressed groups, succeed in creating the coalitions they need to build in order to transform large-scale social structures and cultural norms. Barber builds on the biblical passage stating that "the stone the builders rejected has now become the chief cornerstone" (Matthew 21:42, as cited in Barber, p. 44), to make the case for the possibilities that can occur when coalitions are built across groups that are often divided from one another:

> I want you to know tonight that when the rejected get together, we can in fact redeem America from hate and discrimination. I want you to know tonight that when hands that once picked cotton join the hands of Latinos, join the hands of progressive whites, join faith hands, join labor hands, join Asian hands, and join Native American hands, and join poor hands, and join wealthy hands and join gay hands, and join straight hands, and trans hands—when all those hands get together, when the rejected join hands, our togetherness becomes the instrument of redemption.
>
> (p. 45)

Building solidarity across inter-group and intersectional divides has historically been met with tremendous resistance. As activist Cleve Jones (2016) notes, LGBTQ people were historically excluded from progressive social movements until the late 1960s: "Straight lefties, and particularly labor activists, were notoriously homophobic back then. In the early days of the anti-Viet Nam War protests, gay people were often excluded from demonstrations and marches, sometimes violently" (p. 48), lesbians were purged from the ranks of the National Organization for Women in 1971, and there was "enormous hostility [among certain lesbian activists] to [transgender] women, who were sometimes physically barred from 'women-only' spaces" (p. 50). Carruthers (2018) similarly notes that LGBTQ black activists have sometimes been violently attacked within the Black Lives Matter movement, and that black LGBTQ activist pioneers, such as Marsha P. Johnson and Silvia Rivera, have often been overlooked in histories and media depictions of the LGBTQ movement, which tend to focus on the work of white, cisgender male activists.

Solidarity and Intersectionality

Despite such resistance, activists in many spheres have worked to build coalitions and solidarity within and across social movements for social justice and liberation. One dimension of such solidarity work involves recognition of the degree of *intersectionality* within such movements. Collins and Bilge (2016) define intersectionality as the presence of multiple factors that can contribute to the identity and social location of particular individuals and groups. As they note, "The events and conditions of social and political life and the self can seldom be understood as shaped by one factor. They are generally shaped by many factors in diverse and mutually influencing ways" (p. 2). Building from a recognition of such intersectionality, social change activists are able to bridge gaps among cultural groups often seen as distinct and divided. Audre Lorde (1982) is often quoted as succinctly summing up the meaning of intersectionality, when she said, "There is no such thing as a single-issue struggle because we do not live single-issue lives." Lorde (1982) went on to unpack this meaning in greater specificity: "Each one of us here is a link in the connection between anti-poor legislation, gay shootings, the burning of synagogues, street harassment, attacks against women, and resurgent violence against Black people." Establishing such solidarity within and among such intersecting identities sometimes involves creation and utilization of new language and meanings of existing terms. For example, for Carruthers, the term *Queer* is not solely a reclaimed appellation for those who are lesbian, gay, bisexual, or transgender but rather a general term to describe the historically dispossessed:

> "Queer," as I am defining it here, represents a continuum of possibilities outside of what are considered to be normal sexual or gender identities and behaviors. Affirmation of queerness creates possibility

outside the norm … And in more ways than one, blackness is inherently queer.

(pp. 10–11)

In this way, the term *Queer*, which is already a form of reclaiming an identifier for marginalized groups, can also be used as a term to bridge multiple kinds of intersecting identities, across race and gender/sexuality. Carruthers cites the work of the Chicago-based Black Youth Project 100 (BYP100), a group focused on justice and freedom for Black people, as building solidarity and inclusive coalitions that are developed utilizing a broader Black queer feminist lens that incorporates this understanding of Queerness and intersectionality. In its BYP100 Statement on Radical Inclusivity, the organization includes an affirmation of the necessity of solidarity across oppressed and intersectionally defined groupings: "BYP100 takes a radically inclusive approach to organizing by supporting/creating campaigns that focus on interlocking oppressions of marginalized peoples" (as quoted in Carruthers, 2018, p. 12).

Our Common Humanity as the Ultimate Intersectionality

I would like to conclude with a focus on what I believe to be the ultimate intersectionality: the common humanity among human beings. The idea of intersectionality implies a recognition of the complex heritage and identity of each individual human being. Whether measured through the lenses of race, class, gender, sexual orientation, national origin, or religion, each human being is multidimensional and represents a multicultural identity. Intersectionality thus also implies the necessity of moving from a fractured state of being and back toward wholeness by identifying common sources of oppression, and common pathways toward liberation. If one carries intersectionality to its logical conclusion, one would affirm and embrace each of the unique characteristics of every human being as they combine into making that human being a whole person.

It is important to note that affirming such an all-embracing multicultural and universal understanding of intersectionality does not mean that one affirms a naïve belief that society is on the verge of reaching a post-racial millennium, or has transcended any of the various intersecting oppressions present in contemporary society that have been noted above. A recognition of common humanity should not be seen as glossing over difference, as in the "all lives matter" response to the Black Lives Matter movement. When those who aren't Black respond to affirmations that Black Lives Matter by stating that all lives matter, they state the obvious, but ignore and erase the unique oppression and discrimination faced by Black people in a racist societal context. A conception of universal intersectional identity is not an abstraction. It is the concrete result of engagement with others different from oneself in some ways, while yet recognizing and affirming their common humanity. This engagement is also not abstract. It needs to involve direct participation in ever-widening social, cultural, and political circles, as well as in social movements aimed at overcoming various forms of social oppression, including intersecting social oppression.

The advent of the Internet has created the capacity not only to understand this planetary unity conceptually, but also to manifest it in concrete political organization (Collins & Bilge, 2016). As such, the emergence of truly global social movements for social justice, environmental sustainability, peace, and human rights, including gender and sexual orientation rights, are beginning to occur. On February 15, 2003, the largest international political demonstration in the history of the world took place to protest the oncoming Iraq War (Federman, 2003). This demonstration was organized in meetings earlier that year during the World Social Forum, an international gathering of peace, social justice, human rights, and environmental movements. Similar efforts toward organizing transnational movements for social change have occurred for centuries, notably the movement for the abolition of the transatlantic slave trade, the formation of international human rights solidarity organizations such as Amnesty International, the international LGBTQ movement, successive efforts to create a movement for world peace (Federman, 1982, 1999, 2007), and the Women's March of 2017, which was estimated to have taken place in 673 locations around the world (Bullock, Rennison, Weaver, & Whipp, 2017). Collins and Bilge (2016) note the transnational philosophical themes that are increasingly emergent in seemingly local contemporary social movements across of a variety of issues in various parts of the world:

> These actions illustrate one facet of what social movement literature calls globalization from below. This phrase refers to a *transnational political imaginary*, namely, a way of imagining political action that goes beyond local face-to-face organizing and beyond national politics to encompass a broader transnational focus …. This transnational political imaginary draws from intersectional understandings of the interrelatedness of these protests. The specific histories of disenfranchisement associated with racism, sexism, class exploitation, and ethnic subordination that shape one another in specific social contexts are no longer understood as separate events but, rather, are [understood as] connected.
>
> (pp. 140–141)

In December 1969, the first picture of the planet as a whole was transmitted back to the Earth by Apollo 8 astronauts (Overbye, 2018). This initiated what astronauts have called the "*overview effect*" (Tayag, 2018), the effect that occurs when one is able to see the world as a whole, and to recognize the fact that humanity as a whole is one family living on a single planetary home. Over time, in a subtle way, this overview effect is creating a transformation in the consciousness of newer generations who have never known a world without that image. Just like there are digital natives and digital immigrants, based on generational exposure to the Internet, in the same way, one can conclude that the fact that there are those in the current generations who are native to the overview effect, to the knowledge that everyone is part of one single human family, is having a profound transformation in the thinking of those younger, contemporary generations. Younger generations of global citizen natives recognizing their common humanity across intersecting multicultural dimensions, provide hope for the realization of the common humanity of human beings—not just as a dream, but as a concrete social reality. In summary, two central ideas regarding openness, inclusivity, and multicultural culture animate the analyses and conclusions of this chapter. The first of these is that every human being shares with every other human being a common essence, including a genetic similarity and a common humanity. The second idea is that the combination of characteristics of each individual human being intersect in such a way as to make them wholly unique, and that unique intersection of qualities should be celebrated down to the last person. Universal celebration of the diversity among human beings' unique intersectional essence and expression represents the widest possible application of cultural openness and multicultural inclusion.

References

Africa and the World. (n.d.). African philosophy: Ubunthu a way of life. *Africa and the World.* Retrieved from www.africaw.com/african-philosophy-ubuntu-a-way-of-life

Barber, W. J. (2018). *Revive us again: Vision and action in moral organizing.* Boston, MA: Beacon Press.

BBC Newsbeat. (2017, March 3). *Gilda Wabbit: The face of a liberal future? British Broadcasting Corporation (BBC).* Retrieved from www.bbc.co.uk/newsbeat/article/39158413/gilda-wabbit-the-face-of-a-liberal-future

Bullock, N., Rennison, J., Weaver, C., & Whipp, L. (2017, January 23). Leader takes to Twitter in response to international protests. *Financial Times,* p. 3.

@boubah360. (2017, February 21). *Instagram posting.* Retrieved from www.instagram.com/boubah360/p/BQyIchIAdcl/

Carruthers, C. (2018). *Unapologetic: A Black, queer and feminist mandate for radical movements.* Boston, MA: Beacon Press.

Collins, P. H., & Bilge, S. (2016). *Intersectionality.* Malden, MA: Polity Press.

Federman, J. (1982). Toward a world peace movement. *Humanities in Society, 5*(1, 2), 137–147.

Federman, J. (1999). *The politics of compassion* (Unpublished doctoral dissertation). University of Southern California, Los Angeles, CA.

Federman, J. (2003, October). *Forging an alternative to permanent war: Strategies for peace and justice in the post-9/11 world.* Paper presented at the annual conference of the Peace and Justice Studies Association, Olympia, WA.

Federman, J. (2007, July/August). A movement of movements: First US social forum a historic event [Online]. *Tikkun Magazine*. Retrieved from www.tikkun. org/article.php/socialforum

Heschel, S. (n.d.). Two friends, two prophets Abraham Joshua Heschel and Martin Luther King Jr. *Plough Quarterly Magazine*. Retrieved from www.plough.com/ en/topics/community/leadership/two-friends-two-prophets

Jones, C. (2016). *When we rise: My life in the movement*. New York, NY: Hachette Books.

King, M. L. (1963, August 28). "I have a dream," address delivered at the March on Washington for jobs and freedom. *The Martin Luther King Research and Education Institute*. Palo Alto, CA: Stanford University. Retrieved from https://kinginsti tute.stanford.edu/king-papers/documents/i-have-dream-address-delivered-march-washington-jobs-and-freedom

Kyle, J., & Gultchin, L. (2018, November 7). *Populists in power around the world*. London, UK: Tony Blair Institute for Global Change. Retrieved from https:// institute.global/insight/renewing-centre/populists-power-around-world

Lorde, A. (1982). Learning from the 1960s. Retrieved from www.blackpast.org/ african-american-history/1982-audre-lorde-learning-60s/

Luft, J., & Ingham, H. (1955). *The Johari window, a graphic model of interpersonal awareness*. Proceedings of the western training laboratory in group development. Los Angeles, CA: University of California, Los Angeles.

Overbye, D. (2018, December 21). Apollo 8's earthrise: The shot seen round the world. *The New York Times*. Retrieved from www.nytimes.com/2018/12/21/ science/earthrise-moon-apollo-nasa.html

Rogers, C. (1961). *On becoming a person: A therapist's view of psychotherapy*. Boston, MA: Houghton Mifflin Company.

Shilts, R. (2008). *The mayor of Castro Street: The life and times of Harvey Milk*. New York, NY: St. Martin's Griffin.

Smucker, J. M. (2017). *Hegemony how-to: A roadmap for radicals*. Chico, CA: AK Press.

Tatum, B. D. (1997). *"Why are all the Black kids sitting together in the cafeteria?" and other conversations about race*. New York, NY: Basic Books.

Tayag, Y. (2018, March 27). Six NASA astronauts describe the moment in space when "everything changed". *Inverse*. Retrieved from www.inverse.com/article/ 42902-nasa-astronauts-describe-overview-effect-everything-changed

United Nations Security Council. (1999, December 15). Report of the independent inquiry into the actions of the United Nations during the 1994 genocide in Rwanda. New York, NY: United Nations Security Council. Retrieved from www.securitycouncilreport.org/atf/cf/%7B65BFCF9B-6D27-4E9C-8CD3-CF6E4FF96FF9%7D/POC%20S19991257.pdf

Yip, T., Douglass, S., & Sellers, R. M. (2014). Ethnic and racial identity. In F. T. L. Leong, L. Comas-Díaz, G. C. Nagayama Hall, V. C. McLoyd, & J. E. Trimble (Eds.), *APA handbook of multicultural psychology* (Vol. 1. Theory and research, pp. 179–205). Washington, DC: American Psychological Association.

Afterword

Back to the Future

Ilene A. Serlin

The premise of this book, that humanistic and existential–humanistic psychology must reflect on itself with a multicultural lens if it is going to stay relevant to a fast-changing global world, is very necessary and timely. While most of the issues addressed in this book, such as microaggressions and social change, need to be addressed in contemporary scholarship, there were existentialists such as Sartre and Camus who advocated social action and there were practitioners such as Charlotte Selver who taught about other ways of knowing (Criswell & Serlin, 2015). Some of these people are not taught any longer and should be included in curriculum for the new generation. We can go "back to the future" to build a strong and wide foundation with which to move forward while integrating contemporary scholarship and issues to deepen the relevance for the current times.

Like many of us from the '60s, one of my first influences for knowing myself came from reading Siddhartha, the privileged prince who leaves the palace, encounters suffering in the world, and becomes the Buddha. Many other myths reinforce the image of psychology as the journey of a solitary young hero in search of the holy grail (enlightenment, meaning). However, my foundation teachers were female. Simone de Beauvoir, in *The Second Sex* (2009), opened my eyes to the reality that women's existence is different than that of men, and that women have been "other" to the centrality of men throughout history. Women's consciousness movements flourished during the same time as the emancipatory movements of humanistic psychology; however, when I was president of Division 32 of the American Psychological Association (Society for Humanistic Psychology) in 1996, we were below other divisions in terms of percentage of women in leadership (Serlin & Criswell, 2001). Women typically do not operate as sole heroines, nor do women have the good ol' boy network of men. Other divisions practice and offer training in mentoring for women, but Division 32 has not started a mentoring system.

My first therapist, teacher, and eventually colleague/friend, was Laura Perls, wife of Fritz Perls. Although *Ego, Hunger and Aggression* (Perls, 1969) was written on their dinner table, Laura's name is not on the book. When urged to write, she said that her students were her legacy, and she maintained close relationships around the world for many years. Laura's way of Gestalt was very different than Fritz's; she was subtle, quiet, and supportive rather than confrontive. Fritz was hungry for public acclaim, so he wrote more and is better known. Fritz is famous for his quip: "I'm not in this world to live up to other people's expectations, nor do I feel that the world must live up to mine." While his attitude helped create the stereotype that Gestalt therapy is selfish, Laura studied with Martin Buber and embodied "I–Thou" relationships. Laura's epistemology was not linear male; it was interconnected and relational (Serlin & Shane, 1999). Including her in a humanistic psychology curriculum is important because it corrects and balances the understanding of Gestalt therapy.

Another challenge faced by existential–humanistic psychologists is onto-logical: What does it mean to be human? Some chapters talk about the loss of humanity that comes with microaggression and objectification of those who become "other." The question and experience of what it means to be human will certainly be further challenged with the advent of artificial intelligence and genetic editing. While existential–humanistic psychologists need to be involved in this conversation, they should remember to include all humans in an I–Thou relationship.

Finally, while this book covered many aspects of new multicultural awareness, there are others that would also be valuable and continue to need to be addressed in the evolving humanistic and existential literature. This book provides a foundation for furthering this scholarship. One is a new application for existential–humanistic psychology. As people around the world become more traumatized, people are torn from their commu-nities and sense of place, and existential–humanistic therapists need to understand the meaning of communal pain and suffering in trauma (Serlin & Cannon, 2004). Next is more focus on the suffering of women, and that of Mother Earth (environmental issues). While honoring women's ways of knowing (Goldberger, Tarule, Clinchy, & Belenky, 1996) and somatic awareness, existential–humanistic psychologists should remember and teach those who pioneered these approaches 50 years ago (Thomas Hanna, Eleanor Criswell, Ida Rolf, and Michael Murphy). Finally, as positivist science and scientific methodology is challenged by non-Western and indigenous ways of knowing, existential–humanistic psychology should continue to vigorously promote methodological diversity (Har-away, 1991; Yakushko, Hoffman, Morgan Consoli, & Lee, 2016).

In conclusion, this book provides a much-needed update on humanistic and existential–humanistic psychology. The first step of this update is conscious-raising about areas that are left out, especially ones on multi-culturalism. The next step is to write about these areas, and make sure that the new writing, as well as the historical pieces by existential–humanistic psychologists, is in textbooks and available to psychology students. Finally, existential–humanistic theory needs to be taken out into the world, whether it is clinical (influencing the psychotherapy guidelines at APA), leadership (creating mentoring programs), social (taking action on social or environmental issues), or research (documenting our work). In this way, we can ground our new thinking and writing in concrete action in the real world. This book, *Humanistic Approaches to Multiculturalism and Diversity: Perspectives on Existence and Difference*, is a wake-up call for the need to refresh our thinking and application about the future of humanistic psychology.

References

Criswell, E., & Serlin, I. (2015). Humanistic psychology, mind–body medicine and whole person health care. In K. Schneider, S. F. Pierson, & J. F. T. Bugental (Eds.), *The handbook of humanistic psychology: Theory, research, and practice* (2nd ed., pp. 653–666). Thousand Oaks, CA: Sage.

de Beauvoir, S. (2009). *The second sex* (C. Corde & S. Malovany-Chevallier, Trans.). London: Cape. (*Le deuxieme sexe*, 1949).

Goldberger, N., Tarule, J., Clinchy, B., & Belenky, M. (1996). *Knowledge, difference and power*. New York, NY: Basic Books.

Haraway, D. (1991). Situated knowledges: The science question in feminism and the privilege of partial perspectives. In D. Haraway (Ed.), *Simians, cyborgs, and women* (pp. 183–202). New York, NY: Routledge.

Perls, F. S. (1969). *Ego, hunger, and aggression*. New York, NY: Random House.

Serlin, I. A., & Cannon, J. (2004). A humanistic approach to the psychology of trauma. In Danielle Knafo (Ed.), *Living with terror, working with trauma: A clinician's handbook* (pp. 313–331). Northvale, NJ: Jason Aronson.

Serlin, I. A., & Criswell, E. (2001). Humanistic psychology and women: A critical-historical perspective. In K. Schneider, J. F. T. Bugental, & J. Pierson (Eds.), *Handbook of humanistic psychology: Leading edges of theory, research, and practice* (pp. 29–36). Thousand Oaks, CA: Sage Publications.

Serlin, I. A., & Shane, P. (1999). Laura Perls and Gestalt therapy: Her life and values. In D. Moss (Ed.), *The pursuit of human potential: Sourcebook of humanistic and transpersonal psychology* (pp. 374–384). Westport, CT: Greenwood Press.

Yakushko, O., Hoffman, L., Morgan Consoli, M., & Lee, G. (2016). On methods, methodologies, and continued colonization of knowledge in the study of "ethnic minorities": Comment on Hall et al. (2016). *American Psychologist, 71*, 890–891.

Index

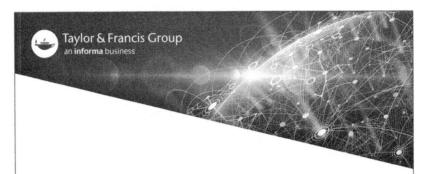

Made in the USA
Monee, IL
17 December 2021

86110017R00138